THE WATERGATE CRISIS

THE WATERGATE CRISIS

Michael A. Genovese

Greenwood Press Guides to
Historic Events of the Twentieth Century
Randall M. Miller, Series Editor

Greenwood Press
Westport, Connecticut • London

Library of Congress Cataloging-in-Publication Data

Genovese, Michael A.
    The Watergate crisis / Michael A. Genovese.
       p. cm.—(Greenwood Press guides to historic events of the
twentieth century, ISSN 1092–177X)
    Includes bibliographical references and index.
    ISBN 0–313–29878–5 (alk. paper)
    1. Watergate Affair, 1972–1974. I. Title. II. Series.
E860.G46   1999
973.924′092—dc21   99–17858

British Library Cataloguing in Publication Data is available.

Library of Congress Catalog Card Number: 99–17858
ISBN: 0–313–29878–5
ISSN: 1092–177X

First published in 1999

Greenwood Press, 88 Post Road West, Westport, CT 06881
An imprint of Greenwood Publishing Group, Inc.
www.greenwood.com

Printed in the United States of America

The paper used in this book complies with the
Permanent Paper Standard issued by the National
Information Standards Organization (Z39.48–1984).

10 9 8 7 6 5 4 3 2 1

Front cover photo: President Nixon waves as he boards the helicopter on the White House lawn
after resigning the presidency and bidding farewell to his staff. UPI/CORBIS-BETTMANN.

*To William Lammers, teacher, friend, mentor,
and gentle man. Bill, you are greatly missed.*

Contents

A photo essay follows page 98

Series Foreword

As the twenty-first century approaches, it is time to take stock of the political, social, economic, intellectual, and cultural forces and factors that have made the twentieth century the most dramatic period of change in history. To that end, the Greenwood Press Guides to Historic Events of the Twentieth Century presents interpretive histories of the most significant events of the century. Each book in the series combines narrative history and analysis with primary documents and biographical sketches, with an eye to providing both a reference guide to the principal persons, ideas, and experiences defining each historic event, and a reliable, readable overview of that event. Each book further provides analyses and discussions, grounded in both primary and secondary sources, of the causes and consequences, in thought and action, that give meaning to the historic event under review. By assuming a historical perspective, drawing on the latest and best writing on each subject, and offering fresh insights, each book promises to explain how and why a particular event defined the twentieth century. No consensus about the meaning of the twentieth century emerges from the series, but, collectively, the books identify the most salient concerns of the century. In so doing, the series reminds us of the many ways those historic events continue to affect our lives.

Each book follows a similar format designed to encourage readers to consult it both as a reference and a history in its own right. Each volume opens with a chronology of the historic event, followed by a narrative overview, which also serves to introduce and examine briefly the main themes and issues related to that event. The next set of chapters is composed of topical essays, each analyzing closely an issue or problem of interpretation introduced in the opening chapter. A concluding chapter suggesting the long-term implications and meanings of the historic event brings the strands of the preceding chapters together while placing the event in the larger historical context. Each book also includes a section of short biographies of the principal persons related to the event, followed by a section introducing and reprinting key historical documents illustrative of and pertinent to the event. A glossary of selected terms adds to the utility of each book. An annotated bibliography—of significant books, films, and CD-ROMs—and an index conclude each volume.

The editors made no attempt to impose any theoretical model or historical perspective on the individual authors. Rather, in developing the series, an advisory board of noted historians and informed high school history teachers and public and school librarians identified the topics needful of exploration and the scholars eminently qualified to examine those events with intelligence and sensitivity. The common commitment throughout the series is to provide accurate, informative, and readable books, free of jargon and up to date in evidence and analysis.

Each book stands as a complete historical analysis and reference guide to a particular historic event. Each book also has many uses, from understanding contemporary perspectives on critical historical issues, to providing biographical treatments of key figures related to each event, to offering excerpts and complete texts of essential documents about the event, to suggesting and describing books and media materials for further study and presentation of the event, and more. The combination of historical narrative and individual topical chapters addressing significant issues and problems encourages students and teachers to approach each historic event from multiple perspectives and with a critical eye. The arrangement and content of each book thus invite students and teachers, through classroom discussions and position papers, to debate the character and significance of great historic events and to discover for themselves how and why history matters.

The series emphasizes the main currents that have shaped the modern world. Much of that focus necessarily looks at the West, especially Europe and the United States. The political, commercial, and cultural expansion of the West wrought largely, though not wholly, the most fundamental changes of the century. Taken together, however, books in the series reveal the interactions between Western and non-Western peoples and society, and also the tensions between modern and traditional cultures. They also point to the ways in which non-Western peoples have adapted Western ideas and technology and, in turn, influenced Western life and thought. Several books examine such increasingly powerful global forces as the rise of Islamic fundamentalism, the emergence of modern Japan, the Communist revolution in China, and the collapse of communism in eastern Europe and the former Soviet Union. American interests and experiences receive special attention in the series, not only in deference to the primary readership of the books but also in recognition that the United States emerged as the dominant political, economic, social, and cultural force during the twentieth century. By looking at the century through the lens of American events and experiences, it is possible to see why the age has come to be known as "The American Century."

Assessing the history of the twentieth century is a formidable prospect. It has been a period of remarkable transformation. The world broadened and narrowed at the same time. Frontiers shifted from the interiors of Africa and Latin America to the moon and beyond; communication spread from mass circulation newspapers and magazines to radio, television, and now the Internet; skyscrapers reached upward and suburbs stretched outward; energy switched from steam, to electric, to atomic power. Many changes did not lead to a complete abandonment of established patterns and practices so much as a synthesis of old and new, as, for example, the increased use of (even reliance on) the telephone in the age of the computer. The automobile and the truck, the airplane, and telecommunications closed distances, and people in unprecedented numbers migrated from rural to urban, industrial, and ever more ethnically diverse areas. Tractors and chemical fertilizers made it possible for fewer people to grow more, but the environmental and demographic costs of an exploding global population threatened to outstrip natural resources and human innovation. Disparities in wealth increased, with developed nations prospering and underdeveloped nations starving. Amid the crumbling of former European colonial empires, Western technology, goods, and culture increasingly enveloped the globe, seeping into, and undermining, non-Western cultures—a process that contributed to a surge of religious fundamentalism and ethno-nationalism in the Middle East, Asia, and Africa. As people became more alike, they also became more aware of their differences. Ethnic and religious rivalries grew in intensity everywhere as the century closed.

The political changes during the twentieth century have been no less profound than the social, economic, and cultural ones. Many of the books in the series focus on political events, broadly defined, but no books are confined to politics alone. Political ideas and events have social effects, just as they spring from a complex interplay of non-political forces in culture, society, and economy. Thus, for example, the modern civil rights and woman's rights movements were at once social and political events in cause and consequence. Likewise, the Cold War created the geopolitical framework for dealing with competing ideologies and nations abroad and served as the touchstone for political and cultural identities at home. The books treating political events do so within their social, cultural, and economic contexts.

Several books in the series examine particular wars in depth. Wars are defining moments for people and eras. During the twentieth century war became more widespread and terrible than ever before, encouraging new efforts to end war through strategies and organizations of international cooperation and disarmament while also fueling new ideologies and instruments of mass persuasion that fostered distrust and festered old national rivalries. Two world wars during the century redrew the political map, slaughtered or uprooted two generations of people, and introduced and hastened the development of new technologies and weapons of mass destruction. The First World War spelled the end of the old European order and spurred communist revolution in Russia and fascism in Italy, Germany, and elsewhere. The Second World War killed fascism and inspired the final push for freedom from European colonial rule in Asia and Africa. It also led to the Cold War that suffocated much of the world for almost half a century. Large wars begat small ones, and brutal totalitarian regimes cropped up across the globe. After (and in some ways because of) the fall of communism in eastern Europe and the former Soviet Union, wars of competing cultures, national interests, and political systems persisted in the struggle to make a new world order. Continuing, too, has been the belief that military technology can achieve political ends, whether in the superior American firepower that failed to "win" in Vietnam or in the American "smart bombs" and other military wizardry that "won" in the Persian Gulf.

Another theme evident in the series is that throughout the century nationalism has continued to drive events. Whether in the Balkans in 1914 triggering World War I or in the Balkans in the 1990s threatening the post–Cold War peace—or in many other places—nationalist ambitions and forces would not die. The persistence of nationalism is yet another reminder of the many ways that the past becomes prologue.

We thus offer the series as a modern guide to and interpretation of the historic events of the twentieth century and as an invitation to consider how and why those events have defined not only the past and present but also charted the political, social, intellectual, cultural, and economic routes into the next century.

Randall M. Miller
Saint Joseph's University, Philadelphia

Preface

After his death in 1994, some government officials and Nixon friends argued that Richard Nixon should be remembered for the totality of his life and career, not simply on the basis of the Watergate scandal. This, of course, is sound advice. But as much as one might wish otherwise, the overwhelming weight of Watergate will always overshadow the successes of the Nixon administration. Opening doors to China, ending the Vietnam War, negotiating détente with the Soviet Union, all add to Nixon's reputation as a skilled foreign policy president, but lurking over his reputation hangs the most grievous scandal in presidential history, a scandal that will always taint the reputation of Richard Milhous Nixon, 37th president of the United States.

This book is not an attempt to understand and evaluate the totality of the Nixon presidency (I have attempted that elsewhere [1]); rather, it is an effort to examine more closely the Watergate crisis, a crisis in leadership and public trust that forced the resignation of Richard Nixon and resulted in the conviction on criminal charges of over a dozen top administration officials. Those who wish to judge the impact and importance of the Nixon presidency must look at the big picture. Nixon *was* more than Watergate. But Watergate overshadows all else.

Why study Watergate? In and of itself, the Watergate crisis is an informative and fascinating case study in corruption, the lust for power, and efforts to control the excesses and abuses of power. But beyond this, the story of Watergate is important because this crisis opened the Pandora's box to an age of cynicism, which even today, over a quarter century later, pollutes the political atmosphere. In the aftermath of Watergate, the press has become more harsh and critical and also committed to "investigative journalism"; public trust in government has remained low; voter turnout has declined; the level of partisan conflict has increased in volume while decreasing in civility and substance to the detriment of the true priorities of the nation; and the use of special prosecutors has changed the politics in Washington and raised constitutional questions about privacy, self-incrimination, use of grand juries, "executive privilege," and the authority of the Justice Department. Thus Watergate is a good place to begin to understand the tribulations of contemporary politics.

In my lifetime, I probably have spent more time with Richard Nixon than is considered healthy. As a graduate student in the late 1970s, I decided that "one day I will write a book about Nixon." He had always intrigued, if also sometimes repulsed me. He was the seminal political figure of his—my—age, who became a metaphor not only for modern politics but also the corruption of power. In many ways, he was the American King Lear. I was determined to discover what made this man tick. In 1990 I published one such effort, *The Nixon Presidency: Power and Politics in Turbulent Times*. Now, a decade later, I am revisiting this still fascinating historical figure. What have I learned in the past decade? Has my view of Nixon changed?

As I have aged, hopefully matured, perhaps mellowed a bit, I find that the emotional intensity attached to my view of Nixon has softened. It is easier for me to be dispassionate, academic about my subject. I continue to be mesmerized by the deft touch Nixon occasionally was able to bring to politics and by the strategic insights he brought to bear on grand strategy. But I also find that time has not altered the sting of Watergate. It remains a profoundly sad and unnecessary scar on the political landscape. In the immediate aftermath of Nixon's resignation, some of his supporters claimed that "in a few years this Watergate thing will seem 'much ado about nothing.' " They were wrong. The legacy of Watergate lingers, a quarter century after the tragic events unfolded. Watergate had a profound and lasting impact on our political system. We are still trying to put Watergate behind us. If this book does not settle all the questions still outstanding about Watergate—for example, how much did Nixon know and when did he know it—it does provide a framework within which to understand the history and legacy of Watergate.

I have benefited from the assistance and support of a number of people in the preparation of this book. Research assistants Kent Jancarik, Pauline Batrikian, Mahira Vallin, and Clare Clamico were thorough and insightful. Neyse Dias' secretarial assistance and typing were greatly valued. Series editor Randall Miller offered useful and timely suggestions. Friends and colleagues lent support and encouragement. My deepest thanks to you all.

NOTE

1. Michael A. Genovese, *The Nixon Presidency: Power and Politics in Turbulent Times* (Westport, CT: Greenwood Press, 1990).

Key Players in the Watergate Crisis

Spiro T. Agnew, Vice President of the United States

Charles W. Colson, special counsel to the President

Archibald Cox, first special prosecutor

John W. Dean, president's counsel

John D. Ehrlichman, director of domestic policy

Sam J. Ervin, Senator, head of Select Committee to Investigate the 1972 Campaign Activities

Gerald R. Ford, Nixon's second Vice President

Alexander M. Haig, chief of staff during Nixon's final days

H. R. "Bob" Haldeman, Nixon's chief of staff

E. Howard Hunt, White House consultant, White House Plumber

Leon Jaworski, second special prosecutor

G. Gordon Liddy, "Plumber," general counsel to the Committee to Reelect the President

Jeb Stuart Magruder, deputy director, Committee to Reelect the President

James McCord, Watergate burglar

John Mitchell, attorney general, head of Nixon's 1968 and 1972 campaigns

Richard M. Nixon, 37th President of the United States

Elliott Richardson, held three Cabinet posts during the Nixon years, including attorney general

John Sirica, federal judge who presided over the Watergate trials

Woodward (Bob) and Bernstein (Carl), *Washington Post* reporters who broke the Watergate story

Ron Ziegler, Nixon's press secretary

Chronology of Events

1969

January 20   Richard M. Nixon is inaugurated the nation's 37th President.

January 21   Attorney General John Mitchell assures America of "vigorous" law enforcement.

March   The United States begins fourteen months of secret bombing of Cambodia, officially recognized as a neutral country.

April 3   The Vietnam War death toll reaches 33,641—more than the Korean War—making Vietnam the third costliest foreign war in U.S. history.

June 13   The Department of Justice reveals that it has wiretapped antiwar activists without court approval, and the government claims it has a legal right to eavesdrop on any domestic group "which seeks to attack and subvert the government by unlawful means."

1970

April 30   In a televised address on the war, President Nixon announces that he sent American troops into Cambodia in hopes of destroying North Vietnamese "headquarters" and "sanctuaries."

May 4   National Guard gunfire kills four students at Kent State University in Ohio after campus protest over the Cambodian invasion.

May 5   Campus demonstrations escalate as students protest the killings at Kent State.

May 8   President Nixon says that U.S. combat forces will start pulling
             out of Cambodia the following week and all will be out by
             mid-June.

May 14   Two black students are killed by police gunfire aimed at a stu-
             dent dormitory at Jackson State College in Mississippi.

June 5   At a secret White House meeting, President Nixon orders an
             interagency committee to make plans for stepped-up domestic
             intelligence.

June 25   The interagency committee on domestic intelligence secretly
             recommends a plan drawn up by White House aide Tom Char-
             les Houston that entails surreptitious entry and other activities
             he recognizes are "clearly illegal."

July 23   President Nixon approves the interagency committee's plans
             for "clearly illegal" covert activities.

July 28   FBI Director J. Edgar Hoover protests the July 23 Nixon deci-
             sion, and the president rescinds his approval of the commit-
             tee's plans.

1971

Early February   Technicians install tape recording equipment in the Oval Of-
             fice of the White House, the President's Executive Office
             Building office, the Cabinet Room, and the Lincoln Sitting
             Room to record conversations for posterity. The recording
             system is not revealed.

May 3   Antiwar protesters disrupt traffic and engage in widespread
             civil disobedience. District of Columbia police arrest 7,000 in
             one day and 5,000 more the next two days.

June 13   The *New York Times* begins publication of the classified Pen-
             tagon Papers, a government history of American involve-
             ment in Vietnam. President Nixon authorizes establishment
             of a "special investigations unit," later known as the Plumb-
             ers, to "stop security leaks and to investigate other sensitive
             security matters." John D. Ehrlichman, the president's chief
             domestic adviser, is appointed to supervise the operation,
             with Egil Krogh, an Ehrlichman deputy, in direct charge.
             David Young, E. Howard Hunt, Jr., and G. Gordon Liddy are
             also members of the unit. H. R. (Bob) Haldeman, the White
             House chief of staff, and presidential counsel John W. Dean
             III are among a select few who know about formation of the
             "Plumbers."

June 28   Daniel Ellsberg, a Defense Department official in the Johnson years, admits he leaked the Pentagon Papers to the press. A federal grand jury indicts him on a charge of stealing the documents.

June 30   The Supreme Court rules, 6 to 3, that the *New York Times* and the *Washington Post* are free to publish articles based on the Pentagon Papers because the government has not proved that national security was endangered.

August 11   Ehrlichman approves a memo written by Krogh and Young that proposes "a covert operation" to get Ellsberg's psychiatric records "if done under your assurance that it is not traceable."

September 3   Hunt, Liddy, Bernard Barker, Eugenio Martinez, and Felipe DeDiego burglarize the Los Angeles office of Ellsberg's psychiatrist. The CIA had given Hunt a special camera, a wig, and a "speech-altering device" for the mission.

September 16   At Charles Colson's suggestion, Hunt begins to compose fake diplomatic cables to implicate the Kennedy administration in the 1963 assassination of South Vietnamese President Ngo Dinh Diem.

1972
January 27   At a meeting in Mitchell's office attended by Mitchell, Dean, and Jeb Stuart Magruder, Liddy describes a $1 million campaign plan, which Mitchell later says included "mugging squads, kidnapping teams, prostitutes to compromise the opposition and electronic surveillance."

February 4   Mitchell, Dean, Magruder, and Liddy meet again to discuss Liddy's downwardly revised $500,000 plan, which includes wiretapping and photography. Mitchell makes no final decision, although later Magruder says Mitchell selected the Democratic National Committee at the Watergate for surveillance.

February 15   Attorney General Mitchell resigns and fifteen days later becomes chief of the Nixon reelection campaign.

March 30   At a Key Biscayne, Florida, meeting, Mitchell, Magruder, and Frederick C. LaRue, a Mitchell campaign aide, listen to Liddy's third campaign proposal. Magruder later says Mitchell approved spending $250,000 to disrupt the Democratic campaign; Mitchell says he did not.

April 4   Four bank drafts totaling $89,000 are issued to Nixon operatives by a Mexico City bank. The money came from Texas contributors to the Nixon campaign, and the donation was moved through Mexico to avoid disclosure (i.e., the money was "laundered").

April 7	The new federal campaign contribution reporting law takes effect, but millions of dollars in secret donations to the president's reelection campaign have been collected before this date.
April 19	A $25,000 check and the $89,000 in Mexican bank drafts are deposited in the Miami bank account of Bernard L. Barker's firm. He later withdraws the money in $100 bills, and it is used in the Watergate operation.
May 2	J. Edgar Hoover, for forty-eight years the FBI's director, dies.
May 3	President Nixon designates L. Patrick Gray II as the acting FBI director.
May 9	President Nixon announces that the United States has mined the North Vietnam harbors of Haiphong and other ports. Hundreds of U.S. bombers continue their massive bombing raids over North Vietnam.
May 22–29	President Nixon arrives in Moscow, becoming the first U.S. President to visit the Soviet Union.
May 28	The Democratic National Committee's headquarters in the Watergate office complex in Washington, D.C., are successfully entered, and eavesdropping devices implanted, by the Hunt-Liddy team.
June 17	James McCord, Frank Sturgis, Barker, Martinez, and Virgilio Gonzalez are arrested by Washington police inside the Democrats' Watergate headquarters, and police confiscate their cameras, eavesdropping equipment, and $2,300 in cash, mostly in $100 bills with serial numbers in sequence.
June 19	The Supreme Court rules that electronic surveillance by the federal government without court approval is unconstitutional.
June 19	White House press secretary Ronald L. Ziegler says he won't comment on the Watergate break-in, calling it "a third-rate burglary attempt."
June 23	Just days after the Watergate burglars are arrested, the president and Bob Haldeman agree to a plan to obstruct the FBI investigation.
June 29	Maurice Stans gives Herbert W. Kalmbach, the president's personal attorney, $75,000 after the lawyer says, "I am here on a special mission on a White House project and I need all the cash I can get." It is the first of about $500,000 used to buy the silence of the Watergate conspirators.

July 1	Mitchell quits as the president's campaign manager, citing personal reasons.
July 6	Gray talks with the president and tells him that "people on your staff are trying to wound you by using the CIA and FBI and by confusing the question of CIA interest in, or not in, people the FBI wishes to investigate." Gray says Mr. Nixon tells him, "Pat, you just continue to conduct your aggressive and thorough investigation."
August 26	The General Accounting Office, Congress's fiscal watchdog, reports "apparent violations" of the Federal Election Campaign Act by the Nixon reelection committee.
August 29	President Nixon says that Dean has conducted a thorough investigation of the Watergate break-in and "I can state categorically that his investigation indicates that no one in the White House staff, no one in this administration, presently employed, was involved in this very bizarre incident. What really hurts is if you try to cover it up." Dean later testifies that he had not heard of his investigation until the president's statement.
September 15	Liddy, Hunt, and the five men caught inside the Watergate on June 17 are indicted by a federal grand jury.
September 16	Attorney General Kleindienst says that the Watergate probe by the FBI and the U.S. Attorney's office in Washington was "one of the most intensive, objective and thorough" in many years.
October 10	The *Washington Post* reveals that the Watergate break-in was part of a massive campaign of political spying and sabotage conducted on behalf of the president's reelection and directed by White House and reelection committee officials.
October 25	Haldeman is revealed by the *Post* as among those authorized to approve payments from a secret espionage and sabotage fund. Ziegler denies the story as "the shoddiest type of journalism . . . that I do not think has been witnessed in the political process for some time."
November 7	Richard M. Nixon and Spiro T. Agnew are reelected in a landslide with 61 percent of the popular vote. They win in every state except Massachusetts.
Late December	Gray burns some Hunt documents along with the Christmas trash.

1973

January 3	Hunt reiterates his demands for more money and executive clemency in exchange for his silence.

January 11   Senator Sam J. Ervin, Jr. (D-N.C.) agrees to lead a Senate investigation of Watergate.

January 11   Hunt pleads guilty to six charges against him in the Watergate case. Four other defendants—Barker, Martinez, Gonzalez, and Frank Sturgis—follow suit four days later. And on January 30, Liddy and McCord are convicted.

January 12   John J. Caulfield, a White House aide and security operative, meets McCord on the George Washington Parkway in Virginia and offers him executive clemency "from the highest level of the White House." McCord refuses.

January 20   President Nixon is inaugurated for a second term and says "we stand on the threshold of a new era of peace."

January 23   President Nixon announces that the Vietnam War, the nation's longest and most divisive, is to end on January 28.

February 2   Judge John Sirica says that he is "not satisfied" that the whole Watergate story has been revealed.

February 7   The Senate votes, 70 to 0, to establish a committee with four Democrats and three Republicans to investigate Watergate and other 1972 campaign abuses.

March 19   McCord writes Judge Sirica a letter charging that perjury was committed at the Watergate trial, that defendants were pressured to plead guilty and keep quiet, that higher-ups were involved, and that "several members of my family have expressed fear for my life if I disclose knowledge of the facts of this matter."

March 21   Within hours of a White House meeting, arrangements are made to pay Hunt $75,000 in hush money.

March 23   Judge Sirica makes McCord's letter public and gives four of the Watergate defendants provisional sentences in an effort to encourage them to talk to the grand jury.

April 5   In San Clemente, Ehrlichman discusses the directorship of the FBI with the federal judge in the current Ellsberg case, W. Matt Byrne, Jr.

April 7   Judge Byrne rejects the FBI directorship.

April 12   Magruder confesses his perjury to prosecutors.

April 17   President Nixon says that a new "intensive" investigation has produced "major developments" and "real progress . . . in finding the truth" about Watergate.

April 17	Presidential press secretary Ziegler says all previous statements about Watergate are "inoperative."
April 27	Judge Byrne discloses a Justice Department memorandum on the break-in at Ellsberg's psychiatrist's office.
April 30	President Nixon accepts the resignations of Haldeman, Ehrlichman, and Kleindienst and fires Dean. Nixon accepts "responsibility" for Watergate.
May 7	The new Attorney General, Elliott Richardson, promises to appoint a special prosecutor in the growing Watergate scandal and give him "all the independence, authority and staff support" he needs.
May 10	Mitchell and Stans are indicted by a federal grand jury in New York on perjury and conspiracy charges in connection with the $200,000 campaign contribution of financier Robert L. Vesco.
May 11	Judge Byrne dismisses all charges in the Pentagon Papers case against Daniel Ellsberg. The judge cites government misconduct as the reason.
May 17	The televised Senate Watergate hearings begin.
May 18	Archibald Cox, former solicitor general of the United States, is named by Richardson as the Watergate special prosecutor.
July 16	White House aide Alexander Butterfield reveals the White House tape recording system.
July 25	The president says that he will not release White House tapes to Cox because it would jeopardize the "independence of the three branches of government."
September 4	Ehrlichman, Krogh, David Young, and G. Gordon Liddy are indicted by a California grand jury in Los Angeles in connection with the break-in at Ellsberg's psychiatrist's office.
October 10	In Federal Court in Baltimore, Vice President Spiro T. Agnew pleads no contest to a charge of income tax evasion, climaxing a lengthy investigation into kickbacks he accepted from contractors while he was Baltimore County executive, governor of Maryland, and Vice President of the United States. He is fined $10,000 and placed on three year's probation.
October 12	President Nixon, in a White House ceremony, nominates House Minority leader Gerald R. Ford of Michigan to be Vice President.
October 20	Cox, in a televised press conference, defends his decision not to compromise with the president on the tapes issue and em-

phasizes that he will not resign. A few hours later, Nixon press secretary Ziegler announces the firing of Cox and abolition of the special prosecutor's office, and the resignations of Richardson and Deputy Attorney General William D. Ruckelshaus for their refusal to fire Cox. The episode comes to be known as the "Saturday Night Massacre."

October 23   The White House says that it will release the tapes Cox sought.

October 30   The House Judiciary Committee starts consideration of possible impeachment procedures.

October 31   The White House says that two of the nine tape recordings scheduled for submission to Judge Sirica do not exist.

November 1   Senator William B. Saxbe (R-Ohio) becomes Nixon's fourth Attorney General, and Houston lawyer Leon Jaworski is appointed as the new special prosecutor.

November 14   White House attorneys learn that there is an 18½-minute gap in the June 20, 1972, tape of a Haldeman-Nixon meeting, and that fact is revealed publicly a week later.

November 17–20 President Nixon, in a series of appearances in the South, seeks public support for his embattled presidency. At one point, he says: "People have got to know whether or not their President is a crook. Well, I'm not a crook."

1974

January 15   A panel of technical experts determines that the 18½-minute gap in the June 20 tape is the result of five separate manual erasures.

February 6   The House votes 410 to 4 to proceed with the impeachment probe and to give the House Judiciary Committee broad subpoena powers.

March 1   Seven key former Nixon administration and campaign officials—Mitchell, Haldeman, Ehrlichman, Strachan, Robert Mardian, Kenneth Parkinson, and Colson—are indicted by a grand jury for allegedly conspiring to cover up the Watergate burglary. The special prosecutor, unsure of his right to indict a sitting president, names Nixon an "unindicted co-conspirator."

March 7   Ehrlichman, Colson, and five others are indicted by a federal grand jury for the break-in at Ellsberg's psychiatrist's office.

April 30   The White House releases 1,239 pages of edited transcripts, and they reveal brutally frank White House discussions on Watergate and administration and political personalities.

May 2   The Maryland Court of Appeals bars former Vice President Agnew from the practice of law, calling him "morally obtuse."

May 7   The president's chief defense lawyer, James D. St. Clair, says no more White House Watergate conversations will be turned over to either the special prosecutor or the House Judiciary Committee.

May 9   The House Judiciary Committee begins formal hearings on the possible impeachment of President Nixon.

May 16   Richard G. Kleindienst becomes the first of the nation's sixty-eight attorneys general to plead guilty to a criminal offense, that he refused to testify accurately during his Senate confirmation hearing. He later was sentenced to a month in jail and fined $100, but both were suspended.

May 21   Jeb Stuart Magruder, once the deputy director of President Nixon's reelection campaign, is sentenced to a prison term of ten months to four years for his part in the Watergate cover-up.

May 24   Special Watergate prosecutor Jaworski appeals directly to the Supreme Court to decide whether the president can withhold evidence in the criminal cases of his former aides. The Supreme Court a week later agrees to hear the case, bypassing the U.S. Court of Appeals.

June 3   Former presidential aide Charles W. Colson pleads guilty to obstructing justice for devising a White House scheme to influence the outcome of Daniel Ellsberg's Pentagon Papers trial by defaming Ellsberg and destroying his public image.

June 21   Colson is sentenced to one to three years' imprisonment and fined $5,000 for obstructing justice in the prosecution of Ellsberg.

July 12   John D. Ehrlichman, once the No. 2 man on President Nixon's White House staff, is convicted of perjury and violating the civil rights of Ellsberg's psychiatrist in connection with the break-in at the doctor's office.

July 24   The Supreme Court, ruling 8–0 that President Nixon has no right to withhold evidence in criminal proceedings, orders him to turn over sixty-four White House tapes of Watergate discussions. The president agrees to turn over the tapes.

July 24   After ten weeks of evidence gathering, the House Judiciary Committee begins debate on articles of impeachment against Richard Nixon.

July 27   The House Judiciary Committee, on a 27 to 11 vote, recommends that President Nixon be impeached because his actions formed a "course of conduct or plan" to obstruct the investigation of the Watergate break-in and to cover up other unlawful activities.

July 29   The committee votes 28 to 10 for a second article of impeachment, alleging the president's repeated misuse of his power to violate the constitutional rights of American citizens.

July 30   The House Judiciary Committee votes 21 to 17 for a third article of impeachment against President Nixon for defying its subpoenas. The committee concluded its inquiry after rejecting two additional articles—one involving the secret bombing of Cambodia (26 to 12), and the other, tax fraud and unconstitutional receipt of improvements from the federal government for his private homes (26 to 12).

July 31   John D. Ehrlichman is sentenced to serve a minimum of twenty months to a maximum of five years in prison. The former White House domestic affairs adviser was convicted July 12, 1974, on charges of conspiracy and perjury growing out of the burglary of the office of Daniel Ellsberg's psychiatrist.

August 2   Judge John J. Sirica sentences former White House counsel John Dean to a minimum of one year to a maximum of four years in prison for conspiracy to obstruct justice in the Watergate case.

August 5   Three new transcripts, recounting conversations on June 23, 1972, between Richard Nixon and H. R. Haldeman, are released by the White House. The tapes reveal that President Nixon personally ordered a cover up of the investigation of Watergate within six days after the illegal entry into the Democrat's national headquarters was discovered. The transcripts completely undermine the president's previous insistence that he was uninvolved in the cover-up and show that he directed efforts to hide the involvement of his aides in the Watergate break-in through a series of orders to conceal details about the break-in. With the transcripts release, the president released a statement about his position and noted, "Although I recognized that these presented potential problems, I did not inform my staff or counsel of it, or those arguing my case, nor did I amend my submission to the Judiciary committee in order to include and reflect it."

August 6   All the Republicans on the House Judiciary Committee who had voted against impeachment turn around and announce they would vote in favor of at least the obstruction of justice article.

August 7   President Nixon meets for a half-hour with Senate Minority Leader Hugh Scott, House Minority Leader John Rhodes, and Senator Barry Goldwater. The president was told that he had about fifteen votes against conviction in the Senate and perhaps only ten votes against impeachment in the House.

August 8   Richard Milhous Nixon announces on television that he would resign his office, effective at noon, August 9. At that time, Gerald Ford, whom Nixon nominated for Vice President on October 12, 1973, would be sworn in as the 38th President, to serve out the 895 remaining days of Nixon's second term.

September 8   President Ford grants Nixon a "full, free, and absolute pardon" for any crimes he may have committed as president.

THE WATERGATE CRISIS
EXPLAINED

I

Historical Overview

Watergate was the most serious scandal in the history of U.S. presidential politics. It was unusual in presidential history because for the first time the president himself was deeply involved in the crimes of his administration. Watergate was a different kind of scandal. Richard Nixon was a different kind of president.[1]

The roots of Watergate extend as far back as the war in Vietnam and the divisiveness it caused at home. Richard Nixon was elected president in 1968 in the midst of that long divisive war. He was elected, in part, on his promise to end the war. But when he became president, he realized that getting out of Vietnam would be no easy task. Public protests against the war exerted much pressure on Nixon to bring the war to an end. But the president could find no way to get out of Vietnam "with honor." The war dragged on, and antiwar protests spread. Out of his determination not to be destroyed by the war, as his predecessor Lyndon B. Johnson was, Nixon proceeded on a path of leak plugging, wiretapping, a secret war in Cambodia, and a series of criminal acts that in the end led to his downfall and fed the already significant erosion of public trust in government.

"Watergate" is a generic term that originally only referred to the break-in of the Democratic National Committee (DNC) headquarters located in Washington, D.C., at the Watergate office complex, but it has come to be an umbrella term, under which a wide variety of crimes and improper acts are included. Watergate caused the downfall of a president. It led to jail sentences for over a dozen of the highest-ranking officials of the administration. It was a traumatic experience for the nation. Why Watergate? How could it have happened? How could someone as intelligent and experienced as Richard Nixon behave so criminally and so stupidly? How could someone so adroit and practiced in the art and science of politics behave so foolishly? How could a "third-rate burglary" turn into a national disaster? How could Richard Nixon have done it to himself?

In essence, Watergate involved three separate, but interconnected, conspiracies. The first conspiracy was the *Plumbers conspiracy*, which took place during Nixon's first term (1969–1973). This involved plugging leaks and "getting" Nixon's political enemies, illegal wiretapping, the break-in of Pentagon Papers distributor Daniel Ellsberg's psychiatrist's office, and other acts, done in some instances for ostensible "national security" reasons and at other times for purely political reasons. The purpose of this conspiracy was to destroy political enemies and strengthen the president's political position.

The second conspiracy was the *reelection conspiracy*. This grew out of lawful efforts to reelect the president but degenerated into illegal efforts to extort money; launder money; sabotage the electoral process; spy; commit fraud, forgery, and burglary; play "dirty tricks"; and attack Democratic front-runners. The purposes of this conspiracy were to (a) knock the stronger potential Democratic candidates (Senators Hubert Humphrey, Edward Kennedy, Edmund Muskie, and Henry "Scoop" Jackson) out of the race; (b) accumulate enough money to bury the Democratic opponent by massively outspending him; and (c) thus guarantee the reelection of Richard Nixon. This conspiracy was conscious, deliberate, and organized.

The third conspiracy was the *cover-up conspiracy*. Almost immediately after the burglars were caught at the Democratic National Committee (DNC) headquarters in the Watergate office complex, a criminal conspiracy began that was designed to mislead law enforcement officers and protect the reelection bid of the president, and then after the election, to keep the criminal investigations away from the White House. To this end, evidence was destroyed, perjury was committed, lies were told, investigations were obstructed, and subpoenas were defied. The purpose of the cover-up was to contain the criminal charges and protect the president. This conspiracy was less conscious, almost instinctive. It was deliberate but poorly organized.

One can divide Watergate activities into four categories: the *partisan* arena, the *policy* arena, the *financial* arena, and the *legal* arena.[2] The *partisan* activities include acts taken against those of the opposition party and those deemed to be "enemies" of the administration. They include wiretapping and break-ins, the establishment of the Huston Plan, the Plumbers and the "enemies list"; forged State Department cables, and political dirty tricks.

Policy activities include the stretching of presidential power beyond legal or constitutional limits. Examples include the secret bombing of Cambodia, the impoundment of congressionally appropriated funds, attempts to dismantle programs authorized by Congress, the extensive use of executive privilege and underenforcement of laws such as the Civil Rights Act of 1964. When Nixon's defenders answer charges against the president by saying that "everybody does it," they are most often referring to this area of behavior.

In the *financial* area, both Nixon's political and personal finances deserve mention. On the political front, the "selling" of ambassadorships, the extortion of money in the form of illegal campaign contributions, and the laundering of money must be included. In Nixon's personal finances, such things as "irregularities" in income tax deductions and questionable "security" improvements in his private Florida and California homes, paid for with tax dollars, are included.

Finally, in the *legal* arena, illegal activities of the Nixon administration include obstruction of justice, perjury, criminal cover-up, interference with criminal investigations, and destruction of evidence. It was the criminal cover-up that eventually led to Nixon's forced resignation.

Categorizing and classifying Watergate behavior does a disservice to the drama and suspense of the unfurling of this political mystery. The story of Nixon's rise and fall, of his choices at several important points in the story, of his ultimate collapse is what makes this drama so poignant and tragic.

THE ROOTS OF WATERGATE

To understand Watergate and the behavior of President Nixon, we must always keep in mind that Watergate did not occur in a vacuum. Context is always important in analyzing events. The series of steps that led to the downfall of Richard Nixon took place in the middle of a divisive war in Southeast Asia, amid domestic protests against that war, during a reorientation of relations between the United States and Soviet Union as well as with China, and during continued troubles in the Middle East and elsewhere. All presidents are compelled to juggle several political balls in the air at one time, and we should keep in mind that as Nixon was making decisions about Watergate, he was also dealing with a vast array of other complex issues.

Vietnam was a war Nixon inherited. At the time Nixon came to the presidency, the war was stalemated, with no victory in sight. It caused domestic strife, protest marches, civil disobedience, the emergence of a counterculture among the young, and a growing distrust of the government and the military. The war was tearing the nation apart. A long, slow, almost unnoticed process got the United States into Vietnam. Decisions by Presidents Dwight D. Eisenhower, John F. Kennedy, and Lyndon B. Johnson brought the United States further and further into a Southeast Asian land war that, in 1969, many Americans saw as unwinnable.

The United States had approximately 520,000 troops in Vietnam when Nixon took office. In fact, a great deal of Nixon's success in the 1968 election was attributed to the failure of Lyndon Johnson and Democrats to win or effectively prosecute the war in Vietnam. This left the Democrats deeply divided and allowed candidate Nixon to talk of a "plan" to end the war. Nixon was, in 1968, the peace candidate. In point of fact, Nixon's "plan" to end the war wasn't much of a plan at all. His early efforts at a negotiated compromise didn't work—North Vietnam wanted victory, not capitulation.

The chief goals of Nixon in Vietnam were to get the United States out of Vietnam, preserve American honor, get the American prisoners of war home, and, he hoped, give South Vietnam a chance for independence from the North. It was the last goal that proved to be America's undoing, because the North Vietnamese would not accept a divided nation. They wanted victory and were determined to achieve it regardless of cost.

Nixon knew that the war had to be ended soon lest he be dragged down by it. "I'm not going to end up like LBJ, holed up in the White House afraid to show my face on the street. I'm going to stop that war fast," he said.[3] Vietnam became the overriding issue of the first term. In effect, everything else internationally and at home was predicated on ending the war in Vietnam.

In late January 1969 Nixon decided that he could not simply pull out of Vietnam, but he could not continue to prosecute the war as Johnson had. He would execute a gradual withdrawal of American fighting forces, thereby diffusing and defusing the antiwar movement at home; he would seek a negotiated agreement with the North, thereby allowing the United States to preserve its honor; and he would dramatically increase the bombing in Southeast Asia, thereby bombing the North into an agreement, while reassuring South Vietnam that American air power could cover the pullout of U.S. combat forces.

THE WAR SPREADS: CAMBODIA AND BEYOND

In 1969, despite Nixon's repeated promises to wind down the war, the president expanded the conflict into Cambodia. Nixon widened the war by secretly bombing North Vietnamese forces based inside the neutral nation of Cambodia. In 1970 Nixon sent troops into Cambodia. It was, for Nixon, a tacit claim of independent war-making powers that suggested an expansive, even imperial, interpretation of presidential power. The secret war in Cambodia was truly a presidential war, conducted by the executive branch on its own, with almost no congressional approval or oversight, little public scrutiny, and no democratic controls. This was Nixon's war.

The president's goal in Cambodia was to disrupt enemy supply lines and attack the North Vietnamese in their "safe" havens inside Cambodia. But to keep this mission secret, the military had to set up improvised command chains outside of normal military channels, file false reports, and create a duel reporting system.

On April 30, 1970, the president went on national television and shocked the nation with his announcement that he had ordered American troops into Cambodia. "The time has come for action," the president said. This decision went to "the heart of the trouble." The president said he was outraged that the enemy had violated the neutrality of Cambodia by setting up sanctuaries there and that "American policy has been to scrupulously respect the neutrality of the Cambodian people." He continued, "Neither the United States nor South Vietnam has moved against these enemy sanctuaries, because we did not wish to violate the territory of a neutral nation."[4]

President Nixon went on to say, "We live in an age of anarchy both abroad and at home. We see mindless attacks on all the great institutions, which have been created by free civilizations in the last five hundred years. Even here in the United States, great universities are being systematically destroyed." With so much in the balance, the president issued a warning. "If, when the chips are down the world's most powerful nation, the United States of America, acts like a pitiful, helpless giant, the forces of totalitarianism and anarchy will threaten free nations and free institutions throughout the world." He added, "We will not be humiliated. We will not be defeated," and "it is not our power but our will and character that is being tested tonight. . . . If we fail to meet the challenge, all other nations will be on notice that despite its overwhelming power, the United States, when real crisis comes, will be found wanting."

Because of the Cambodian invasion, the war at home heated up beyond anything the president expected. The campuses immediately erupted. Nixon's comment about "bums blowing up campuses" was published and further fired up the already outraged protesters. Four hundred forty-eight colleges declared themselves "on strike." Many rioted. Police had to protect the White House from the over 100,000 protesters who converged on Washington.

The mood in the White House was tense. A siege mentality captured the president and his top aides. Then on May 4 tragedy struck. At an antiwar demonstration at Kent State University in Ohio, National Guardsmen opened fire on a group of protesters and bystanders. Nine people were wounded; four were killed.

The biggest student strikes in U.S history followed. On May 9, over 250,000 demonstrators descended on Washington, and across the country campuses shut down. Dr. Clark Kerr, who chaired a Carnegie Commission study on higher education, reported that 89 percent of all independent universities and 76 percent of all public universities held demonstrations.[5]

The president's response was brief and insensitive. In a statement read to the press by Press Secretary Ron Ziegler, Nixon said that "this should remind us all once again that when dissent turns to violence, it invites tragedy. It is my hope that this tragic and unfortunate incident will strengthen the determination of all the nation's campuses administrators, faculty, and students alike to stand firmly for the right which exists in this country of peaceful dissent and just as strongly against the resort to violence as a means of such expression."[6] Less than two weeks later, two more students were killed at Jackson State College in Mississippi.

The public pressure on Nixon was enormous. The expanded war with only a marginal hope for an honorable settlement, domestic turmoil, and dissension within his own administration—all ate at the president. Nixon seemed near the breaking point on May 8 when a series of bizarre incidents occurred. He spent nearly the entire evening and early morning on the telephone, calling officials, friends, relatives; some he called several times. (According to White House logs, the president called his chief of staff Bob Haldeman seven times and his national security adviser Henry Kissinger eight times, the last call taking place at 3:38 A.M.) He wanted to know what they thought of him, how they viewed events of the past weeks. In all, Nixon made fifty-one calls the evening and morning of May 8–9.

The president had trouble sleeping that night, so just before 5:00 A.M. he ordered his limousine, and he and valet Manolo Sanchez drove to the Lincoln Memorial where a group of antiwar protesters were camping out. Upon arriving at the Lincoln Memorial, the president got out of the car and began talking to the protesters. Nixon defended the invasion of Cambodia, saying that he hoped it would bring a quicker end to the war. Then he began to reminisce about his youth, urged the young people to travel, and then he was gone. From there, Nixon ordered his driver to go to the Senate Building, where, upon finding the building locked, Nixon went to the House, where a custodian let the president in. Nixon went to the seat he had occupied as a congressman and told Manolo Sanchez to sit in the Speaker's chair and make a speech. Then Nixon went to the Mayflower Hotel for breakfast, after which the returned to the White House at 7:30 A.M.

In the long run, the bombing and the invasion of Cambodia backfired on the president. A limited military success, the event sparked a storm of domestic protest and led to a major political setback as Congress passed a resolution prohibiting funds from being used in Cambodia. With the invasion, Vietnam became "Nixon's War." Nixon overreacted to the criticism. The secret bombing of Cambodia set into motion a series of events that would lead the administration down a path of illegality and impropriety that culminated in Watergate and the resignation of a president.

THE WAR AT HOME

The domestic upheaval created by the war in Vietnam had a profound impact on the Nixon administration. As the war dragged on, the general public became increasingly dissatisfied with the way Lyndon Johnson and Richard Nixon had handled the war. Johnson was driven from office, declining to run for reelection in 1968 because of opposition to his Vietnam policies among the public. When Richard Nixon won the presidency as the "peace candidate" promising to end the war, hopes that his plan could quickly be implemented soon gave way to frustration and anger among the public. And as the war dragged on and on, the antiwar movement picked up numbers with each passing day.

Richard Nixon seemed to take the antiwar marches personally. Politically, he knew that the growing antiwar movement was narrowing both his time and his options in Southeast Asia. But on a personal level, Nixon felt a special uneasiness about the demonstrators. The opponents of the war seemed to tap something dark and menacing within Nixon. He felt threatened by the protesters, and would not, could not, sit idly by while the protesters dragged him down as they had done to his predecessor. Nixon was determined not to be their victim. He would act. But these acts planted seeds of illegal and immoral activities that would eventually lead to the president's downfall.[7]

Vice President Agnew became the administration point man in its "war" against antiwar protesters. In May 1969 Agnew said, "In my judgment, the war in Vietnam would be over today if we could simply stop the demonstrations in the streets of the United States." Later Agnew said that "a society which comes to fear its children is effete. A sniveling, hand-wringing power structure deserves the violent rebellion it encourages. If my generation doesn't stop cringing, yours will inherit a lawless society where emotion and muscle displace reason." Agnew promised that the Nixon administration would "separate them from our society with no more regret than we should feel over discarding rotten apples from a barrel."

To prosecute the war successfully, Nixon needed a stable base of domestic support, which the antiwar movement was clearly undermining. Nixon could not accept this. So began a series of domestic activities aimed at stifling dissent and protest. It was the beginning of the end of the Nixon presidency. H. R. Haldeman wrote, "I firmly believe that without the Vietnam War there would have been no Watergate."[8]

PLUGGING LEAKS

The failure of the president's Vietnam policy, the mounting pressure of domestic protest, the seeming disloyalty of some administration officials, Nixon's predisposition to see adversaries as enemies, and the leaks of information to the press all came together and helped create a siege mentality in the White House. Indeed, a form of paranoia began to creep in and distort the judgment of administration officials.

One of the most serious irritants to Nixon and Kissinger was the profusion of information being leaked to the press. Leaking information was an art deftly used by Nixon and especially Kissinger. At his first staff meeting in January 1969, Kissinger declared, "If anybody leaks anything, I will do the leaking." But others were leaking information, and both Nixon and Kissinger believed that some of the leaks endangered national security and undermined the administration's position. Consequently the president and his national security adviser set out to plug the leaks.

From the first months in office, top Nixon people were complaining of leaks, and the president was furious about them, repeatedly complaining to Bob Haldeman at their daily meetings. In an effort to stop the leaks, Nixon ordered investigations, interviews, lie detector tests, sworn affidavits, and depositions; finally, the administration engaged in wiretaps and break-ins. As the president wrote, "It was decided that when leaks occurred Kissinger would supply [FBI director] Hoover with the names of individuals who had had access to the leaked materials and whom he had any cause to suspect. I authorized Hoover to take the necessary steps including wiretapping to investigate leaks and find the leakers." And the president wanted "maximum secrecy on this wiretap project."[9]

THE WIRETAPS

The president's legitimate need to protect the privacy of executive branch information and Nixon's near paranoia about loyalty and secrecy—real needs and false fears—led to acts of illegality, a series of warrantless wiretaps in 1969. In early May 1969 in an article in the *New York Times*, William Beecher revealed the secret of the bombing of Cambodia. The revelation, according to Nixon speech writer William Safire, "drove Henry Kissinger up his basement office wall."[10] Nixon and Kissinger were furious. Kissinger spoke to FBI director J. Edgar Hoover several times that day, insisting that the FBI find the source of the leak. According to a Hoover memorandum, the White House would "destroy whoever did this if we can find him, no matter where he is."[11]

Nixon and Kissinger were so outraged at the leak of information that after only three months in office, they took matters into their own hands and instituted a series of wiretaps aimed at discovering the source of the Beecher leak. The fact that so early in his first term the president had decided to bypass the FBI and act independently of the other agencies of the government speaks volumes to Nixon's distrust of others, even the FBI. Newspaper reporters, (e.g., Beecher), Nixon administration officials (e.g., NSC staffer Morton Halperin), and others (e.g., Defense Department aides) were tapped with the approval of the president. Kissinger and NSC aide Alexander Haig supplied the names of suspected leakers to the FBI, and at least one of the taps (Halperin's) was installed before Attorney General John Mitchell signed the authorization for the wiretap (the Halperin wiretap remained active for twenty-one months).

Kissinger danced around his own role in the ordering of wiretaps, but there can be no doubt of the central role he and the president played in this affair. All the participants were aware of the need to keep the wiretaps a secret, and each knew of the danger if the existence of the taps was revealed. In notes taken by Bob Haldeman at a 1969 meeting with the president, John Ehrlichman, and Kissinger, Ehrlichman gives the following cautionary advice:

> Re taps impt. for K. To get the files out of his office
> Thru E & Mitchel find someone to read taps
>   Maybe use Huston etc. for this
> Work out a scheme minimize what done thru Hoover
>   esp. newsmen shld be done outsider
> K. shldn't be reading these[12]

Soon, other reporters were added to the list to be wiretapped (e.g., Hedrick Smith, Marvin Kalb, Joseph Kraft). All the taps were installed *without warrants*. But afterwards, when the wiretaps were revealed, the president, Kissinger, and Haig had conflicting stories about who ordered what, and all had partial memory lapses concerning the events.

THE HUSTON PLAN

In his speech on the Cambodian invasion, the president spoke of being in the "age of anarchy," and Nixon was determined not to let the age get the best of him. In his memoirs Nixon wrote of 1970 as a time when the nation was faced with an "epidemic of unprecedented domestic terrorism" and of "highly organized and highly skilled revolutionaries dedicated to the violent destruction of our democratic system."[13] Thus, in June 1970, the president ordered a reassessment of the government's domestic intelligence gathering capacity. Haldeman assigned aide Tom Huston, a former defense intelligence officer, to oversee the project.

On June 5, 1970, CIA director Richard Helms, FBI director Hoover, National Security Agency head Vice Admiral Noel Gayler, Defense Intelligence Agency head Lieutenant General Donald Bennett, Haldeman, Ehrlichman, and the president met to coordinate their activities against domestic disturbances. After several subsequent meetings, the group (called the Intelligence Evaluation Committee) arrived at a plan, called the Huston Plan.

This plan, which Senator Sam Ervin later described as evidence of a "Gestapo mentality," called for opening of mail and tapping of telephones without warrants, breaking into homes and offices, and spying on student groups. Huston admitted to Nixon and the others that "covert [mail] coverage is illegal and there are serious risks involved," and that surreptitious entry "is clearly illegal; it amounts to burglary. It is also highly risky and could result in great embarrassment if exposed."[14]

On July 14, 1970, Bob Haldeman sent Huston a memo that read:

The recommendations you have proposed as a result of the review, have been approved by the President. He does not, however, want to follow the procedure you outlined on page four of your memorandum regarding implementation. He would prefer that the thing simply be put into motion on the basis of this approval.[15]

The president approved the plan.

But it was not long before J. Edgar Hoover raised objections. "The risks are too great," Hoover told Nixon through Huston, "these folks are going to get the President into trouble." Nixon reluctantly withdrew his approval.

Nixon would defend his approval of the Huston Plan with an "everybody does it" defense. In response to a Senate interrogatory in 1976, Nixon said his approval was based on what previous administrations had done and claimed inherent powers that, he argued, were legal when the president acted for national security reasons.

While the Huston Plan died, the idea of developing an expanded domestic intelligence operation run out of the White House did not. Through the Justice Department and John Mitchell, a new Intelligence Evaluation Committee was formed, and through the CIA, domestic intelligence gathering, which is illegal under the CIA charter, expanded, in the form of Operation Chaos. The web of illegal activities was spreading.

MONDAY MELEE AND TEAMSTERS THUGS

As the antiwar demonstrations grew, a fortress was erected around the White House, and the administration felt besieged. In May 1971, antiwar activists scheduled a demonstration for Washington, D.C., with the ambitious goal of "stopping the government." The demonstration did succeed in stopping D.C. traffic and interfering with daily commuters as they tried to get to work, but the government was not shut down.

Initially, the D.C. police acted with restraint and flexibility. But on instructions from the president, who was at the "Western White House" in San Clemente, California, Attorney General Mitchell was put in charge of dealing with the protesters. With the help of the National Guard, the army, and the Marines, the D.C. police conducted a massive and indiscriminate arrest operation. On Monday, May 3, 7,200 people, protesters as well as innocent bystanders, reporters, and people trying to get to work were incarcerated, the most ever incarcerated in the United States in a single day. Over a four-day period, 13,400 people were arrested.

The jails could not accommodate so many people; 1,700 were taken to a practice field around RFK Stadium, where they were locked up; few of those arrested were read their rights or charged with any crime, normal arresting procedures were ignored, and some were kept locked up over twelve hours with no toilet facilities, unable to make any phone calls, and unable to contact lawyers. The inevitable consequence of these wholesale arrests and violations of civil liberties was that of the over 13,000 people who were incarcerated, all but about two dozen had their cases thrown out of court.

Nixon returned to the White House from San Clemente in the midst of the May Day demonstrations. Infuriated at the protesters, Nixon wanted a firmer, more-forceful response on the part of the government. On May 5, the demonstrators marched on the Capitol. Twelve hundred people were taken into custody. In the White House, Nixon and Haldeman discussed ways to deal with the protesters.

A tape recording of the May 5, 1971, conversation reveals a bizarre and frightening discussion between the president and his chief of staff. Perhaps nowhere is the dark side of Nixon more clearly seen than in this tape. The president, angered by the activities of the antiwar protesters, endorsed a suggestion that "thugs" from the Teamsters Union be used to attack demonstrators. According to the president, the Teamsters were to "go in and knock their heads off." "Sure," Haldeman replied, "murderers. Guys that really, you know, that's what they really do. . . . It's the regular strikebusters-types and all that . . . and then they're gonna beat the [obscenity] out of some of these people. And, uh, and hope they really hurt'em. You know . . . smash some noses."[16] The thought of the president of the United States demeaning his office by advocating that Teamster thugs go after American citizens and "knock their heads off" is shocking. But this is not the first time the president discussed roughing up American citizens. On Air Force One, on a trip to California, Haldeman's notes of a July 24, 1970, in-flight meeting with the president contain the following note:

> Get a goon squad to start roughing up demo's
> VFW or Legion no insults to P.
> use hard hats

On May 26, Nixon met with a group of construction workers and long-shoremen who had attacked some antiwar marchers in New York. The president told the group he found their actions "very meaningful." There is nothing to suggest that in this particular case the president or Haldeman directly ordered or encouraged these men to attack the marchers.

THE PENTAGON PAPERS

Slightly more than one month after the May Day melee, another shock hit the administration: the publication of the Pentagon Papers. It led to an unprecedented effort by the administration to exercise prior restraint and censorship against the press.

On June 13, 1971, the *New York Times* began to publish excerpts of a top-secret study of the origins and conduct of the war in Vietnam. The study was begun in 1967 by Secretary of Defense Robert McNamara. It was given to the *Times* by Daniel Ellsberg, a former employee of McNamara who had become disillusioned with the war.

The study, a forty-seven-volume report entitled "History of U.S. Decision-Making Process on Vietnam Policy," became known as the Pentagon Papers. It included a detailed account of how President Johnson had misled the Congress and public about Vietnam. The Nixon administration, through the Justice Department, got the Federal District Court for the Southern District of New York to issue a temporary injunction, based on national security grounds, ordering the *Times* to cease publication of stories based on the Pentagon Papers.

But other papers also received copies of the Papers, and began to publish them. These newspapers were also ordered to cease publication. The case very quickly got to the Supreme Court, and on June 30, 1971, the Court ruled against the government, allowing publication of the Pentagon Papers. The court's vote was 6 to 3, and it rejected the administration's claim of an inherent power to prevent publication of material on national security grounds.

In the arguments of the Nixon administration, there developed an expansive notion of a powerful "National Security State," with rights and powers that went far beyond the Constitution and laws. The sweeping claim of inherent powers and the covert "national security" apparatus set up by the Nixon administration distorted the impact of the Constitution and created the framework for an increase of presidential power, as well as the abuse of presidential power.

Although the Pentagon Papers did not deal directly with the Nixon administration, the president believed that publishing the papers would undermine his efforts to control Vietnam policy. To indicate the importance of this case to the Nixon administration, there was serious consideration given to having the president argue the case before the Supreme Court. In the end, it was decided that this was too risky.

Charles Colson has called the events surrounding the Pentagon Papers issue "the beginning of the end." It was here that the administration really began to "cross the line."[17] Indeed, the events that followed the release of the Pentagon Papers relate directly to the downfall of the Nixon presidency.

As the administration went to court to try to halt publication of the Pentagon Papers, a secret effort to discredit and defame Daniel Ellsberg was also going on. Colson, who pleaded guilty to obstructing justice in the Ellsberg trial, said on June 24, 1971: "The president on numerous occasions urged me to disseminate damaging information about Daniel Ellsberg, including information about Ellsberg's attorney and others with whom Ellsberg had been in contact."[18]

Nixon's urgings led Colson to contact his longtime friend Howard Hunt to discuss the possibility of "nailing Ellsberg." Colson taped his conversation with Hunt and gave Ehrlichman a transcript along with the recommendation that he hire Hunt. The seeds that would grow into the Plumbers were planted.

THE PLUMBERS

Frustrated by the Supreme Court decision to allow publication of the Pentagon Papers; frustrated by the FBI's inability to stop information leaks; suspicious of the loyalty of the FBI, CIA, and other government agencies; unhappy with the lack of response to their overtures to the bureaucracy on security matters; paranoid about events surrounding the antiwar movement and domestic dissent; and generally displeased with the quality of government work—the Nixon administration decided to take matters into its own hands. In 1971 a special White House secret apparatus was organized to deal with such matters as plugging leaks. The Special Investigations Unit, known as the Plumbers, because their job was to plug leaks, met in Room 16 of the Old Executive Office Building. This clandestine group began to do more than originally charged.

On June 17, 1971, only four days after the *New York Times* published its first story about the Pentagon Papers, Kissinger, Haldeman, Ehrlichman, and the president met in the Oval office to discuss Daniel Ellsberg. Kissinger was worried that Ellsberg might have other material and described him (according to John Ehrlichman) as a drug user, a genius, and a threat to national security. He had to be discredited, prosecuted, and stopped.

Because Nixon felt that the FBI and other agencies were inept, uncooperative, and disloyal, the only recourse was for the White House to set up its own intelligence gathering and covert operations capacity. To head this secret unit, David Young, a former NSC associate of Kissinger's, and Egil ("Bud") Krogh, a lawyer on Ehrlichman's Domestic Council staff, were chosen. Neither man had experience in covert operations, but their loyalty was unquestioned. Young and Krogh hired more-experienced hands such as E. Howard Hunt (CIA) and G. Gordon Liddy (FBI).

Krogh, who emerged as leader of the group dubbed the Plumbers, saw his role in somewhat expansive terms. "We were going after an espionage ring, not just Daniel Ellsberg!"[19] And indeed, such steps as firebombing the Brookings Institution and burglaries were seriously discussed. One of the first acts of the Plumbers, though, showed how small and petty the Nixon people could be. In 1971 E. Howard Hunt and Chuck Colson forged top-secret State Department cables in an effort to falsely link President John Kennedy to the assassination of South Vietnam's president Ngo Dinh Diem. They then tried, unsuccessfully, to get *Life* magazine to run stories based on these fake cables.

One of the biggest of the known jobs of the Plumbers related to the Pentagon Papers and efforts to embarrass and discredit Daniel Ellsberg. On June 28, 1971, Ellsberg was indicted for theft of government property and violation of the Espionage Act. The Nixon administration was determined to convict Ellsberg, but more than that, it wanted to discredit him and, if possible, link his activities to the Democrats (the 1972 election was only a short time away). To accomplish these goals, the clandestine arm of the administration had to be expanded and invigorated.

In late August, Hunt and Liddy went to Los Angeles to "case" the office of Daniel Ellsberg's psychiatrist, Dr. Lewis J. Fielding, located in Beverly Hills. On Labor Day weekend, Hunt and Liddy, and "three Cubans" (Bernard Barker, Eugenio Martinez, and Felipe DeDiego) broke into Fielding's office in the hope of finding information that would prove damaging to Ellsberg. Nothing of use was found. In his memoirs, Nixon argues that he was not aware of the break-in, but nonetheless defends it on national security grounds, admitting that it was part an outgrowth of Nixon's own sense of urgency about undermining Ellsberg.

Who ordered the Fielding break-in? John Ehrlichman had ordered a "covert operation" (he was convicted for ordering the break-in), with the stipulation that it be "done under your assurance that it is not traceable." There is no clear-cut evidence that Nixon knew of the break-in beforehand. In his memoirs, Bob Haldeman relates in detail a post-presidency conversation with Nixon concerning the break-in. As Haldeman recounts the conversation, Nixon spoke as if he *had* ordered the break-in, saying at one point, "I was so damn mad at Ellsberg in those days. And Henry was jumping up and down. I've been thinking and maybe I did order that break-in." Haldeman then recounts how Nixon took steps that set in motion a "devious attack on Ellsberg and leakers," at one point telling Chuck Colson, "I don't give a damn how it is done, do whatever has to be done" and "I don't want excuses. I want results. I want it done; whatever the cost."[20]

John Ehrlichman recalls that after repeated frustration over the job the FBI had been doing in its—in Nixon's view—meager efforts to pursue Ellsberg and stop leaks, Nixon finally gave a vague order for the Plumbers to proceed. As Ehrlichman writes, "Nixon authorized Krogh to use 'his people,' Howard Hunt, G. Gordon Liddy, et al., to find out what Ellsberg was up to."[21] Even if the president had not ordered, or even known the specifics of, the break-in of Ellsberg's psychiatrist's office, it is clear that Nixon set a tone, or a mood, and put great pressure on those around him to "get Ellsberg." The president's wish was their command, and clearly many of those who worked for the president felt confident that these covert and illegal methods would meet with the president's approval. They were correct.

So obsessed were the Nixon people with getting Daniel Ellsberg, that at a San Clemente meeting between Nixon and Matthew Byrne, the judge in the Ellsberg case, John Ehrlichman called Byrne aside and tentatively "offered" him the directorship of the FBI, if he handled the Ellsberg case in the right way (Byrne later threw the case out of court). The impropriety of the Fielding/Ellsberg break-in was emphasized by U.S. District Court Judge Gerhard Gesell, who called the break-in "clearly illegal."

At a conference on the Nixon presidency held at Hofstra University in 1987, Chuck Colson discussed the impact of the Pentagon Papers on the behavior of the Nixon administration. Colson said that he saw the release of the Pentagon Papers as "the pivotal point" of the Nixon years. "When that happened," the ground rules began to change. That was when the Nixon people had, in Colson's words, "crossed that line." Egil Krogh agreed, citing the events surrounding release of the Pentagon Papers as "the seminal event of the Nixon term that resulted in the downfall of that administration." It sparked both legitimate national security fears and illegitimate personal fears, which animated behavior of an illegal nature. Internally, the process of moral deterioration became accelerated.

Krogh concluded his Hofstra University commentary by saying that "what was done in 1971 set a precedent, a pattern that I think those who went on to work for the committee to Re-Elect later on felt was appropriate conduct. They felt that if the White House would be willing to condone that kind of activity for national security purposes in 1971, it wouldn't be much of a stretch to condone it in 1972, 1973, for political purposes, and that's exactly what took place."[22]

THE 1972 ELECTION

As the 1972 election approached, things looked very good for President Nixon. But the optimism over the president's election prospect was not based solely upon Nixon's style or policy successes; it rested also upon a strategy that successfully eliminated all the president's top Democratic challengers. In effect, the president tried to pick his opponent in the 1972 race.

The Nixon team developed a two-pronged strategy that was (1) proactive and (2) predatory. The proactive side was designed to highlight the president's accomplishments. The predatory side was designed to attack and destroy the Democratic front-runners.

Nixon had an inordinate fear of losing. His insecurities combined with past experiences to lead Nixon to overkill in campaigns. After all, in 1960 he lost the presidency by the thinnest of margins in a race he believed had been stolen from him (the president spoke of this frequently in the early campaign strategy sessions). In 1968, after a huge early lead, Nixon beat Hubert Humphrey by only one half of one percent. The president vowed not to let this happen again. He would win, and win "big."

As the primary season got under way, Senator Edmund Muskie (D., Maine) appeared to be Nixon's main challenger. Muskie, a popular and seasoned campaign veteran, rated close to and sometimes ahead of the president in early polls. Nixon feared a campaign against Muskie and set out to tilt the race.

The campaign organization, the Committee for the Reelection of the President, known as CREEP, was first run by Jeb Magruder, but the real head was Attorney General John Mitchell. In close contact with the White House, Mitchell called most of the shots from the outset. He, along with chief fundraiser Maurice Stans, established one of the most highly organized, and up to that time the most well funded presidential campaign in American history.

In addition to the normal and expected work of the president's reelection effort, a subterranean operation of illegal money collecting and "dirty tricks" was employed. In an effort to accumulate enough money to run the campaign, the president's money collectors went beyond the bounds of pressuring potential donors to the murky world of extorting funds.

Though Nixon continually claimed that he did not know about the dirty tricks campaign (he was, he maintained, working on issues such as peace and prosperity, and had no time for the details of campaigning), a May 5, 1971, tape recording indicates otherwise. One and one half years before the election, the dirty tricks campaign was already underway. Nixon and Haldeman were discussing some of Colson's tricks against Muskie, laughing and joking about oranges sent in Muskie's name to some protesters, when the conversation turned to more serious tricks. Haldeman told the president Colson "got a lot done that he hasn't been caught at," adding, "We got some stuff that he doesn't know anything about, too."

Haldeman then responded to a question from Nixon, saying that Dwight Chapin, Nixon's appointments secretary, had established a link with "a guy that nobody, none of us knows except Dwight . . . who is just completely removed. There's no contact at all. He's starting to build it now. We're going to use it for the campaign next year." (They were almost certainly referring to Donald Segretti.)

"Are they really any good?" asked Nixon. Haldeman replied that "this guy's a real conspirator type . . . thug-type guy. . . . This is the kind of guy that can get out and tear things up." Clearly Nixon was aware of the dirty tricks operation at the early stages of the campaign.

Part of the Nixon predatory strategy involved attempts to sabotage the campaigns of the top Democratic candidates in hopes of destroying their campaigns and thereby running against one of the weaker Democrats in the November general election. The predatory strategy involved the use of political "dirty tricks" that often went far beyond the bounds of ethics and the law.

In the 1972 campaign, Nixon was determined to use all the tools available to him to "get" his political opponents. As early as July 1969, Nixon, in White House notes taken by Bob Haldeman, discusses the use of dirty tricks:

> req. mts dirty tricks dept.
> use power of WH more ruthlessly
> in deadly battle use all weapons

To engage in the battle of dirty tricks, Nixon's appointment secretary Dwight Chapin hired college chum Donald Segretti. Segretti was in charge of "Operation Sedan Chair," the effort to harass the Democratic candidates with what were called "black advances." Of course, almost all this sprang out of Nixon's "us versus them" attitude, his notion of confrontational politics, his view that politics was the law of the jungle—get them before they get you.

Nixon was a man haunted by memories of past failures, of fears of enemies. He saw the world as a hostile place and politics as a dirty, harsh business. One had to be tough to survive, and Nixon wanted to be the winner in this game. Thus, Nixon could approve the dirty tactics and "hardball" politics of his campaign team. As John Dean's memo of August 1971 stated: "This memorandum addresses the matter of how we can maximize the fact of our incumbency in dealing with persons known to be active in their opposition to our Administration. Stated a bit more bluntly how can we use the available federal machinery to screw our political enemies?"[23]

Because Muskie was the front-runner, the Nixon people went after him. A memo written by Pat Buchanan reads, "We ought to go down to the kennels and turn all the dogs loose on Ecology Ed." Buchanan added, "The President is the only one who should stand clear, while everybody else gets chewed up."[24]

The predatory strategy worked beyond the administration's wildest dreams. Muskie, who had trouble getting his campaign on track, dropped out of the race shortly after the New Hampshire primary; Jackson, Humphrey, and the rest followed until Senator George McGovern, whom Nixon considered his weakest potential opponent, got the nomination. McGovern was very liberal and had only marginal support from mainstream Democrats. The president could not have been more pleased if he had picked his opponent, which in a way, he had.

The result of the 1972 campaign seemed a foregone conclusion even before it had begun. Nixon had several significant foreign policy victories to point to and seemed to be ending the war in Vietnam. McGovern on the other hand had nothing but trouble. His choice as vice president, Senator Thomas Eagleton of Missouri, it was revealed, had experienced severe depression on several occasions and had been hospitalized. He had also received electric-shock treatment for his depression. When this became public, Eagleton was forced off the ticket and R. Sargent Shriver, former Peace Corps director and ambassador to France, was put on the ticket. But the damage had been done, and the McGovern campaign never recovered.

THE WATERGATE BREAK-IN

As McGovern self-destructed, the Nixon camp moved forward. But a curious event took place in mid-June. In the early morning hours of June 17, five men were arrested inside the office of the Democratic National Committee headquarters in the Watergate office complex. A young security guard making his rounds discovered a piece of tape horizontally covering the lock on the door. He removed the tape, but did not call the police. Later, while on another set of rounds, he discovered *another* piece of tape on the same door. This time he called the police.

A short time later the D.C. police arrived and arrested five men in the sixth-floor offices of the DNC. The men were wearing rubber surgical gloves, and carrying walkie-talkies, electronic eavesdropping equipment, cameras, and other tools. One of the men, James McCord, a former employee of the CIA, was the security chief of CREEP. Later, two others, who were in the Howard Johnson hotel across the street, were arrested in connection with the Watergate break-in: a former CIA operative and consultant to the Nixon White House, E. Howard Hunt, and G. Gordon Liddy, general counsel to CREEP. The White House and CREEP denied any connection to the break-in, but among the belongings of those arrested at the Watergate were papers linking the suspects to the White House.

While the newspapers reported the story, and links between the burglars and the Nixon White House seemed possible, the break-in had little impact on public opinion (due in part to a cover-up of the crime by the White House). If the public had suspicions, they did not run deep. On November 7, 1972, Richard Nixon was reelected in an enormous landslide. In spite of the "minor annoyance" value, the Watergate story did not damage the president. He won a reelection victory, getting 97 percent of all electoral votes, and over 60 percent of the popular vote. It was biggest landslide in presidential history.

The jubilation at containing damage from the Watergate story was short lived. Shortly after the election, a slow stream of news stories built up to an avalanche of bad news that revealed a wide range of criminal and unethical acts committed on behalf of the president.

On January 8, 1973, the trial of the Watergate burglars began. The White House was hoping for continued silence from the conspirators. On January 12, James McCord and CREEP "undercover agent" John Caulfield met in the evening on an overlook of the George Washington Parkway, and Caulfield assured the burglars of executive clemency "from the highest level of the White House." Nixon lawyer and fundraiser Herbert Kalmbach later admitted that on January 19, Mitchell, John Dean, and Fred LaRue asked him to raise hush money for the defendants. At the trial itself, Magruder and Herbert Porter, Magruder's assistant, perjured themselves, testifying that Liddy was given money only for legitimate political intelligence gathering. On January 25, McCord, who was resisting the clemency offer, met for a third time with Caulfield, who told McCord he was "fouling up the game plan." But the game plan was starting to collapse under pressure from several directions.

DIRTY MONEY

> "I made my mistakes, but in all of my years of public life, I have never profited, never profited from public service. I have earned every cent. And in all of my years of public life, I have never obstructed justice. And I think, too, that I could say that in my years of public life, that I welcome this kind of examination because people have got to know whether or not their President is a crook. Well, I'm not a crook, I have earned everything I have got."
>
> —Richard M. Nixon
> Walt Disney World, November 17, 1973

"Money," as former California Assembly Speaker Jesse Unruh used to say, "is the mother's milk of politics," and the Nixon team collected and spent more money (over $60 million) than any previous campaign in presidential history. "Remember 1960," Nixon told Haldeman, "I never want to be outspent again."

The effort not to be outspent was led by former Commerce secretary Maurice Stans, with Nixon's longtime personal lawyer Herbert Kalmbach as chief fundraiser. The money was collected in two stages, reflecting changes in the campaign reform laws. Money collected *before* April 7, 1971, did not fall under the stricter reporting requirements of the new regulations, so there was a major effort to get the money in "pre-April 7."

In spite of frantic efforts to get as much money as possible before the reporting requirements went into effect, some money came in "late." On April 10, a former Republican State senate majority leader named Harry L. Sears gave Stans an attaché case containing $200,000 in $100 bills. The money was illegally treated as "pre-April 7" money and proved an even greater embarrassment when it was revealed that the money was a contribution from Robert Vesco, the international financier and fugitive from American justice.

Stans and his fundraising associates sought contributions from corporations dependent on the largesse of the government. Campaign contributions from corporations are illegal, but this did not deter Stans. The pitch made to these corporate executives was "finely calibrated depending on who they were and how much fund-raisers thought they could get."[25]

This approach brought in millions. By politely hinting that corporate contributions would help and that failure to contribute would hurt badly, the president's reelection team was able to extract political tithes from some of the biggest and most respected companies in the nation. Even a partial list is impressive: American Airlines, $55,000; Braniff Airways, $40,000; Ashland Oil, $100,000; Goodyear Tire and Rubber, $40,000; Gulf Oil, $100,000; Northrop, $150,000; and Phillips Petroleum, $100,000. This who's who of corporate America illegally contributed to the Nixon reelection effort, and all were convicted after the 1972 campaign.

In an effort to hide the money, that is, to prevent tracing it to the source, most of this money was laundered. The laundering took several forms. American Airlines sent money from a U.S. bank to a Swiss account of an agent in Lebanon, back to another U.S. bank, then to CREEP. Still other firms gave money from slush funds, and some airlines sold bogus tickets and sent the cash to CREEP. By far the most common route to launder money was through Mexico. In fact, it was to protect the money-laundering operation in Mexico that President Nixon first became actively involved in the criminal conspiracy to obstruct justice on June 23, 1972, less than a week after the Watergate break-in. Illegal corporate contributions proved to be an excellent source of money, as did the "selling" of ambassadorships. Several big donors were promised ambassadorships in exchange for campaign money. J. Fife Symington gave over $100,000, but the promised post of Spain or Portugal fell through (Herbert Kalmbach plead guilty to a charge of promising a federal job to Symington in exchange for money). Vincent P. de Roulet paid over $100,000 for Jamaica. Walter H. Annenberg received Great Britain after a $250,000 contribution. Mrs. Ruth Farkas, after donating $250,000 and being promised Costa Rica, complained to Kalmbach, saying, according to the grand jury testimony, "Well, you know, I am interested in Europe, I think, and isn't two hundred and fifty thousand dollars an awful lot of money for Costa Rica?" After giving a total of $300,000, Mrs. Farkas was appointed ambassador to Luxembourg. The president was well aware of the "ambassadorial auction." As notes taken by H. R. Haldeman at a meeting with the president and Maurice Stans on March 21, 1972, indicate, Stans and Nixon discussed possible appointments and how much money each donor gave. The notation on Farkas was: "Mrs. Farks 250?-where's the play on her?"

DIRTY TRICKS

In 1971 a file entitled "Political Enemies Project" (the "enemies list") was kept by the president's special counsel Charles Colson. Along with John Dean, Colson compiled a list (released on December 10, 1973) that, according to congressional investigations, contained 575 names. On September 9, 1971, Colson came up with twenty names for "go status." The list included

United Automobile Workers leader Leonard Woodcock, Congressman John Conyers, journalist Daniel Shorr, actor Paul Newman, and others. The White House tried, with very limited success, to get the IRS to audit the taxes of those on the list. Nixon was involved directly in this, as a tape of a conversation between the president, Haldeman, and Dean, on September 15, 1972, dealing with *Washington Post* attorney Edward Bennett Williams indicates.

President Nixon: I would not want to be in Edward Bennett Williams' position after this Election. . . . We're going after him.

Haldeman: That is a guy we've got to ruin.

President Nixon: You want to remember, too, he's an attorney for the *Washington Post*.

Dean: I'm well aware of that.

President Nixon: I think we are going to fix the son of a bitch. Believe me. We are going to. We've got to, because he's a bad man.

Dean: Absolutely . . . I've tried to . . . keep notes on a lot of the people who are emerging . . . as less than our friends.

President Nixon: Great.

Dean: Because this is going to be over someday, . . . We shouldn't forget the way some of them have treated us.

President Nixon: I want the most comprehensive notes on all of those that tried to do us in. . . . They didn't have to do it. . . . I mean if . . . they had a very close election everybody on the other side would understand this game. But now they are doing this quite deliberately and they are asking for it and they are going to get it. We have not used this power in this first four years. . . . We have never used it. We haven't used the Bureau and we haven't used the Justice Department, but things are going to change now. . . . They're going to get it right.

Dean: That's an exciting prospect.

President Nixon: It's got to be done. It's the only thing to do.[26]

The larger enemies list included Senators Ted Kennedy, Edmund Muskie, and Walter Mondale; the presidents of Yale and the Harvard Law School; the heads of the World Bank, Ford Foundation, and Rand Corporation; four ex-cabinet members; two ex-ambassadors; a Nobel Prize winner; and actors Carol Channing, Steve McQueen, Burt Lancaster, Shirley McLaine, and Gregory Peck; along with football player Joe Namath.

On August 16, 1971, John Dean sent Bob Haldeman a memo entitled: "How to Deal with Our Political Enemies and How We Can Use the Available Political Machinery to Screw Our Political Enemies." Dean wanted to address "the matter of how we can maximize the fact of our incumbency in dealing with persons known to be active in their opposition to our Administration."[27]

The word *enemy* is unusual in American politics. Normally one thinks of adversaries, opponents, or rivals, but not *enemies*. Yet to Nixon, the word *enemy* fit. He did indeed see his opponents as enemies and attempted to move the machinery of government against them. The Nixon administration made government into an instrument of revenge and retaliation. Nixon and his circle of supporters attempted not just to defeat their rivals but to destroy their enemies. Along the way they broke the law and subverted the democratic process.

Members of the administration were involved in other subterranean tricks such as fake-letter-writing campaigns to inflate the level of support for the president's policies, alleged discussions of plots to murder newspaper columnist and Nixon critic Jack Anderson, and plots to sneak LSD into Daniel Ellsberg's soup prior to a speaking engagement. One of the most amazing and insidious activities in the campaign of dirty tricks and sabotage was what became known as the "Liddy Plan." As chief legal counsel for CREEP, G. Gordon Liddy cast his net over a wide array of activities, most notorious of which was the plan that bears his name. In an effort to further disrupt and divide the Democrats, Liddy was to develop an intelligence-gathering/undercover operation. On January 27, 1972, at four o'clock in the afternoon, Liddy went to the office of Attorney General John Mitchell and presented a plan that was frightening, or should have been.

At the meeting with Liddy and Mitchell were John Dean and Jeb Magruder. Liddy, with charts and an easel, presented a plan, code-named "Gemstone," of sabotage and surveillance of unprecedented proportions.

Carrying a $1 million price tag, the Liddy Plan called for mugging squads to beat up demonstrators at the Republican Convention, teams to kidnap leaders of the demonstrations and hijack them to Mexico until the Republican Convention was over, electronic surveillance against the Democrats at their Washington headquarters and convention sites, prostitutes to be employed to lure prominent Democrats onto a yacht equipped with hidden cameras and recording equipment, break-ins to obtain and photograph documents, shorting-out the air conditioning at the arena in Miami where the Democrats were to have their convention, and other sordid acts.

John Dean called the plan "mind-boggling." The attorney general, the highest-ranking law enforcement official in the land, rather than throwing Liddy out of his office, as he later admitted he should have done, rejected the plan, not on its merits, but as too expensive, and asked Liddy to draw up a new, scaled-down version. As John Dean testified before the Senate Watergate Committee, Mitchell "took a few long puffs on his pipe," and told

Liddy, "the plan . . . was not quite what he had in mind and the cost was out of the question, and suggested to Liddy he go back and revise his plan, keeping in mind that he was most interested in the demonstration problem."

On February 4, 1972, Liddy returned to Mitchell's office with a scaled-down plan costing only half a million dollars. But again the attorney general demurred. Liddy was to come up with another proposal. Almost two months later, on March 30, 1972, a third meeting with Mitchell was held in Key Biscayne, Florida. Dean and Liddy were not present, but Magruder and Fred LaRue were in attendance. Toward the end of a wide-ranging meeting, Mitchell, who by that time had resigned as attorney general to become director of CREEP, turned to the revised Liddy plan. While everyone at the meeting expressed reservations, Mitchell finally approved the plan, but gave Liddy only $250,000. Among the targets was Larry O'Brien, chair of the Democratic National Committee, whose office was located in the Watergate office complex.

Within a week, Liddy was off and running. He received $83,000 in cash from CREEP's Finance Committee, purchased bugging and surveillance equipment, and began planning the first break-in of Watergate. In attempting to figure out why Mitchell approved the revised Liddy plan, and why so many others in the administration and CREEP went along with it, Jeb Magruder offers that it was "the result of a combination of pressures that played upon us at that time." First, Liddy "put his plan to us in a highly effective way"; second, Mitchell was distracted by other matters in his job as Attorney General; third, Mitchell's wife, the high-strung Martha, was putting a strain on her busy husband; and fourth, "Liddy's plan was approved because of the climate of fear and suspicion that had grown up in the White House, an atmosphere that started with the President himself and reached us through Haldeman and Colson and others, one that came to affect all our thinking, so that decisions that now seem insane seemed at the time to be rational." He continued, "It was all but impossible not to get caught up in the 'enemies' mentality."[28]

THE BREAK-IN

Out of this atmosphere of dirty tricks, dirty money, and dirty politics came the plan to break into and bug offices in the headquarters of the Democratic National Committee. While the roots of the DNC break-in can be found in the legitimate need for campaign intelligence, things got so out of hand, sank so low, that the dirty tricks and break-ins were eventually seen as a necessary part in the reelection of the president.

Early efforts at gaining political and campaign intelligence led John Dean, at the instruction of Haldeman, to contact Jack Caulfield to set up such a capability. Caulfield developed what he called "Operation Sandwedge, "an intelligence-gathering operation" that would have "black bag" (illegal activities) capability. Caulfield's plan never got off the ground, and Dean continued to feel the pressure from Haldeman. Dean would later testify before the Senate Watergate Committee that the White House had an insatiable appetite for political intelligence.

As part of Liddy's intelligence-gathering plan, information was to be obtained by what Liddy called a *Nacht und Nebel* (Night and Fog) operation. One such operation, code-named Gemstone, was to get information on what the Democrats had on the Republicans, and more specifically on Nixon. The fear was that Larry O'Brien, Chairman of the DNC, might possess material that could be particularly damaging to the president. The "primary purpose of the break-in was to see if O'Brien had embarrassing information linking President Nixon's close friend Bebe Rebozo to loans from Howard Hughes" that went to Nixon. "It was a planned burglary," said Magruder.[29] Thus, while most political professionals scoffed at the break-in in its aftermath, suggesting that it had to be a renegade operation because everyone knew that there was nothing of value at the DNC, there was a reason: the fear that Larry O'Brien had the goods on a Hughes-Nixon deal.

To get this information, Liddy and his accomplices first broke into the DNC headquarters on May 27, 1972, and installed wiretaps. When the taps did not work properly, a second surreptitious entry was required. On the night of June 16 and morning of the 17th, Liddy and his cohorts returned.

Did President Nixon *know* about Gemstone, the Liddy Plan, the effort to bug the DNC? There is no evidence to suggest that he knew of the plan in advance. Even though Nixon may not have ordered the break-in, he had created an atmosphere in which planning such crimes was tolerated and even encouraged. Haldeman gives us an indication of the atmosphere when he recounts an example of what he calls "classic Nixonian rhetorical overkill" when the president ordered him to get the tax files of leading Democrats: "There are ways to get it," Nixon said, "Goddamnit, sneak in, in the middle of the night."[30] On January 14, 1971, Nixon had sent Haldeman a memo suggesting that they needed more information on DNC chairman Lawrence O'Brien. The memo read in part: "It would seem that the time is approaching when Larry O'Brien is held accountable for his retainer with Hughes," and "perhaps Colson should make a check on this." Though Nixon had an interest in O'Brien, there is no direct evidence pointing to the president having advance knowledge of the break-in. But he was actively involved in the cover-up from the beginning.

THE COVERUP BEGINS

The arrests at the Watergate, occurring less than five months before the 1972 election, might have been a political embarrassment, perhaps even a serious scandal, but the White House quickly went to work to cover-up the crime, and contain political damage from the president and his reelection.

Initially, the story of the arrests at the Watergate attracted very little attention. On June 18, the day after the arrests, the story appeared on page 30 of the *New York Times*. Few seemed to notice or care. The president and Haldeman were in Key Biscayne, John Mitchell and Jeb Magruder in California, and John Dean in Manila. But within hours of the break-in, the cover-up began. On the morning of the 18th, G. Gordon Liddy called Magruder in Los Angeles and told him of the arrests at the Watergate.

Liddy informed Magruder that "the four men arrested with McCord were Cuban freedom fighters, whom Howard Hunt recruited. But don't worry; my men will never talk." The cover-up was immediate and reflexive. Magruder told the Senate Watergate Committee, "The cover-up began that Saturday when we realized there was a break-in." Or, as John Mitchell said, "What'd they expect us to do—advertise it?"

The cover-up, in Magruder's words, "was immediate and automatic; no one even considered that there would *not* be a cover-up. It seemed inconceivable that with our political power we could not erase this mistake we had made."[31] Upon hearing the news of the arrests from Liddy, Magruder immediately informed John Mitchell, and the cover-up was under way. In a flurry of activity, steps were taken to sever whatever links could be established between the burglars and the White House. Magruder had one of his assistants remove the Gemstone file from his office. Liddy also removed files from CREEP headquarters. Haldeman aide Gordon Strachan used the White House shredder to destroy incriminating documents. Liddy even went so far as to volunteer to John Dean that he, Liddy, would wait on a corner and be killed if it became necessary! As Dean recalled: "He told me that he was a soldier and would never talk. He said if anyone wished to shoot him on the street, he was ready."[32]

E. Howard Hunt's name was expunged from the White House phone directory. Hunt removed $10,000 from his White House safe. John Ehrlichman ordered that Hunt's safe be opened and the contents removed. Dean ordered Hunt to leave the country but later rescinded the order. A quick payment scheme for the burglars was put into action. But the frenetic activity lacked coherence and guidance. According to Magruder, the guidance began with a June 19 meeting with Mitchell, LaRue, Assistant Attorney General Robert Mardian, Dean, and himself. At the meeting, Magruder asked what to do with the Gemstone file. Mitchell suggested that it might be a good idea if Magruder had a fire in his home that evening.

At the June 19 meeting, according to Magruder, it was agreed that the president's reelection would suffer if the truth about the break-in and bugging became known, and a plan to cover up this act evolved out of the meeting. All top-level CREEP officials would deny, deny, and they agreed on false stories to tell the FBI and prosecutors. Shortly thereafter, John Dean was assigned to keep the cover on the story and contain the damage.

On Saturday afternoon, June 17, John Ehrlichman called presidential press secretary Ron Ziegler, who was with the president and Haldeman in Florida, and told him that Howard Hunt was arrested at the Watergate and that Hunt could be traced to the White House. On the 18th, Ehrlichman again called Florida and discussed McCord and Hunt's involvement in the break-in with Haldeman. Ehrlichman was worried that it could open a can of worms, which could lead prosecutors to Haldeman, Mitchell, himself, and a host of embarrassing and illegal activities that could not stand the light of day.

On June 18 the president, then in Key Biscayne, called Chuck Colson. Nixon had reason to believe that Colson knew of, or was involved in, the DNC break-in. After all, Colson was considered the administration's hit man. According to testimony given by Colson, Nixon was so upset at McCord's involvement in the break-in that Nixon threw an ashtray across the room. Nixon knew that McCord was a link to CREEP and the White House, and ultimately to Nixon himself. Also on June 18 Nixon put Ehrlichman in charge of Watergate, and Ehrlichman assigned Dean to the operational role in handling the problem.

The following day Nixon telephoned Colson, and they spoke for an hour about the break-in. According to Colson's testimony to the House Judiciary Committee, he told the president that administration officials were holding meetings in Washington to determine how best to handle the problem.

When the President returned to Washington on June 20, the cover-up was already in motion. That morning, the *Washington Post* ran a story that proclaimed: "White House Consultant tied to bugging figure." The Howard Hunt link was being pieced together. If Hunt could be linked to his sponsor, Colson, it was a very short step to the president.

June 20 was the first time Nixon had the opportunity to meet with the top people involved in the break-in and cover-up. On that day, the president held meetings or discussions with Haldeman, Mitchell, Colson, and others. He discussed Watergate with these aides, and when the White House taping system was revealed during the House investigation, a search for tapes of these meetings proved fruitless. Meetings with Mitchell were, according to a

White House spokesman, not recorded; there was a mysterious 18½-minute gap in a Haldeman conversation on Watergate, and a 38-second gap in the Dictabelt recording Nixon made of his daily recollections. On this, the most important day for the president, the day when he first discussed Watergate with the top principals, the recorded evidence is mysteriously gone.

By June 23, less than a week after the arrests, the president was directly leading a criminal cover-up. In a discussion between Haldeman and Nixon, the substance of which was not revealed until August 5, 1974, in a released tape, the president's chief of staff informed Nixon that the break-in occurred because Liddy was under pressure (probably from Mitchell) to "get more information," to which the president responded, "All right, fine. I understand it all. We won't second-guess Mitchell and the rest. Thank God it wasn't Colson." Haldeman then informed Nixon that the FBI was beginning to close in on the source of money used for the illegal activities, saying "the FBI is not under control," and suggested that "the way to handle this now is for us to have Walters, [deputy director, CIA] call Pat Gray [acting director, FBI] and just say 'stay to hell out of this' . . . Pat wants to [end the investigation] . . . he doesn't have the basis for doing it. Given this, he will then have the basis" (all quotes from Watergate tapes).

The president then ordered Haldeman to tell CIA director Richard Helms that "the President believes that it is going to open the whole Bay of Pigs thing up again. And . . . that they [the CIA] should call the FBI in and [unintelligible] don't go any further into this case period!"

Later that day in another meeting with Haldeman, Nixon ordered Haldeman to tell Helms that "Hunt . . . knows too damned much. . . . If it gets out that this is all involved . . . it would make the CIA look bad, it's going to make Hunt look bad, and it is likely to blow the whole Bay of Pigs things which we think would be very unfortunate—both for the CIA and for the country . . . and for American foreign policy. Just tell him [Helms] to lay off. . . . I would just say, look it, because of the Hunt involvement, whole cover basically this."

At 1:30 P.M. on June 23, Haldeman and Ehrlichman met with Helms and Vernon Walters of the CIA and persuaded them to approach Gray in an effort to limit the FBI investigation into the break-in. Later that afternoon, Haldeman again met with the president to report on his meeting with Helms and Walters. He told the president that though he didn't mention Hunt, he did tell the CIA officials that "the thing was leading into directions that were going to create potential problems because they were exploring leads that led back into areas that would be harmful to the CIA and harmful to the Government," and that Helms "kind of got the picture." He said, Helms told him, "We'll be very happy to be helpful [unintelligible] to handle anything you want. . . . Walters is going to make a call to Gray."

At almost the precise moment Haldeman was having this conversation with the president, Vernon Walters called L. Patrick Gray and told him that if the FBI pursued its investigation into Mexico, it would be jeopardizing some of the CIA's covert operations. He suggested that the investigation be limited to the suspects already under arrest. Gray complied. Thus, the criminal conspiracy to obstruct justice, to interfere with an FBI investigation, began less than a week after the arrests in the Watergate. This put the president right in the middle of a criminal conspiracy to obstruct justice. The national security excuse was a ruse. The top people in the administration were covering up a crime.

In his memoirs, Richard Nixon explained the events surrounding the June 23 meeting as the first steps towards the end of his presidency. Admitting that he did enlist the CIA's help in limiting the FBI investigation, Nixon nonetheless defends his actions as a pragmatic way of dealing with a potential problem, not as a criminal cover-up.[33]

On June 30 John Mitchell abruptly resigned as head of CREEP for "personal reasons." But Mitchell was not out of the picture. He simply moved across the hall to rejoin his old law firm and from there continued to lead the cover-up. Meetings frequently took place involving Mitchell, Magruder, and LaRue in which, as Magruder recalls, "We did not discuss the Watergate affair in terms of perjury or burglary or conspiracy. We would refer, rather, to 'handling the case' and 'making sure things don't get out of hand.' "[34]

From the day after the burglars were caught in DNC headquarters, until the November presidential election, President Nixon and his top aides conducted a plan of concealment, cover-up, and containment. The goals were to prevent any damaging information from getting to the prosecutors and to make sure that no potentially explosive scandals interfered with the reelection of the president.

Within weeks, in an effort to contain and cover up, efforts were made to buy the silence of the defendants in the Watergate break-in case with promises of executive clemency and money. (John Dean testified that he told Mitchell of "the need for support money in exchange for the silence of the men in jail." Liddy and his associates eventually received over $500,000.) Officials of CREEP were pressured to commit perjury, and an elaborate effort was under way to interfere with the FBI investigation.

In early July, suspicion grew of a possible connection between the burglars and administration officials. U.S. District Court Judge John Sirica, who was overseeing the Watergate grand jury, raised a number of questions, but his prodding seemed to be going nowhere.

In public, the president tried to distance himself from the break-in, denying any complicity for himself or any White House officials in the illegal acts, and on the whole he was believed. On August 29, at a press conference, Nixon, responding to a question on Watergate, said that "what really hurts, is if you try to cover it up." When, on September 15, an eight-count indictment in the Watergate case was handed out, the charges were limited to Hunt, Liddy, and the five burglars. The charges included stealing documents, tapping telephones, and planting eavesdropping devices. The president's strategy was working; no one in the White House was implicated.

Why a cover-up? Why didn't the president come clean early and cut his losses? Why was there virtually no discussion of *not* covering up? According to Jeb Magruder, on the Monday after the break-in, he met with Mitchell and suggested that they come clean on Watergate immediately. But Mitchell, after a discussion with Haldeman and Ehrlichman, told Magruder that they could not come clean on Watergate because they had "other reasons" to keep the lid on the story.

Indeed, "other reasons" made the cover-up so important and necessary. Covering up the break-in itself was not the key; what was important was to keep a lid on all the other illegal and unethical activities that might be revealed if the "can of worms" were opened. The real enemy was an enemy from within. That is what had to be kept hidden, the dirty tricks and dirty money and crimes of the past several years: warrantless wiretaps, the Fielding break-in, the extortion of campaign funds, sabotage of elections, campaign crimes, and a host of other crimes. There simply could not *not* be a cover-up.

UNCOVERING THE COVER-UP

While most of the press played down the Watergate story in the early phase, two reporters for the *Washington Post*, Carl Bernstein and Bob Woodward, began to piece the story together, finding many loose ends that pointed toward involvement by higher-ups in the Nixon administration. On October 10, they published a story linking John Mitchell to illegal campaign acts. In spite of scathing attacks from the president's men, the *Post*, on October 25, published another damaging article, this one linking Bob Haldeman to the scandal. Slowly things were closing in on the president himself.

On July 6, 1972, Pat Gray warned the president that "people on your staff are trying to mortally wound you by using the CIA and FBI." Gray didn't know that it was the president who was leading the cover-up.

In an effort to control the Watergate investigation, the president, through John Dean, closely monitored the Justice Department's investigations. Dean was allowed to sit in on questioning of White House and CREEP officials, and as Dean later told the president, "I was totally aware what the bureau was doing at all times. I was totally aware what the grand jury was doing. I knew what witnesses were going to be called. I knew what they were going to be asked." When Nixon asked why Henry Peterson (the assistant attorney general who was in charge of the Watergate investigation) was "so straight with us," Dean replied, "Because he is a soldier."

This greatly aided the administration in its efforts to keep the investigation limited. Thus, witnesses could be encouraged to commit perjury and conceal information, and Dean could keep track of how well the cover-up was holding together. Additionally, Peterson kept reporting to the president on the status of the investigation. Peterson did not know that the information he gave Nixon was going to aid in the cover-up because he did not know that the president was involved in the cover-up. At one point, Nixon told Ehrlichman and Ziegler, "I've got Peterson on a short leash." Following pressure from Nixon, Peterson and his colleague Earl Silbert kept the investigation on a very narrow course. Again, the cover-up seemed to be working. But the defendants were threatening to go "off the reservation."

By late December James McCord sent John Caulfield a letter warning: "If the Watergate operation is laid at the CIA's feet, where it does not belong, every tree in the forest will fall. It will be a scorched desert. The whole matter is at the precipice now. Just pass the message that if they want it to blow, they are on exactly the right course."[35]

Shortly after the election, the defendants began to fear that they were vulnerable, that Nixon did not need their silence as much as he did prior to the election, and that they might be "forgotten." Hunt began pressuring Colson. He spoke of financial needs of the defendants. But Colson, who was taping the call, tried to get Hunt to back away. Hunt refused. Colson gave the tape to Dean, who played it for Haldeman and Ehrlichman. The threat was clear. Dean was told to "tell Mitchell to take care of all these problems." Hunt wrote a nine-hundred-word indictment of the way they were being handled by the administration. The defendants, he wrote, had committed the burglary "against their better judgment," but the administration was guilty of "indecisiveness at the moment of crisis." They failed to "quash the investigation while that option was still open," and leveled a laundry list of other charges, including "failure to provide promised support funds on a timely and adequate basis; continued postponements and consequent avoidance of commitments."

Then Hunt listed some of the potentially damaging information he possessed: "Mitchell may well have perjured himself"; the Watergate crime was "only one of a number of highly illegal conspiracies engaged in by one or more of the defendants at the behest of senior White House officials. These as yet undisclosed crimes can be proved"; that "immunity from prosecution

and/or judicial clemency for cooperating defendants is a standing offer";
and that "congressional elections will take place in less than two years." The
deadline given Colson was extended until November 27, but the defendants
would meet before that time to "determine our joint and automatic response
to evidence of continued indifference on the part of those in whose behalf we
have suffered the loss of our employment, our futures, and our reputations as
honorable men. The foregoing should not be interpreted as threat. It is
among other things a reminder that loyalty has always been a two-way
street."[36] The president of the United States was being *blackmailed*.

The threat worked. Almost immediately, $50,000 was delivered by La-
Rue to Hunt's lawyer. Shortly thereafter, LaRue said he needed more money.
Haldeman told Dean to give LaRue "the entire damn bundle, but make sure
we get a receipt."

On December 8, Hunt's wife, Dorothy, was killed in a plane crash. She
was carrying $10,000 in $100 bills. Hunt became increasingly despondent,
and wanted clemency. Charles Colson began to push for clemency to Ehrlichman, who, according to Dean, took the matter up with the president and
then gave Colson an assurance that the president had promised clemency for
Hunt. A few days later, the president and Colson discussed Hunt's clemency.

Nixon endorsed the idea for Hunt and Liddy but said he "would have difficulty with some of the others." Colson pointed out that the others "can't hurt
us." But Hunt and Liddy could: "direct meetings, discussions are very incriminating to us. . . .They're both good healthy right-wing exuberants."

On January 8, 1973, it appeared that the administration would be able to
hold the cover-up together. As the Watergate trial approached, Dean, in a
meeting with the president, laid out the scenario for the trial. According to
notes taken by Haldeman (Haldeman's notes are available for public reading
at the National Archives), Dean told the president:

    Hunt take guilty 3 counts
        After Silbert opening stmt
        w/say no higher-ups involved
        rest w/go to trial-Rothblatt wild man
            w/Cubans
    Liddy go-hope for error-lots of procedures
        etc.
        All will sit mute
            and if immunized after-w/take contempt
            better cause won't take stand
    McCord will testify-but he has no firsthand knowledge
    Grt concern that commitments won't be honored
        prob w/funds-LaRue on this

Three days later, the Watergate trial began. Everyone was back on the reservation; just in time. The defendants all pleaded guilty except for Liddy and McCord.

After deliberating only ninety minutes, the Watergate jury, on January 30, found Liddy guilty on all six counts and McCord guilty on all eight counts. Sentencing was postponed. On February 2 Judge Sirica said that he was "not satisfied" that the full story on Watergate had been disclosed. In spite of Sirica's skepticism, the cover-up was holding.

But as each problem was temporarily solved, a new one sprang up. On February 7, by a 70–0 vote, the Senate established a select committee, headed by North Carolina's Sam Ervin, to investigate Watergate and related campaign abuses. In response to the committee, the president, Haldeman, Ehrlichman, Dean, and aide Richard Moore met at the LaCosta resort in California on February 10 and 11. In meetings that lasted between eight and fourteen hours, the group agreed on a strategy; CREEP, not the White House, would assume primary responsibility for Watergate defense matters, John Mitchell would coordinate this, and, as Dean later recalled, they would "take a posture of full cooperation but privately . . . attempt to restrain the investigation and make it as difficult as possible to get information and witnesses. . . . The ultimate goal would be to discredit the hearings." H. R. Haldeman's notes of February 11 reflect this:

> public stance of cooperation
> but stand ready to quietly obstruct
> paint as partisan but not from W. H.

The "La Costa strategy" became part of the cover-up attempt.

Starting on February 27, John Dean began a series of meetings with the president to discuss the cover-up. Dean warned the president that the containment policy might not hold up forever. (The tape of this conversation was subpoenaed during the House Judiciary Committee's impeachment inquiry, but the White House could not find the tape.)

On the morning of February 28, John Dean told the president, "We have come a long road on this already. I had thought it was an impossible task to hold together . . . but we have made it this far and I am convinced we are going to make it the whole road and put this thing in the funny pages of the history books rather than anything serious." But on that very day, Pat Gray's confirmation hearings to be director of the FBI began. Gray ended up telling much more than anyone had intended. In what proved to be a major embarrassment, Gray admitted that he repeatedly turned over FBI files on the Watergate investigation to John Dean, in spite of the fact that Dean and other

White House officials were suspects in the investigation. Gray also admitted that Dean had been allowed to sit in when the FBI questioned witnesses, and that Dean "probably lied." Almost out of nowhere, John Dean became a central figure in the Watergate drama, and the Senate Judiciary Committee, which was conducting the Gray confirmation hearings, wanted to talk to this previously little-known figure.

But Nixon did not want Dean to testify. Dean knew too much. Thus, executive privilege was invoked. Nixon's view of executive privilege, the constitutionally questionable "right" of a president to refuse to answer or have his staff answer to the Congress, was unusually broad, almost absolute. The president stated on March 12: "Under the doctrine of separation of powers, the manner in which the President personally exercises his assigned executive powers is not subject to questioning by another branch of government. If the President is not subject to such questioning, it is equally appropriate that members of his staff not be so questioned, for their roles are in effect an extension of the Presidency."

The Judiciary Committee was unpersuaded, and voted unanimously to demand Dean's appearance. The president could not afford to have Dean testify, and he eventually withdrew Gray's nomination.

As Dean's role became more exposed, he began to have doubts about whether the cover-up could be maintained. On March 13, he warned the president, "There are dangers. . . . There is a certain domino situation. If some things start going, a lot of other things are going to start going." The president, as usual, was more graphic: "Sloan starts pissing on Magruder and then Magruder starts pissing on who, even Haldeman." Everyone, Dean noted, was looking to "cover his own ass."

Each passing day seemed to bring a new damaging revelation. By mid-March the president spent more and more time dealing with, or—more accurately—reacting to, each new problem. The criminal investigation continued, the Senate was about to start its hearings, the press dug deeper and deeper, and the public was turning slowly against the president. A new public relations line was needed.

On March 17, the president pressured Dean to write a report that "basically clears the President," in which Dean could "make self-serving goddamn statements." But John Dean could not, or at least did not, write his Watergate report clearing the president. Dean feared that he was being set up. He was right.

The March 21 meeting between the president and John Dean was pivotal in the Watergate saga. In what has been called the "Cancer on the Presidency" meeting, Dean gave Nixon a comprehensive overview of the complicity of Mitchell, Haldeman, Ehrlichman, Magruder, Colson, Kalmbach,

Strachan, and himself in the Fielding and Watergate break-ins and the cover-up, telling the president, "A lot of these people could be indicted." Dean told the president of the danger and reviewed the genesis of Watergate:

Dean: I think, I think that, uh, there's no doubt about the seriousness of the problem we've got. We have a cancer-within-close to the Presidency that's growing. It's growing daily. It's compounding, it grows geometrically now, because it compounds itself. Uh, that'll be clear as I explain, you know, some of the details, uh, of why it is, and it basically is because (1) we're being blackmailed; (2) uh, people are going to start perjuring themselves very quickly that have not had to perjure themselves to protect other people and the like. And that is just—And there is no assurance—

President: That it won't bust.

Dean: That that won't bust.

President: True.

Dean went on to give the president details of the Watergate crimes, many of which Nixon already knew. Dean described the Liddy Plan, Mitchell's role, the Ellsberg break-in, the dirty tricks, the Watergate break-in, and perjury by administration officials. Then Dean turned to the cover-up, reminding the president he "was under pretty clear instructions not to really . . . investigate this." Dean went on to discuss the money demands of the Watergate defendants. These payoffs were, to Dean,

Dean: The most troublesome post-thing, uh, because (1) Bob is involved in that; John is involved in that; I am involved in that; Mitchell is involved in that. And that's an obstruction of justice.

President: In other words the fact that, uh, that you're, you're, you're taking care of witnesses.

Dean: That's right. Uh . . . But, now, here, here's what's happening right now.

Dean then briefed the president on some of the other problems they faced.

In the March 21 meeting, the president was fully informed on Watergate, its roots, and the continuing cover-up. He was told of potential criminal liability among his top people and was warned that the cover-up was cracking. The cancer on the presidency was growing, warned Dean. But rather than clean up the mess, Nixon got deeper into a cover-up. He instructed in how to commit perjury, approved of hush money to maintain the silence of the Watergate defendants, and orchestrated a new cover-up plan. Nixon was now in charge of the management of the Watergate cover-up.

The following day, the president, Dean, Haldeman, Ehrlichman, and Mitchell met in the Oval Office to devise a way of dealing with the upcoming

Senate hearings. They discussed a way to limit testimony, using executive privilege as a means to get the committee to compromise on the method of questioning White House officials.

The meeting moved to the subject of the "Dean report," with Dean saying, "I really can't say if I can do it." But the president continued to pressure Dean, with Ehrlichman telling Dean to say that "nobody [in the White House] was involved," to which Nixon adds, "That's right."

The discussion returned to the use of executive privilege, and the president, responding to a suggestion by Mitchell, said, "All that John Mitchell is arguing, then, is that now we use flexibility in order to get on with the cover-up plan." All the participants knew that they could not fully testify. As Nixon said to Mitchell, "I know we can't make a complete cave-in and have the people go up there and testify. You would agree on that?" "I agree," responded Mitchell.

Toward the end of the March 22 meeting, Nixon assured everyone, "We will survive it," and complimented Dean for being a "son-of-a-bitching tough thing," and the president added: "I don't give a shit what happens. I want you all to stonewall it, let them plead the Fifth Amendment, cover-up or anything else, if it'll save it—save the plan. That's the whole point."

Then the president, commenting to Mitchell, said, "Up to this point the whole theory has been containment, as you know, John," and Mitchell answered, "Yeah."

The following day, everything changed.

On Friday, March 23, an unexpected crack in the cover-up developed. In open court, Judge John Sirica dropped a bombshell when he made public a letter written to him by convicted Watergate burglar James McCord. McCord's letter charged that the Watergate defendants were under "political pressure" to plead guilty and remain silent, that perjury had been committed, and that higher-ups were involved.

The following week McCord testified for four hours in a closed-door session before the Senate Watergate Committee. He declared that Colson, Dean, Magruder, and Mitchell had prior knowledge of the Watergate break-in.

Dean began to feel the noose closing around his neck. The McCord letter and his fear that Nixon was setting him up, plus the continued pressure to write a "Dean report," led Dean to consider a trip to the prosecutors in hopes of getting a deal. Finally, on March 26, when Haldeman told Dean that the White House was cutting Magruder and Mitchell loose, he realized that everyone except the president was expendable. Dean, fearing that Magruder would crack, called criminal lawyer Charles Shaffer. On April 2, Dean's lawyers told the prosecutors that their client was ready to cooperate. On

April 8, Dean began to talk. Magruder, seeing the writing on the wall, also decided to cooperate with the prosecutors.

ALL FALL DOWN

April was a particularly bad month for the president. With Dean and Magruder talking to the prosecutors, he had to see that the cover-up might collapse on his shoulders. In mid-April the world began to shatter for Nixon. He called April 14 "the day when everything began to fall apart." The president had devised an "hors d'oeuvre strategy," as Nixon told Haldeman and Ehrlichman, "Give 'em an hors d'oeuvre and maybe they won't come back for the main course." But who would be a tasty hors d'oeuvre? John Mitchell, of course. On April 14 Nixon, Haldeman, and Ehrlichman decided to try to get Mitchell to take the fall for Watergate. He refused. Ehrlichman's unsuccessful effort to persuade Mitchell to take the rap for the president led Mitchell to conclude that he was "too far out" and would not take the fall. Mitchell defended himself by pointing out that the genesis of Watergate came from pressure exerted from within the White House, not from his office.

If Mitchell would not shoulder blame and protect Nixon, who would? It was decided that John Dean would be made a presidential scapegoat, the sacrificial lamb. The new strategy devised by Nixon, Haldeman, and Ehrlichman was to have Dean write a report that "basically clears the President and the White House staff of involvement." If Dean would submit such a report, the president could go public and say, "Look, this is what I relied on. Dean deceived me." But Dean refused, suspecting that he was being set up, and instead continued to talk to the Justice Department in hopes of getting a deal from the prosecutors. At the same time, Magruder continued to meet with government prosecutors and tell all.

On April 14, the president, Haldeman, and Ehrlichman discussed their own complicity in the cover-up. The president began by saying that "Dean only tried to do what he could to pick up the pieces, and everybody else around here knew it had to be done." "Certainly," Ehrlichman said. Later Ehrlichman, the only one of the three who was not aware of the taping system then in operation, said, "There were eight or ten people around here who knew about this [the totality of the criminal activities], knew it was going on, Bob knew, I knew, all kinds of people knew."

"Well, I knew it, I knew it," Nixon added.

The management of Watergate, up to now scattered and only semi-coordinated, began to frustrate the president. Aware that the edges of the cover-up were unraveling and that it was in danger of completely falling apart and engulfing him, he suggested getting "everyone" together, "They've gotta have a straight damn line."

The president's desperate efforts to save the cover-up seemed doomed the following day, April 15, when Attorney General Richard Kleindienst informed Nixon that Haldeman and Ehrlichman were "being drawn into the criminal case," and that John Dean was their chief accuser. Kleindienst advised the president to dismiss his two top aides.

At 9:00 on the evening of the 15th, Dean met with the president and told him, according to Dean's testimony to the Senate, that he "had gone to the prosecutors," told them of his own involvement and that of others, but had not discussed with them the president's role in Watergate. The president asked Dean a number of leading questions that made Dean think the conversation was being taped, and Nixon said of his March assurance to Dean that he could get $1 million "to maintain the silence of the defendants," that "he had, of course, only been joking."

The president knew Dean had to go, but he was still hoping to put the blame on Dean. When they met on April 16, Nixon gave Dean two draft letters, one requesting a leave of absence, the other a letter of resignation. Dean refused to sign either, again fearing he was being set up for a fall.

The following morning the president discussed the John Dean problem with Haldeman and Ehrlichman. Dean has "decided to save his ass," the president said. And on April 17, Haldeman records in his notes that he told Nixon, "I must admit the guy (Dean) has really turned into an unbelievable disaster for us." "I'm trapped," the president concluded, "I've trapped myself."

In an April 30 television address, the president, bowing to the inevitable, announced the resignations of Haldeman and Ehrlichman. He also announced John Dean's dismissal. He denied any personal involvement in the break-in or cover-up but conceded that "there had been an effort to conceal the facts." Nixon claimed that he was misled by subordinates into believing that no one from his administration or campaign organization was involved.

In his memoirs, Nixon admits that the April 30 speech was less than truthful, giving the impression that he was unaware of the cover-up until March 21. Instead of "exerting presidential leadership," Nixon admitted embarking upon an "increasingly desperate search for ways to limit the damage."[37]

The president was unprotected; his "Berlin Wall" of Haldeman and Ehrlichman was gone. If Nixon was isolated before, he was even more alone and isolated in May as the Senate Watergate hearings began. At this time, the Nixon high command took a new shape. General Alexander Haig assumed Haldeman's role as chief of staff. And, bowing to pressure to appoint a special prosecutor in the Watergate case, new Attorney General Elliot Richardson announced that former solicitor general and Harvard law professor

Archibald Cox would serve in that capacity. Cox immediately went to work accumulating evidence.

SENATOR ERVIN'S COMMITTEE

When the Senate Select Committee on Presidential Campaign Activities (usually referred to as the Ervin Committee, or Watergate committee) opened its hearings on May 17, the president was already in a precarious position: Dean, Magruder, and McCord were talking, Haldeman and Ehrlichman had been jettisoned from the administration, the president's popularity was slipping, and the press was pursuing lead after lead on Watergate. The fact that the Senate hearings would be televised nationally only worsened matters.

The hearings got off to a slow start, with the committee initially calling witnesses on the periphery of power. Everyone was waiting for John Dean. Finally, on June 25, John Dean took the chair and began to read his prepared opening statement in a monotone voice: "To one who was in the White House and became somewhat familiar with its interworkings, the Watergate matter was an inevitable outgrowth of a climate of excessive concern over the political impact of demonstrators, excessive concern over leaks, an insatiable appetite for political intelligence, all coupled with a do-it-yourself White House staff, regardless of the law."

Thus began a 245–page statement in which Dean blew the lid off the administration. The portrait Dean painted was devastating: wiretapping, burglary, enemies lists, secret funds, money laundering, dirty tricks, Plumbers, intelligence surveillance, character assassination, obstruction of justice, cover-up. But all Dean had was his word—no documentation, no corroboration. Dean's assertion that the president was right in the middle of the mess came down to his word against the president's. How would the dilemma be resolved?

The answer fell into the lap of the committee on July 16 after several staff members had questioned Nixon staffer Alexander Butterfield in preparation for his appearance before the committee. In that questioning, Butterfield revealed the existence of a White House taping system. Butterfield was rushed to give testimony. Minority counsel (now U.S. Senator) Fred Thompson asked, "Mr. Butterfield, are you aware of the installation of any listening devices in the Oval Office of the President?" "I was aware of listening devices, yes, sir," was Butterfield's reply. "Are you aware of any devices that were installed in the Executive Office Building office of the President?" asked Thompson. "Yes, sir."

The president had secretly tape-recorded all conversations in the Oval Office, the president's office in the Executive Office Building, the Lincoln Room, and at Camp David. Another bombshell. The tapes could confirm or shatter Dean's charges against the president. It was no longer Dean's word against the president's. There was proof.

The Senate immediately requested the tapes, as did the special prosecutor. Nixon refused. The Senate and special prosecutor subpoenaed several of the tapes, and Nixon still refused, citing executive privilege. The Senate Watergate Committee and Archibald Cox took the president to court over the tapes. On August 29, Judge John Sirica ruled that the president must turn over the subpoenaed tapes. The president appealed the ruling, and on October 12, the U.S. Court of Appeals upheld Sirica's order. The president decided to appeal to the Supreme Court.

As the battle for the tapes began, the Senate committee continued to hear from witnesses. Mitchell, Ehrlichman, and Haldeman all contradicted Dean and pointed the finger at Dean as being the real culprit in the cover-up. But as the Senate's investigation wound down, the battle for the tapes heated up.

As if things weren't bad enough for President Nixon, the Justice Department was also investigating charges of corruption against Nixon's vice president, Spiro Agnew. Allegedly, Agnew had taken cash payments—bribes—in exchange for government contracts while Agnew was an official in and later governor of Maryland. According to the charges, Agnew was accepting bribe money while he was vice president.

An investigation by the U.S. attorney in Baltimore found approximately fifty possible criminal violations, including bribery, extortion, conspiracy, and tax evasion. After reviewing the evidence, Agnew's attorneys negotiated a plea bargain: Agnew would resign as vice president, plead *nolo contendere* (no contest) to a single charge of income tax evasion, the Justice Department would enter the evidence into the public record, and Agnew would escape a prison sentence. Walter Hoffman, the judge in the case, told Agnew that the no-contest plea was "the full equivalent of a plea of guilty." On October 10, 1973, Spiro Agnew resigned as vice president. Two days later, President Nixon nominated Gerald Ford as vice president. Ford was easily confirmed and was sworn in on December 6, 1973.

The battle for the tapes continued, with the president insisting that Archibald Cox, who was technically part of the executive branch, cease from pressing the president to produce the tapes. In an effort to get a compromise, Nixon offered Cox a surprise deal: The Stennis Plan. Under this plan, Nixon would let the seventy-two-year-old conservative Democrat Senator John Stennis of Mississippi, who was still recovering from a gunshot wound, verify the accuracy of a transcript of the tapes, but not turn them over to Cox. Part of the deal included an insistence that Cox ask for no more tapes.

Cox refused, and on October 20, in what came to be known as the "Saturday Night Massacre," Attorney General Richardson, ordered by Nixon to fire Cox, refused to do so and resigned. Deputy Attorney General William Ruckelshaus refused as well and also resigned. Finally Solicitor General Robert Bork was named acting attorney general, and he carried out Nixon's order to fire Cox, abolish the special prosecutor's office, and have the FBI seal Cox's offices to prevent removal of any files. (Bork's role in this affair came to haunt his reputation and was a key element in the Senate's refusal to confirm his nomination to the Supreme Court in 1987.)

A tremendous public outcry followed, as did the introduction of twenty-two bills in Congress calling for an impeachment investigation. On October 30, the House Judiciary Committee began consideration of possible procedures in the event of an impeachment. The process of impeachment was made cumbersome by the framers of the U.S. Constitution. The House Judiciary Committee holds hearings and makes a recommendation to the full House, who then votes on impeachment. If Articles of Impeachment are approved, the president is tried in the Senate. Nixon finally agreed to turn over some of the tapes. On November 1, 1973, Leon Jaworski was appointed as a new special prosecutor. He too sought the tapes. As pressure on the president mounted, calls for his resignation appeared. On November 17, the president, in a televised press conference, said, "People have got to know whether or not their President is a crook. Well, I'm not a crook."

The president was determined to try one last public relations offensive; this one called "Operation Candor." In this operation, Nixon would publicly promise to deliver everything, but stall, stall, and stall. Although the president promised on November 20 that there were no more Watergate "bombshells" waiting to explode, on the very next day Nixon's lawyers told John Sirica of a "gap" problem in the tapes. Operation Candor was dead when Judge John Sirica revealed that there was an 18½-minute gap in the important June 20, 1972, tape of a conversation between Nixon and Haldeman, a meeting held three days after the Watergate break-in.

Alexander Haig, Nixon's chief of staff, blamed the gap on "some sinister force," but a panel of experts concluded that it was the result of five separate manual erasures. Judge Sirica recommended a grand jury investigation into "the possibility of unlawful destruction of evidence and related offenses," adding "a distinct possibility of unlawful conduct on the part of one or more persons exists." The 18½-minute gap caused another public outcry. Nixon dug in. As the Ervin Committee and special prosecutor continued to battle Nixon for more tapes, the president announced that he would not hand over any more tapes because it would violate confidentiality and could have an adverse effect on the Watergate trials.

On February 6, with only four dissenting votes, the House of Representatives adopted H.R. 803, which directed the House Committee on the Judiciary, under Chairman Peter Rodino (D-New Jersey), to begin an investigation into whether grounds existed for the House to impeach President Nixon.

Watergate was moving closer and closer to the president. On March 1, the federal grand jury indicted seven former top presidential aides—Mitchell, Haldeman, Ehrlichman, Colson, Mardian, Parkinson, and Strachan—for attempting to cover up the Watergate investigation by lying to the FBI and to the grand jury, and for paying hush money to the original defendants. The grand jury also turned a briefcase over to Judge Sirica, the contents of which were kept secret, but which related to the president's role in the scandal. Based on this material, the grand jury named Richard M. Nixon, president of the United States, as an "unindicted co-conspirator" in the case.

The House joined the Senate and special prosecutor in seeking White House tapes, but the president continued to resist. Finally, on April 29, in a national television address, Nixon announced that he would supply the Judiciary Committee with "edited transcripts" of the subpoenaed conversations. Nixon said this action would "at last, once and for all, show that what I knew and what I did with regard to the Watergate break-in and cover-up were just as I have described them to you from the very beginning. As far as the president's role with regard to Watergate is concerned, the entire story is there."

But the entire story *was not* there. The transcripts later proved to be incomplete and inaccurate. At the time, however, they appeared impressive indeed. The president, in his speech, had the camera pan to a table containing stack upon stack of binders that appeared to contain thousands upon thousands of pages. In reality, this was a public relations ploy. Many of the large binders contained only a few pages of text.

Among the many White House omissions is this portion of the March 22, 1973, conversation between Nixon and Mitchell. The president says: "I don't give a shit what happens. I want you all to stonewall it, let them plead the Fifth Amendment, cover up or anything else, if it'll save it—save the plan. That's the whole point. . . . Up to this point, the whole theory has been containment, as you know, John." This incriminating material *does not* appear in the White House transcript but is in the House Judiciary Committee's version. There were many other inaccuracies. Nixon's sanitized version was not acceptable, and the fight for the tapes themselves continued.

Leon Jaworski was methodically building a criminal case against administration officials, but a problem remained: What to do about the president? The charges against Mitchell, Haldeman et al. hinged upon a conspiracy in which the president was actively involved. But could the president of the United States be indicted in a criminal case, or was impeachment the only avenue with which to deal with charges of presidential criminality?

Jaworski asked for legal memoranda from his staff relating to this question. The conclusion reached was that while there was a question of "propriety," there was "no explicit or implicit constitutional bar to indictment."[38] In the end, Jaworski, though admitting that there was clearly enough evidence to indict Nixon, could not bring himself to indict a sitting president. Instead, the grand jury unanimously voted to name Richard Nixon an "unindicted co-conspirator."

THE MEDIA: FROM LAMBS TO LIONS

During the 1972 campaign, the press was somewhat neutral regarding the president. But as the story of Watergate and its related horrors picked up steam, and as the trickle of negative stories built into an avalanche that eventually buried Richard Nixon, the press had an increasingly important role in shifting public opinion against the president. The cumulative impact of day after day of revelations, day after day of TV coverage of Senate and House hearings, the unrelenting pressure of investigative reporting, and the almost daily discovery of bombshell after bombshell, eventually led to Nixon's downfall.

Nixon claimed he "had the most unfriendly press in history, it has never bothered me." Actually it did bother Nixon, as it would any president. Nixon did face a hostile press, but *not* in the campaign of 1972. And while administration officials kept complaining about "excessive press coverage" of a "third rate burglary," there was actually very little coverage of Watergate during the campaign.

A study by Ben Bagdikian revealed that only 15 out of the 433 Washington-based reporters were assigned to the Watergate story, and some on only limited bases. Robert Maynard of the *Washington Post* found that of the approximately 500 articles written by national columnists during the 1972 campaign, less than two dozen dealt with Watergate. And Edwin Diamond reviewed all network TV newscasts during the campaign, and found "a straight, unquestioning serving of 'news' that it is clear, in hindsight advanced the cover-up." CBS gave Watergate the most coverage of the TV networks, but as their White House correspondent Dan Rather noted, "CBS News was putting some stories about Watergate on the air, more than our broadcast competitors, but pitifully few." Rather blames this on "the deadly daily diet of deceit sent us from the White House. . . . They lied, schemed, threatened, and cajoled to prevent network correspondents from getting a handle on the story. And they succeeded."[39]

After the 1972 election, the Watergate story seemed to take on a life of its own. Day after day, story after story, Watergate news seemed to engulf the president. Nixon's aides insisted that the press was being unfair and that Nixon was "hounded from office" by a hostile press. Nixon himself claimed that the press had "built this [Watergate] into a federal case." But did the press *create* Watergate, or merely help *uncover* it? Edwin Diamond writes: "The record of the Watergate coverage discloses no hounding of the president. Quite the contrary. The press did not speak as a chorus with one voice. The president had his own defenders . . . equally important, his [campaign] in 1972 initially came across louder than the message of Watergate."[40]

THE HOUSE FACES IMPEACHMENT

In this highly charged atmosphere of eroding public confidence in the president, in which every day seemed to bring a new, more-damaging revelation, the House Judiciary Committee prepared to open the public phase of its impeachment inquiry. The case against the president had been building for over a year, but the case was made up primarily of circumstantial evidence linking the president to the scandal, with accusations from Dean, Magruder, and others. The direct evidence was still fairly thin.

As committee counsel John Doar accumulated material against Nixon, it became clear that the full weight of the accumulated evidence was devastating. But before impeachment proceedings against the president could begin, a very important question had to be answered: What is an impeachable offense?

At one end of the spectrum of thought (the president's position) was the view that impeachment could *only* be for serious crimes. Nixon's was a strictly *legalistic* view. At a March 6, 1974, press conference, Nixon, answering a question, said that "impeachment should be limited to very serious crimes committed in one's official capacity." Nixon added, "When you refer to a narrow view of what is an impeachable crime, I would say that might leave in the minds of some of our view. The Constitution is very precise." At the other end of the spectrum was the view that impeachment was primarily a *political* device for potentially removing a president, and one need not find violations of the law to vote for impeachment.

The Constitution, as it is in many areas, is rather vague regarding impeachment. The Constitution says that public officers "shall be removed from office on impeachment for, and conviction of, treason, bribery, or other high crimes and misdemeanors" (Article II, sect. 4). The founders' original proposal on impeachment first presented at the Constitutional Convention provided for impeachment for "malpractice or neglect of duty." The Committee on Detail changed the wording to read "treason, bribery, or corruption," and still later changed it to "treason or bribery." George Mason recommended that "maladministration" be added to the list, but James Madison objected on grounds that it was too vague. Finally, the wording was changed to the old British term, "high crimes and misdemeanors." What then, did the founders understand by this phrase?

In general, the founders, following the British common law tradition, did not understand "high crimes and misdemeanors" in the narrow, legal sense, or in the strictly criminal sense. Constitutional scholar Raoul Berger concludes that the founders had a fairly wide view of the grounds for impeachment that included misapplication of funds, abuse of official power, neglect of duty, encroachment on or contempt of Parliament's prerogatives, corruption, and betrayal of trust.[41]

The history of impeachment in the United States offers few precedents, as only a handful of cases have reached the Senate. Several of these cases, however, *did not* involve indictable criminal offenses. In the only other attempted case of presidential impeachment, that of Andrew Johnson in 1868, the charges were almost strictly political.

On February 21, John Doar submitted a report to the committee entitled, "Constitutional Grounds for Presidential Impeachment," which reviewed the history of impeachment and its application to the case at hand. Doar concluded that impeachment was a remedy to be applied in cases of "serious offenses against the system of government."

A long, emotional, often heated, sometimes eloquent debate over the evidence against the president ensued. Under the glare of national television, Chairman Peter Rodino of New Jersey guided the hearings through these difficult times with even-handedness. He knew that if the impeachment of Richard Nixon were to be legitimate and appropriate, it would require a bipartisan vote in favor of impeachment.

On July 19, John Doar summarized the case against Nixon for the committee. "Reasonable men," he said, "acting reasonably would find the President guilty." Doar spoke of Nixon's "enormous crimes" and accused the president of "the terrible deed of subverting the Constitution." Minority counsel Albert Jenner supported Doar's conclusion.

On July 27, the committee voted on Article I of impeachment, which accused the president of engaging in a "course of conduct" designed to obstruct justice in attempting to cover up Watergate. This article passed by a 27-11 vote, with 6 Republicans joining all 21 Democrats in the majority. The following day, Article II, charging Nixon with abuse of power, passed 28-10, and on the following day, the third article of impeachment, charging the president with unconstitutionally defying a congressional subpoena for White House tape recordings, passed 21-17. Two other articles, dealing with concealing the bombing of Cambodia and with income tax evasion, both failed by a 26-12 vote.

The vote against the president—especially on Articles I and II—was bipartisan (see Table 1.1). Rodino was able to get enough Republicans to vote against a president of their own party to ensure that the public would see that the case against Nixon crossed party loyalties. The Judiciary Committee would recommend to the full House that it vote to impeach Richard M. Nixon, 37th president of the United States. On only one other occasion, in the impeachment of Andrew Johnson over 100 years earlier had the House faced such a situation.

THE BATTLE FOR THE TAPES

Everyone seemed to want Nixon's White House tapes. The Senate, the special prosecutor, then the House, all wanted the recorded record to see who was telling the truth. But the president refused to part with the tapes, citing variously executive privilege, the need for confidentiality, and other reasons.

Judiciary Committee chairman Peter Rodino wanted the tapes, and by a vote of 20-18 (essentially along partisan lines) the Judiciary Committee rejected Nixon's offer of written transcripts instead of the actual tapes, and in-

Table 1.1
Vote on Impeachment Articles

Article		For		Against		
		Dems.	*Reps.*	*Dems.*	*Reps.*	*Total*
I	Obstruction of Justice	21	6	0	11	27-11
II	Abuse of Power	21	7	0	10	28-10
III	Contempt of Congress	19	2	2	15	21-17
IV	Bombing of Cambodia	12		9	17	12-26
V	Income Tax Evasion	12		9	17	12-26

Source: Adapted from *Impeachment of Richard Nixon*, Report of the Committee on the Judiciary, House of Representatives, August 20, 1974.

formed the president that he had "failed to comply with the Committee's subpoena." After battles by the Judiciary Committee and Jaworski to get the tapes from the president, the Supreme Court agreed to hear the case.

President Nixon refused to comply with the Committee's subpoena, invoking a claim of "executive privilege." Although there is no mention of executive privilege in the Constitution, the claim derives from a belief that it is part of the implied power of the executive function of the president. The president's claim was not entirely self-serving. Not only is there a considerable history of presidential claims of privilege and confidentiality, but it is clear that some stages of the policy-making process must remain outside the glare of public scrutiny.

Taking the case placed the Court in the center of a legal *and* political battle. It was not a foregone conclusion that the president would obey a Court ruling. He already had warned that he would only obey a "definitive" ruling, and Charles Alan Wright, Nixon's lawyer, said, "The tradition is very strong that judges should have the last word, but," he added, "in a government organized as ours is, there are times when that simply cannot be the case."

The case, *United States of America v. Richard Nixon*, revolved around the question of who decides whether a president obeys a subpoena—the Congress, the courts, or the president himself? Leon Jaworski argued that the president must comply with a subpoena in criminal case, that our system of law is based on no man being above the law:

Who is to be the arbiter of what the Constitution says? Now, the president may be right in how he reads the Constitution. But he may also be wrong. And if he is wrong, who is there to tell him so? . . . This nation's constitutional form of government is in serious jeopardy if the President, any President, is to say that the Constitution means what he says it does, and that there is no one, not even the Supreme Court to tell him otherwise.

Nixon's lawyer, James St. Clair, thought otherwise: "The president is not above the law. Nor does he contend that he is. What he does contend is that as President the law can be applied to him only one way, and that is by impeachment."

On July 24, in an 8-0 decision (Justice William Rehnquist, who at one time worked in the Nixon administration, withdrew from the case), the Supreme Court ruled that President Nixon must give to Judge Sirica (who was presiding in the Watergate cover-up trial) the tapes, which were evidence in a criminal case. While acknowledging a heretofore-unrecognized constitutional basis for the claim of executive privilege, the Court ruled that in this case, the president was required to turn over the tapes. The decision read in part:

A President and those who assist him must be free to explore alternatives in the process of shaping policies and making decisions and to do so in a way many would be unwilling to express except privately. . . . The privilege is fundamental to the operation of government and inextricably rooted in the separation of powers under the Constitution. . . . Nowhere in the Constitution . . . is there any explicit reference to a privilege of confidentiality, yet to the extent this interest relates to the effective discharge of the President's power, it is constitutionally based.

But this privilege was not without limits. As the Court noted:

Neither the doctrine of separation of powers, nor the need for confidentiality of high level communications, without more, can sustain an absolute, unqualified presidential privilege of immunity from judicial process under all circumstances. The President's need for complete candor and objectivity from advisers calls for great deference from the courts. However, when the privilege depends solely on the broad undifferentiated claim of public interest in the confidentiality of such conversations, a confrontation with other values arises.

On August 5, Nixon finally released the tapes, and his fate was sealed. The June 23, 1972, tape became known as the "smoking gun," providing undeniable evidence of Nixon's criminal complicity. When its content became known, the president's defense collapsed. When he released the tapes, the president admitted that some of the tapes "are at variance with certain of my previous statements." Nixon *had* lied, covered up, obstructed justice, not for national security reasons, but to protect himself. There was no way Nixon could survive. Even his staunchest supporters turned on the president. It was over.

Impeachment in the House and conviction in the Senate were now certainties. Public opinion, which had been turning against the president since January, was now overwhelmingly against him. Gallup Poll data (see Table 1.2) reveals the quick, sharp shift in public opinion.

The June 23 tape not only revealed that Nixon was directing a criminal cover-up in the first week after the break-in but also showed Nixon to be a small, petty person. This tape, and others, contained revealing personal glimpses into Nixon the man, and much of what was revealed showed a dark side of Nixon never before seen by the public.

THE RESIGNATION

The final days were a nightmare for Nixon. He became progressively alone and isolated. He began to drink heavily. Son-in-law Edward Cox later remarked "the president was up walking the halls last night, talking to pic-

Table 1.2
Percent Believing in Nixon's Complicity (in Watergate)

May 11–14	56
June 1–4	67
June 22–25	71
July 6–9	73
August 3–6	76

tures of former presidents—giving speeches and talking to the pictures on the wall." Theodore H. White said the president was "an unstable personality" and "a time bomb which, if not defused in just the right way, might blow the course of all American history apart." Chief of Staff Haig ordered the president's doctors to deny Nixon all pills.[42]

In the final days a virtual coup took place. With the president behaving in an unstable manner, Haig took over day-to-day operations of the White House, and Secretary of Defense James Schlesinger ordered all military commanders to accept *no orders* from Nixon unless Schlesinger himself countersigned the order!

As those around the president began to see resignation as the only viable alternative, a slow, delicate process of coaxing Nixon to accept the inevitable began. With his popularity in the low 20 percent range and falling, with impeachment and conviction a certainty, all that remained was for the final decision to be made.

In the late afternoon of August 7, Hugh Scott, minority leader in the Senate, John Rhodes, minority leader in the House, and Barry Goldwater, elder statesman of the Republican party, met with Nixon in the Oval office. Al Haig warned them, "He is almost on the edge of resignation and if you suggest it, he may take umbrage and reverse." In the meeting, the word *resignation* never came up. Instead, the three Republican leaders assessed Nixon's waning support in the Congress. Scott told Nixon the situation was "gloomy." "It sounds damn gloomy," Nixon replied. Goldwater said it was "hopeless." Without using the words, the three visitors made it clear that Nixon would be impeached and convicted. When they left, Nixon went upstairs in the White House to tell his family it was over. The president broke the news to his family and, according to his daughter Julie, asked, "Was it worth it?"[43]

In a fifteen-minute television address delivered on the evening of August 8, 1974, the president announced that "I shall resign the presidency effective at noon tomorrow." In the speech, Nixon showed little remorse, and cited as his reason for leaving that: "In the last few days it has become evident to me that I no longer have a strong enough political base in the Congress to justify continuing in office." He added, "I regret deeply any injuries that may have been done in the course of the events that led to this decision. I would say only that if some of my judgments were wrong—and some were wrong—they were made in what I believed at the time to be in the best interest of the nation." Nixon neither protested his innocence nor admitted guilt. It was a controlled, carefully crafted speech.

The next morning, the Nixon family went to the East Room for a farewell to the president's staff. In an emotional talk, Nixon rambled almost uncontrollably, then pulled himself back together, rambled, then controlled himself. He spoke about his father.

I think they would have called him sort of a little man, common man. He didn't consider himself that way. You know what he was? He was a streetcar motorman, first, and then he was a farmer, and then he had a lemon ranch. It was the poorest lemon ranch in California, I can assure you.

Then his mother:

Nobody will ever write a book, probably, about my mother. Well, I guess all of you would say this about your mother—my mother was a saint. And I think of her, two boys dying of tuberculosis, nursing four others in order that she could take care of my older brother for three years in Arizona and seeing each of them die, and when they died, it was like one of her own. Yes, she will have no books written about her. But she was a saint.

Nixon spoke of his background, of sorrow and hatred, of troubles and heartaches, and he wept.

He then walked to his helicopter for the first leg of a journey that would take him to San Clemente, California. When the plane was midway across the American heartland, he was no longer president of the United States.

On August 9, 1974, shortly before noon, Nixon's letter of resignation was delivered to Secretary of State Henry Kissinger. It read in its entirety: "Dear Mr. Secretary: I hereby resign the office of President of the United States. Sincerely, Richard Nixon." He was the first president ever to resign from office. Upon being sworn in as president, Gerald Ford said, "Our long national nightmare is over," and said that the wounds of Watergate were "more painful and more poisonous than those of foreign wars."

The Judiciary Committee filed its report with the full House. In the end, *all* thirty-eight members recommended impeachment. On August 20, the House accepted the committee's report and recommendations by a vote of 412-3, without taking any action on it. The ten Republicans on the Judiciary

Committee who earlier voted against all the impeachment articles issued the following statement:

Our gratitude for his having by his resignation spared the nation additional agony should not obscure for history our judgment that Richard Nixon, as President, committed certain acts for which he should have been impeached and removed from office.

They added:

We know that it has been said, and perhaps some will continue to say, that Richard Nixon was "hounded from office" by his political opponents and media critics. We feel constrained to point out, however, that it was Richard Nixon who impeded the FBI's investigation of the Watergate affair by wrongfully attempting to implicate the Central Intelligence Agency; it was Richard Nixon, who created and preserved the evidence of that transgression and who, knowing that it had been subpoenaed by this Committee and the Special Prosecutor, concealed its terrible import, even from his own counsel, until he could do so no longer. And it was a unanimous Supreme Court of the United States which, in an opinion authored by the Chief Justice, whom he appointed, ordered Richard Nixon to surrender that evidence to the Special Prosecutor, to further the ends of justice.

The tragedy that finally engulfed Richard Nixon has many facets. One was the very self-inflicted nature of the harm. It is striking that such an able, experienced and perceptive man, whose ability to grasp the global implications of events little noticed by others may well have been unsurpassed by any of his predecessors, should fail to comprehend the damage that accrued daily to himself, his Administration, and to the Nation, as day after day, month after month, he imprisoned the truth about his role in the Watergate cover-up so long and so tightly within the solitude of his Oval Office that it could not be unleashed without destroying his Presidency.

THE PARDON

Would Nixon, as ex-president, have to face criminal charges? After all, the charge of conspiracy to obstruct justice named Nixon as an "unindicted co-conspirator." The answer came less than a month after Nixon left office.

On Sunday, September 8, 1974, President Gerald Ford called a news conference in which he announced that he had granted former President Nixon "a full, free, and absolute pardon . . . for all offenses against the United States which he, Richard Nixon, has committed, or may have committed, or taken part in during the period" of his presidency.

Some suggested that Ford and Nixon, or Ford and Haig, made some sort of deal: resignation in exchange for a pardon. But no proof exists, and all parties to the decision deny that any deal, implicit or explicit, was made. But the pardon, granted in the absence of criminal charges, leaves some unanswered questions and creates disconcerting problems. To what extent was Nixon criminally guilty? Is a president above the law? How does one accept a pardon for acts he claims never to have committed?

The Republicans took a beating in the mid-term elections following Richard Nixon's resignation. Fighting an uphill battle against the recent legacy of Watergate, the Republicans had little hope of doing well. In the House, the Republicans lost forty-eight seats, and in the Senate lost five seats. Numerically this may not seem drastic, but one must remember that the Democrats already had large majorities in both chambers. Given their already clear control of the Congress, these numbers are indeed impressive.

But the story was not over. The United States would now have to contend with the dark legacy of Watergate.

NOTES

1. Much of the material in this chapter is taken from Michael A. Genovese, *The Nixon Presidency: Power and Politics in Turbulent Times* (Westport, CT: Greenwood Press, 1990).

2. Paul J. Halpen, in his edited volume, *Why Watergate?* (Pacific Palisades, CA: Palisades, 1975), 1–3, provides the first three categories; I have added the fourth.

3. George C. Herring, *America's Longest War* (New York: Wiley, 1979), 217–51.

4. When the president spoke these words, American B-52s had been flying bombing missions over Cambodia for over thirteen months.

5. Les Evans and Allen Myers, *Watergate and the Myth of American Democracy* (New York: Pathfinder, 1974).

6. Rowland Evans, Jr., and Robert D. Novak, *Nixon in the White House* (New York: Random House, 1971), 227–85.

7. In November 1969, the My Lai massacre—in which American soldiers killed more than 350 South Vietnamese villagers—became public knowledge. Although the massacre took place in 1968, Nixon had to deal with the public outrage. His response was to spy on Ronald Ridenhour, who made the massacre known to the army and later to Congress. The revelation of the My Lai massacre proved to be a turning point in public opinion as the "middle class" began to turn against the war. See Seymour M. Hersh, *The Price of Power* (New York: Summit, 1983), 135; and Clark R. Mollenhoff, *Game Plan for Disaster* (New York: Norton, 1976), chap. 9.

8. H. R. Haldeman, *The Ends of Power* (New York: Times Books, 1978), 79.

9. Richard M. Nixon, *RN: The Memoirs of Richard Nixon* (New York: Grosset and Dunlap, 1978), 387–88.

10. William Safire, *Before the Fall: An Inside View of the Pre–Watergate White House* (Garden City, NY: Doubleday, 1975), 166.

11. Hersh, *The Price of Power*, 86–87.

12. All references to notes taken by H. R. "Bob" Haldeman who served as the president's chief of staff, are taken from the National Archives holdings of presidential material, Arlington, Virginia.

13. Nixon, *RN*, 469–71.

14. William Shawcross, *Sideshow: Kissinger, Nixon and the Destruction of Cambodia* (New York: Simon and Schuster, 1979), 157–69; Jonathan Schell, *The Time of Illusion* (New York: Random House, 1975), 111–16; and Tad Szulc, *The Illusion of Peace* (New York:Viking, 1978), 294–96.

15. Quoted in Barry Sussman, *The Great Cover-up: Nixon and the Scandal of Watergate* (New York: Signet, 1974), 207–9.

16. Seymour M. Hersh, "1971 Tape Links Nixon to Plan to Use Thugs," *New York Times,* September 24, 1981, p. 1.

17. Charles Colson, comments at Hofstra University Conference on the Nixon Presidency, November 1987.

18. Sussman, *The Great Cover-up*, 213.

19. Quoted in Hersh, *The Price of Power*, 397.

20. Haldeman, *The Ends of Power*, 114–16.

21. Ehrlichman, *Witness to Power* (New York: Simon and Schuster, 1982), 165.

22. Commentary by Charles Colson and Egil Krogh, Hofstra University Conference on the Nixon Presidency, November 1987.

23. Stanley I. Kutler, *The Wars of Watergate* (New York: Knopf, 1990), 4, 104–7.

24. Quoted in Schell, *The Time of Illusion*, 146.

25. J. Anthony Lukas, *Nightmare: The Underside of the Nixon Years* (New York: Viking, 1973; Penguin, 1988), 128.

26. All direct quotations of presidential conversations, unless otherwise noted, are taken from the White House recordings of the president, usually referred to as "the tapes."

27. Theodore H. White, *Breach of Faith: The Fall of Richard Nixon* (New York: Atheneum, 1975), 135–36.

28. Jeb Magruder, *An American Life: One Man's Road to Watergate* (New York, Atheneum, 1974), 185.

29. Jeb Magruder, comments at Hofstra University Conference, November 1987.

30. Haldeman, *The Ends of Power*, 170.

31. Jeb Magruder, Hofstra University, November 1987.

32. See Fred Emery, *Watergate* (New York: Touchstone, 1994), 165.

33. Nixon, *RN*, 646.

34. Magruder, Hofstra University, November 1987.

35. *New York Times* Staff, *The End of a Presidency* (New York: Bantam, 1974), 161.

36. Lukas, *Nightmare*, 257–59.

37. Nixon, *RN*, 850.

38. Richard Ben-Veniste and George Frampton, Jr., *Stonewall: The Real Story of the Watergate Prosecution* (New York: Simon and Schuster, 1977).

39. Edwin Diamond, *The Tin Kazoo* (Cambridge: MIT Press, 1975), 217. See also chap. 11, "Myths of Watergate." Dan Rather, "Watergate on TV," *Newsday*, December 16, 1973, p. 9.

40. Diamond, *The Tin Kazoo*, 218.

41. Raoul Berger, *Impeachment: The Constitutional Problems* (New York: Bantam, 1973).

42. Carl Bernstein and Bob Woodward, *The Final Days* (New York: Simon and Schuster, 1976), 395 and 100–2, 204, 230–70, 437–39, and 498.

43. Bernstein and Woodward, *The Final Days*, 441–46.

2

What Manner of Man? Watergate and the Development of Nixon's Political Personality

Happy people don't make history.

—French proverb

Who is Richard Nixon? Behind the public persona, the politician's mask, who is this man whose administration proved the most corrupt in U.S. history? What moved and motivated him, what forces animated his behavior?

Perhaps this incident, related by Ellen K. Coughlin, best captures Nixon the man and the politician:

When his father died in 1956, Richard Nixon was campaigning for the vice-presidency of the United States. Soon after attending the funeral, the candidate was off again on a swing through upstate New York.

The first stop was Buffalo. He began a speech there with the words, "My father . . ." and then his voice faltered and he clung to the podium as if deeply moved.

He began again. "I remember my father telling me a long time ago: 'Dick . . . Dick, Buffalo is a beautiful town.'"

"It may have been his favorite town."

Later, he moved on to Rochester, where he told the same story, substituting only the name of the city: "Dick, Rochester is a beautiful town." And then to Ithaca, where the performance was repeated once again.[1]

Richard Milhous Nixon was a complex, multidimensional figure, a man of many contradictions. There were, as cartoonist Herblock oversimplified, two Nixons—the good Nixon and the bad Nixon—and they existed side by side within the man.

Simple, easy descriptions do not apply to Richard Nixon. Longtime Nixon friend and speechwriter Raymond Price saw his former boss as something of a paradox. Theodore White also noticed the paradoxical quality of Nixon when he wrote of "the essential duality of his nature, the evil and the good, the flights on panic and the resolution of spirit, the good mind and the mean trickery." And former White House aide William Safire described Nixon as a complex man with multiple layers, best seen as a layer cake, with the icing (Nixon's public face) "conservative, stern, dignified, proper. But beneath the icing one finds a variety of separate layers which reveal a complex, sometimes contradictory, paradoxical human being." Price perceptively observed that one part of Nixon was exceptionally considerate, exceptionally caring, sentimental, generous of spirit, kind, while another part was coldly calculating, devious, craftily manipulative, and yet, a third part was angry, vindictive, ill-tempered, mean-spirited. According to Price, those close to Nixon often referred to his "light side" and his "dark sides," and over the years, the light side and the dark side "have been at constant war with one another." Because of this, Price opined, "he has always needed people around him who would help the lighter side prevail." "Interestingly," Price added, "the extent to which the dark side grew not out of his nature, but out of his experiences in public life." The light side-dark side assessment of Nixon is frequently referred to, especially by Nixon insiders. Some staffers (e.g., Robert Finch) appealed to Nixon's better side, while others (e.g., Charles Colson and H. R. Haldeman) appealed to the dark side. For the most part, the latter dominated in the White House. This light side-dark side quality of Nixon made him a sort of Dr. Jekyll, Mr. Hyde.

Nixon's chief of staff, Bob Haldeman, once described Nixon as "the weirdest man ever to live in the White House," and John Ehrlichman described his former boss as "the mad monk." Nixon has been a fascinating subject for analysis precisely because he is so puzzling. As columnist Hugh Sidey has said, "He is an absolutely sinister human being, but fascinating. I'd rather spend an evening with Richard Nixon than with almost anybody else because he is so bizarre. He has splashes of brilliance. He is obscene at times, his recall is almost total; his acquaintanceship with the world's figures is amazing. He is a fascinating human being."

In trying to answer the question "Who is Richard Nixon?," one runs into the problem inherent in all efforts at psychobiography.[2] After all, in trying to probe the inner workings of presidents or other public figures, we would be better served by "getting them on the couch" so as to probe, in a serious and analytical way, the psychological makeup of our subjects. But we have no such opportunity. Ours is the task of psychobiography at a distance; of trying to take the measure of our subject without evidence sufficient for validation.

Yet another complicating factor stems from the fact that we are dealing with controversial figures, and it is difficult to withdraw emotions and give an objective assessment of our subject. Further, in attempting to tease out what factors in childhood or elsewhere caused a certain pattern of behavior, we run into the problem of causality: Did the fact that "X" did not get a pony as a child lead him to hate his parents, which led him to hate authority, which led him to become a revolutionary?

If handled carefully, these problems can be dealt with, and we should not abandon our efforts because the mountain seems—and is—so hard to climb. Personality is important, and though while it is difficult to study presidential personality, it is also necessary to do so. In presidential politics, both the individual and the institution mold and shape behavior. In this chapter, we examine the role of individual personality on political behavior. This essay is an attempt to come to grips with a complex, often contradictory man, but not as a strict and analytically precise psychological exploration. The only conclusions we can reach are tentative ones. The presidency is an institution shaped to a large extent by individual presidents. Especially in crises, unstructured or ambiguous situations, or times when role conflict or no clearly defined role behavior is in place, personality can have (and has had) a significant impact on presidential behavior.

Presidents face pressures to conform to certain role expectations, but as an institution, the presidency is less bound by role and is more responsive to variations of individual presidents than most offices. As former Lyndon Johnson aide George Reedy once observed, "The office neither elevates nor degrades a man. What it does is to provide the stage upon which all of his personality traits are magnified and accentuated."

CHILD IS FATHER TO THE MAN—NIXON'S YOUTH

One can see in Nixon's childhood certain recurring patterns or themes, which may have led to the development of psychological traits later affecting his adult behavior. The extent to which the traits and characteristics developed early in life impacted upon Nixon's behavior as president is shown in Nixon's relationship to his father and mother, the role illness and death played in his childhood, and the view of the world Nixon developed out of his childhood experiences. In many ways, Garry Wills's comment that "Nixon's background haunts him" rings true.

From his relationship with his parents, young Richard's early development was, in David Abrahamsen's words, a tug-of-war between "two contrasting emotional antagonists, one parent unusually quiet and unyielding, the other often unruly and violent." As a boy, Nixon was caught in the middle. This forced him to walk a "tightrope" emotionally. Several psycho-biographers characterize the home and family environment in which he grew as unhealthy and not conducive to the development of high self-steem. The relationship of Frank and Hannah Nixon was described by Nixon biographer Stephen Ambrose as "a union of opposites." Nixon's relationship to his parents rests at the center of many interpretations of the roots of Richard Nixon's problems.

Nixon's father, Frank, is variously described as "gloomy and argumentative" and "tyrannical" (Wills); as "a chronically angry man, ulcer-ridden from the early years of his marriage, who invited hatred in his own family," who "punished his sons savagely," as "volatile, unpredictable and explosive," (Brodie); and as "a tyrant who intimidated his children. He spanked them on the slightest pretext." He was "unpredictable." "His children feared him" (Abrahamsen). In his autobiography, *RN*, Nixon writes of his father as a man with a "quick tongue and a ready pair of fists" who was a "natural fighter." When Frank was in one of his "black moods," young Richard knew to avoid him. Frank, his son Richard wrote, "had a brusque and bristly exterior."

Nixon's mother Hannah was almost the direct opposite of Frank. Hannah Nixon is remembered as "saintly" (Wills); "shy and quiet" (Barber); "the epitome of self-control" (Di Clerico); and Nixon himself, on the eve of leaving the presidency, spoke of his mother as "a saint." A devout Quaker and pacifist, Hannah Nixon was the source of almost all of young Richard's security and affection in childhood. But this security was interrupted when Hannah was forced to leave Richard with his father while Hannah took their tubercular sons to Arizona. Also, at the age of twelve, Richard was sent to live with an aunt for six months for reasons that are still unclear. These separations had a deep impact on young Richard Nixon.

These two parents of vastly different style, temperament, and outlook pulled Nixon in two different directions. This was complicated by the extended periods of separation from his mother Nixon was forced to endure. David Abrahamsen sees the result of this tug-of-war in Richard producing confusion, ambivalence, and identification problems for Nixon. As Abrahamsen writes, "Nixon had a double personality, a person who simultaneously seems to display entirely different thoughts, feelings, attitudes, and character." These behavior traits were imprinted on Nixon in childhood and extended into his adult life. It created, in Abrahamsen's terms, "an emotional conflict therein." There was "an abyss between his higher, noble intentions and his aggressive, lower inclinations."

Death also had a profound affect upon young Richard Nixon. Two of his brothers died of tubercular meningitis: the first, seven-year-old Arthur, with whom Richard was very close, died when Richard was twelve; the second, twenty-three-year-old Harold, died when Richard was twenty. Both had lengthy periods of illness that necessitated their mother Hannah taking her sons to Arizona in an effort to find a climate that might help them recover. During these times, Richard stayed at home with his father, and away from his mother.

Some psychohistorians note Nixon's reaction to the death of his two brothers as "survival guilt." This guilt may have led to an unconscious wish for injury or even a "death wish," a self-destructiveness that may have resulted in Nixon behaving during the Watergate affair in a way that invited his own demise. He becomes, in David Abrahamsen's terms, "his own executioner. He punishes himself by arranging his own failures." His own doctor, at the height of the Watergate crisis, said that the president had a "death wish," and his head Secret Service guard said "You can't protect a President who wants to kill himself." The seeds of Nixon's low self-esteem and insecurity were sewn early in his life and would come back to haunt him as president. Essentially, Richard Nixon had a warm, loving mother who abandoned him from time to time, and a tough, harsh father whom he could never please. This seems to have taught Nixon that the soft and the nurturing are unreliable, that toughness and aggression are manly, and the world is a harsh and cold place. Unable to attain a self-image that gave him satisfaction in what he was, he seemed constantly striving, compensating, and working hard to attain a sense of achievement based on what he did. He would face a hard world always ready to do battle. He attempted to attain a sense of self in outside achievements: winning. Or so the psychobiographical argument goes.

Nixon is portrayed as a man of inadequacy. His lack of trust in people stemmed from a "view of human nature which was jaundiced" and reflected in Nixon's comment that "Most people are good not because of love but because of fear. You won't hear that in Sunday School, but it's true."

Throughout his rise in politics, Nixon ran confrontational and aggressive campaigns. His attack style, developed in the early campaigns for the House and Senate seats, and later in his vice-presidential years, proved highly successful. Nixon seemed a natural at the politics of confrontation.

Throughout the many psychobiographies of Richard Nixon several themes seem to dominate (see Table 2.1).[3] A childhood marred by sickness and deaths in the family, a self-image of insecurity and low self-esteem developing from his relationship to a stern, demanding father and a saintly mother, led to a personality development that most psychobiographers see as unhealthy. From James Barber's active-negative categorization, to Bruce Mazlish's characterization of a boy unloved, to Eli Chasen's compulsive-obsessive personality diagnosis, to David Abrahamsen's conclusion that Nixon has a "psychopathic personality and character disorder," to Fawn

Table 2.1
Richard Nixon's Psychological Characteristics

Author	Characteristics	Source
Abrahamsen	*Psychopathic Personality Type* Orally and anally fixated, obsessive-compulsive longings, passive-aggressive, secretive, egocentric, manipulative, paranoid personality, suffers from character disorders	Childhood
Barber	*Active-Negative Type* Vague self-image, insecure, low self-esteem, lack of trust, need to manage aggressiveness, driven to compensatory behavior, feelings of inadequacy	Childhood
Brodie	*Man of Paradox* Self-loathing, paranoid? Sense of being unloved, impulse toward self-destruction, severally defective conscience, self-hatred	Childhood
Chesen	*Compulsive-Obsessive Type* Feeling of uncertainty, need to prove manliness, need to control	Childhood
Mazlish	*Fear of Being Unloved, Self-Absorption* Capacity for denial, low self-esteem, compensatory behavior, feelings of inferiority; compulsiveness, need for control, projection, repressed hostility, lack of trust, death wish	Childhood

Brodie's view of Nixon as "self-loathing," and "paranoid," we see a psychiatric profile both disturbing and, perhaps, frightening.

If Nixon possessed these pathological characteristics, how did he rise to such heights, how did he achieve so many personal and political successes? In general, Nixon's psychobiographies argue that many of Nixon's psychological characteristics aided him in his political career! He was, by all accounts, a brilliant, hard-working man, and those "negative" psychological characteristics drove him to achieve, to succeed, to win. Thus he sought in politics to compensate for his feelings of weakness by winning, and by ambitious striving to succeed, by beating an opponent. In this way politics served as a temporary way of satisfying his feelings of insecurity and low self-esteem. Politics gave Nixon a way to attain, through outward gratification, some of the things he lacked internally. Politics satisfied a need.

NIXON THE POLITICIAN

"There they go: See-No-Evil, Speak-No-Evil and Evil," said Senator Bob Dole on seeing Gerald Ford, Jimmy Carter, and Richard Nixon boarding an airplane together. How can one see Nixon's personality affecting upon his behavior in politics? Nixon's operating style was deeply rooted in his personality—he had a tendency to overpersonalize politics, and the operations of the White House began to function as an extension of President Nixon's character. He often was unable to differentiate between disagreement and disloyalties; he had a tendency to see political opponents as enemies; and he looked upon the political world as an excessively hostile environment full of people out to get him. Aide Tom Charles Huston once remarked, "No one who has been in the White House could help but feel he was in a state of siege."

This led to a discernible, distinct, operating style that guided Nixon's behavior as president. Richard Nixon developed a "Paranoid Style," which, while obscured at first, became more and more prevalent as his administration progressed. This style of operation can be seen in Nixon's relations with his staff and, in the development and execution of policy, and in the end it contributed to the downfall of the Nixon presidency.

Nixon, who noted that he was an "introvert in a highly extroverted profession," never felt comfortable with politicking. Generally uncomfortable in interpersonal relationships, Nixon entered politics as an outsider who never quite fit in. He viewed politics as a battle. He wrote:

I believe in the battle, whether it's the battle of the campaign or the battle of this office, which is a continuing battle. It's always there wherever you go. I, perhaps, carry it more than others because that's my way.[4]

If politics is a battle, one must have enemies, and Nixon had a tendency to view political opponents as enemies. In March 1973 Nixon told John Dean, "Nobody is a friend of ours. Let's face it." The view that the world around them was full of enemies pervaded the Nixon White House. And eventually a siege mentality took over, creating an isolated fortress around the president. He was not rich, or good looking, or from the Eastern establishment and Ivy League, as was John Kennedy. He was not as sophisticated, athletic, or graceful as Kennedy. This led to a sense of inferiority for which Nixon seemed always to be compensating. He never really felt he had made it, and even as president, he was always the outsider fighting against a world out to get him.

Nixon speechwriter William Safire, discussing the "us versus them" attitude that pervaded the White House, suggested that even though it may have been based on sound political reasoning, "it all got out of hand." Safire referred to Nixon as "the first political paranoid with a majority!" In some senses, Nixon did have enemies—as all politicians do. But this is part of the governmental process. Nixon's real "enemies": a Congress controlled by the Democrats; a bureaucracy staffed mostly by Democrats; an antiwar protest movement picking up steam; and the political legacy of the New Deal/Great Society—all worked against Nixon, but not in the way the president felt and saw. Nixon took real political adversaries and turned them into enemies, saw political conflicts as battles to the death.

In seeing his political opponents as enemies, Nixon had a tendency to overpersonalize every slight or insult. He harbored grudges and remembered every hurt. Abrahamsen calls him "an injustice collector." Evans and Novak, echoing this theme, wrote of Nixon's "invisible ledger of past wrongs," which was meticulously kept by Nixon himself. If you were in the ledger, Nixon would get you. John Dean told President Nixon that he was keeping notes "on a lot of people, who are emerging as less than our friends," to which Nixon responded:

They are asking for it and they are going to get it. We have not used this power in this first four years, as you know. We have never used it. We have not used the bureau and we have not used the Justice Department, but things are going to change now. And they are going to do it right or go.

Dean then said to Nixon, "What an exciting prospect!"[5]

In Nixon's memoirs, one finds repeated references to people out to get him: to journalistic reporting as "all prejudicial," to the "ferocity of reporting," to the media as "a vigilante squad" taking "the law into their own hands," to "the McGovern media," to enemies who "crucify us," to "opponents" who "are savage destroyers, haters," to a "Republican conspiracy to force me out of office," to Archibald Cox who was determined "to get me," and how there "has to be a line drawn at times with those who are against us; and then we have to take the action to deal with them effectively."[6] Nixon also deeply resented the Kennedy's because they seemed to have, or be, everything Nixon was not. Thus, one can find nearly a dozen critical (and unnecessarily small) comments about the Kennedys scattered throughout Nixon's memoirs.[7] What is so revealing about these references—and there are many—is that they emerge from a work over which Nixon had complete control. These were not accusations wildly thrown out in a fit of anger, but the result of a carefully written book intended as a defense of and record of his presidency.

All this is part of Nixon's often-noted crisis mentality. Throughout his career he faced—and sometimes created—crises, which served as tests of his strength, character, and resolve. His 1962 book *Six Crises* is a tale of someone whose life has been a series of ongoing crises, tests, or challenges that had to be overcome. As Nixon wrote:

One of the most trying experiences an individual can go through is the period of doubt, of soul-searching, to determine whether to fight the battle or to fly from it. It is in such a period that almost unbearable tensions build up, tensions that can be relieved only by taking action, one way or the other. . . . A leader is one who has the emotional, mental and physical strength to withstand the pressures and tensions . . . and then, at the critical moment, to make a choice and to act decisively. The men who fail are those who are so overcome by doubts that they either crack under the strain or flee. . . . Those who have known great crises—its challenges and tension, its victory and defeat—can never become adjusted to a more leisurely and orderly pace. They have drunk too deeply of the stuff, which really makes life exciting and worth living to be satisfied with the froth.[8]

This need to face crises may have been linked to the oft-mentioned tendencies toward self-destruction Nixon seemed to possess. Faced with repeated crises, Nixon sought to play the heroic role, often at great personal risk. His trip to the Middle East in June of 1974 at the height of the Watergate investigation, while suffering from phlebitis, is but one of many examples of Nixon putting himself in danger—both personal and political—to test, push, and perhaps punish himself. Facing enemies in crisis situations allowed Nixon to justify using falsehoods and other unsavory tactics against his enemies. After all, they were "playing hardball," and he would too. It was a tough world, and to be a man meant playing tough.

Nixon was the most "political" man imaginable. Though he was a conservative by instinct and temperament, he had no deep-rooted ideological core, no guiding principles, beliefs, or ideals. This allowed him to shift policies so dramatically on such major issues as wage and price controls, China, the Soviet Union, communism. This helped Nixon become a master of realpolitick, although one often didn't know where it was leading.

To Nixon, politics was not so much a battle over ideas and ideals, as a battle over power. He saw everything through the lens of power and from the perspective of politics in the narrowest sense of that word.[9] Nixon was amoral, in the Machiavellian sense. He had no real internal gyroscope to guide him morally. Power was the guide, winning his god. Thus, Nixon did not see himself acting immorally; rather, he saw himself maximizing his power in a hostile and aggressive world.

Nixon was a loner who had few friends and preferred it that way, or so he said. "I never wanted to be buddy-buddy . . . even with close friends. I don't believe in letting your hair down, confiding this and that and the other thing. . . . I believe you should keep your troubles to yourself. That's just the way I am. Some people think it's good therapy to sit with a close friend and, you know, just spill your guts. Not me. No way."[10] Such a cautious, rigid closed attitude suggests a lack of trust in others and a fear of revealing one's self. People didn't like him for the simple reason he didn't like people.[11]

Nixon's personality tendencies were fed by a political atmosphere of mistrust and confrontation. The politics of protest that marked the 1960s, the legacy of mistrust left behind by Lyndon Johnson and the "credibility gap," the increased executive branch secrecy as a consequence of the rise of the national security state, and the constant threats posed by the Cold War and the growing isolation of the presidency, all contributed to an increase in Nixon's less admirable tendencies.

Nixon's fears, insecurities, repressed anger, even paranoia produced a world image of Nixon standing alone, pitted against a hostile environment. In response, he became excessive, and self-righteous, and he played the game with one goal in sight—to win, by any means necessary. In the end, Nixon's paranoid style defeated him.

Personality played, and plays such an important role in presidential politics because the modern presidency is in many ways unmoored from the constraints of traditional checks such as political parties, or even political bosses. Campaigns are not run through parties, but as individualistic, entrepreneurial, and episodic events. Each candidate develops a personal campaign, raises funds largely outside the party structure, and is not beholden to party regulars or party leaders for support. The weakness of party relative to the president's campaign, means that the candidate, and later the president, can govern apart from and above the constraints of party. In this atmosphere, the personality of the president becomes increasingly important and one of the few remaining internal constraints upon presidential behavior.

NOTES

1. See Ellen K. Coughlin, "Putting Richard Nixon on the Couch," *The Chronicle of Higher Education*, February 13, 1979, p. 3.

2. In a 1988 discussion with Archibald Cox, I confessed that I was trying not to write a Nixon psychobiography, but that so much of what Nixon did seemed to emanate from who he was, to which Cox replied, "Of course, with Nixon character is everything." (Loyola Marymount University, April 22, 1988).

3. See James D. Barber, *The Presidential Character* (Englewood Cliffs, NJ: Prentice-Hall, 1985); David Abrahamsen, *Nixon vs. Nixon: An Emotional Tragedy* (Farrar, Straus, and Giroux, 1977); Fawn Brodie, *Richard Nixon: The Shaping of His Character* (New York: Norton, 1984); Eli Chesen, *President Nixon's Psychiatric Profile* (New York: Peter H. Wyden, 1973); and Bruce Mazlish, *In Search of Nixon: A Psychohistorical Inquiry* (Baltimore: Penguin, 1972).

4. Quoted in Erwin C. Hargrove, *The Power of the Modern Presidency* (New York: Knopf, 1974), 177.

5. House Judiciary Committee, Recordings of Nixon White House, (see Watergate chapter for more comprehensive review of contents of the Nixon tapes).

6. Richard M. Nixon, *RN: The Memoirs of Richard Nixon*, 582, 664, 676, 682, 971, 978, 912.

7. Ibid., 509, 515, 542–43, 633, 645, 654, 677, 688, 775, 872.

8. Richard M. Nixon, *Six Crises* (New York: Pyramid Books, 1968), 461.

9. Brodie, *Richard Nixon*, 25.

10. Quoted in Bob Greene, "Reflections in a Wary Eye," *Esquire Magazine*, February 1981, p. 15.

11. See Bryce Harlow, "The Man and the Political Leader," in Kenneth W. Thompson, ed., *The Nixon Presidency* (Lanham, MD: University Press of America, 1987), 9–10.

3

Is the President Above the Law?

"When the President does it, that means that it is not illegal."
—Richard M. Nixon to David Frost, May 1, 1977

Watergate marked a period of presidential lawlessness unprecedented in American history. But other presidents also went beyond the letter of the law. Each president takes an oath to "faithfully execute" the law, but who is to say what the law means? Is there a time when a president may go beyond the law? Or, put more starkly, is the president above the law? The events of Watergate raise a variety of questions about constitutional and democratic government in the United States: Who shall determine what the law means? When, if ever, can the president go beyond the law? And can a constitutional system designed for the eighteenth century function in the twenty-first?

The Constitution was written over 200 years ago in an age when trade and communication were slow, weapons were of limited destructive force, few citizens had much education, and fewer still could even vote. The Constitution established a system based on limited government, the rule of law, and separation of powers. All this "limited" the power of the government to act. It set up roadblocks on leadership.[1]

The framers wanted a cautious deliberative system, not one-man rule. Having just fought a revolution against what they believed to be the arbitrary power of the king, they were determined to chain the impulse towards tyranny and thus place limits on the power of the president.

NIXON'S DEFENSE

President Nixon claimed that (a) a presidential act (order) cannot be illegal; (b) there are times when a president must move beyond the law; and (c) interpreting the Constitution is not the sole province of the Court—presidents too can interpret the meaning of the Constitution. Leaving aside for a moment the inherent contradiction in these first two positions, we can and should dismiss the first argument. The president is not above the law.

But Nixon's second point merits serious attention. Are there times when a president is justified in moving beyond the limits of legality? In extraordinary times, during emergencies, can a president—for protection of the nation—go beyond the law?

There is evidence to suggest that the framers foresaw only one instance when this might be permitted: in the event of a surprise attack against the United States that required a quick military response to ensure the survival of the nation. Apart from such an occurrence, the president was empowered to execute the law and exercise some amount of administrative discretion, but little else. Otherwise, the government, including the president, could only legitimately act on the basis of law. It was, 200 years ago, a rather novel concept, but it was designed to protect liberty from governmental intrusion. By making it difficult for the government, either in the form of the Congress or the president, to act unilaterally, the Constitution made it difficult for the government to trample on liberty.

President Nixon claimed that he was acting in extraordinary circumstances that allowed (even demanded) him to skirt the technicalities of the law. Extraordinary times called for extraordinary actions. With a war in Vietnam and mass protests at home, the president was convinced that the United States faced a crisis that threatened the nation's very existence. He believed that the Congress was idly sitting by while the United States crumbled. Nixon believed that he represented "the silent majority" of citizens who supported "peace with honor" in Vietnam, and "law and order" at home.

As ammunition for his case, the president could cite the emergency actions of Abraham Lincoln during the Civil War and Franklin Roosevelt during the depression and World War II. Were these valid comparisons that justified Nixon's actions, or merely self-serving rationalization? This leads us to Nixon's third argument.

WHO INTERPRETS THE CONSTITUTION?

The president's claim rested on a dispute over who could and should interpret the Constitution: the president or the Court. Nearly all legal scholars insist that the power to interpret the Constitution rests ultimately (though perhaps not exclusively) with the Supreme Court, but it must be added that the president and Congress are not disinterested observers. After all, the separation of powers requires each branch vigorously to defend the powers and prerogatives of their respective institutions. When there is conflict—especially over political and policy questions—the president may be expected to try and protect the institutional parameters of his office.

Because the Constitution is vague on many things and silent on others, there is room for disagreement. Must the president succumb to the decisions of the Court at all times? Why is the Court's view of the Constitution more valid than his?

It is within the self-interest of a president to assert that he has as much right to interpret the constitutionality of competing claims as does the Court. But it also may be within the president's *right* to do so. After all, the Constitution is unclear on this subject, and though some insights can be gleaned from the words of the framers, an argument can be made that, on the basis of the separation of powers, one branch (the judiciary) cannot decide on the scope of powers of another branch (the presidency) when these two institutions disagree. Of course, someone's view of constitutionality must prevail in such disputes, and though most scholars believe the courts are the legitimate and appropriate "final word" on the Constitution, the ambiguity of the issue leaves some room, however thin, for a president to press his claims in this area.

MOVING BEYOND THE LAW

In the aftermath of World War II, the United States, as the dominant power of the West, emerged as leader of what was called the "Free World." The Soviet Union challenged the West and sought to expand its international sphere of influence. A Cold War developed a bipolar conflict that dominated the fifty-year period following World War II.

In response to the constant crisis, amid growing fears not only about communist ability to attack the United States and its interests directly by military means including the use of nuclear weapons but also about communist infiltration of American institutions and government the United States developed a national security state with the president as the central policymaker. Presidential power expanded as American influence increased and as the need for prompt action in times of crisis became more important. Congress was too slow and unyielding. Only the president, so the argument went, could respond with the speed and certainty necessary to meet these crises. The president became the central figure in politics, and soon an "imperial presidency" (a presidency seemingly above the law) began to emerge. Presidents, accustomed to getting their way in foreign affairs, became frustrated by many checks on their power domestically. Ambitious and goal-oriented presidents became extremely frustrated as other actors blocked their way. An obstreperous Congress, demanding special interests, an uncooperative business community, an adversarial press, and others can at times seem to gang up on a president, preventing him from achieving his policy goals. The separation of powers and the checks and balances were set up so that ambition could counteract ambition and power could check power. The model of decision making was decidedly cooperative, not executive. But as the frustrations of high demands, high expectations, limited power, and falling public approval eat away at presidents, they often cannot resist the temptation to go beyond the properly prescribed limits of the office. Rather than accept defeat on a key issue, presidents are tempted to cut corners, go beyond the law, and stretch the constitutional limits. When all else fails, as it often does, some presidents—knowing that their future political success, not to mention their historical reputation, is at stake—simply cannot resist going beyond the law. Presidents who are not well grounded in the virtues of the American system may see the system itself as the enemy and thus feel justified in going beyond the law. Richard Nixon with Watergate and Ronald Reagan with the Iran-Contra scandal are but the two most pronounced recent examples.[2]

As government became more complex, and as policy-making during the Cold War became more insulated from public scrutiny in the interests of national security, an attitude of arrogance overtook the president and his top staff. "We know best" and "they are blocking progress" slid into the conceit that the "slight" abuse of power was being done for the greater good. Such an attitude leads to the *Imperial Presidency* and the further abuses of power.[3]

Is the president above the law? Of course not. Such a notion violates all precepts of the rule of law.[4] But are there certain prescribed circumstances that can justify a president's going beyond the law? Are there times when the president may exceed his constitutional powers?

THE PRESIDENT'S EMERGENCY POWER

While the word *emergency* does not appear in the Constitution, there is some evidence to suggest that the founders did envision the possibility of a president exercising "supraconstitutional powers" in a time of national emergency.[5] The Constitution's silence, some suggest, leaves room for presidents to claim that certain constitutional provisions (e.g., Article 2, Section 1, the executive power clause, and the "faithfully execute" the law clause, along with Article 2, Section 2, the commander-in-chief clause) grant the president *implied powers* attendant to the performance of his job. Claims of such powers become especially pressing in times of crisis.

During a crisis, the president often assumes extraconstitutional powers.[6] The separate branches—which, under normal circumstances, are designed to check and balance a president—will usually defer to the president in times of national emergency. The president's institutional position offers him a vantage point from which he can more easily exert crisis leadership, and the Congress, the Court, and the public usually accept the president's judgments.

The notion of one set of legal and constitutional standards for normal conditions and another for emergencies raises some unsettling questions regarding democratic governments and constitutional systems.[7] Can democratic regimes function in any but prosperous, peaceful circumstances? Or must the United States constantly rely upon the strength of a despot or "constitutional dictatorship" to save it from disaster? Are constitutional governments incapable of meeting the demands of crisis? In short, can democracy work in the modern age, or is it a relic of quieter times?

The problem of emergency situations in democratic systems is not easily answered. If the potential power of the state is used too little or too late, the democratic state faces the possibility of destruction. If used arbitrarily and capriciously, this power could lead the system to accept a form of permanent dictatorship. In a contemporary sense, the constant reliance on the executive to solve the many "emergencies" (usually self-defined by the executive) facing America could very well lead to the acceptance of the overly powerful executive and make the meaning of the term "emergency" shallow and susceptible to executive manipulation.

With each new "emergency" in American history, the public and our political institutions seemed to become more accustomed to accepting a broader definition of presidential power to meet each new crisis. In the twentieth century, it seems hardly a debatable point to say that a president is expected to assume responsibility and added powers to meet both domestic and foreign crises.

During times of war, the Court has conceded that the emergency allows the president to assume additional powers, if only temporarily. But the president must recognize the limits of his responsibilities. Franklin D. Roosevelt, in 1942, after claiming/requesting of Congress a grant of an unusually large amount of power, assured the legislature that "When the war is won, the powers under which I act automatically revert to the people—to whom they belong."[8] The expectation was that executive would return the extraordinary powers he was granted during the crisis back to their rightful place once the crisis had passed. But serious questions remain as to (1) whether presidents have in fact returned this power, and (2) whether, even if the president desired to do so, a complete or even reasonable return to normality is possible after dictatorial or quasi-dictatorial power is placed in the hands of the executive. In sum, can a democracy survive without a strong executive, and conversely, can a democracy exist with one?

PRESIDENTIAL ACTION IN TIMES OF EMERGENCY

The American political system regularly has met crises with an expansion of presidential power. The necessity for quick, decisive, often extraconstitutional actions that the crisis may demand places a heavy burden upon the president. Because he is the only leader able to move quickly, the burden of meeting the crisis "must" fall on his shoulders. According to Richard Longaker, "In time of crisis constitutional limitations bend to other needs."[9]

Abraham Lincoln during the Civil War and Franklin Roosevelt during the Great Depression serve as examples of presidents who, when faced with a crisis, acted boldly, assumed power, became what some have called "constitutional dictators."[10] But what distinguishes the constitutional dictator from the imperial president? What separates the actions of Lincoln and Roosevelt, generally considered to be appropriate, from those of Nixon, generally considered inappropriate or imperial?

Essentially, for the crisis presidency to be valid, (1) the president must face a genuine and a widely recognized emergency; (2) the Congress and public must—more or less—accept that the president should exercise supraconstitutional powers; (3) the Congress may, if it chooses, override presidential acts; (4) the president's acts must be public so as to allow Congress and the public to judge them; (5) there must be no suspension of the next election; and (6) the president should consult with Congress where and as soon as possible (even calling Congress into special session as Roosevelt did soon after his inauguration in 1933). Lincoln and Roosevelt met (more or less) all these requirements; Nixon, very few of them.

Even when the requirements are met, however, one should not be sanguine about presidential usurpations of power. As the Supreme Court warned in *Ex parte Milligan* (4 Wall. 2, 1866): "Wicked men, ambitious of power, with a hatred of liberty and contempt of law, may fill the place once occupied by Washington and Lincoln."[11]

NOTES

1. Thomas E. Cronin and Michael A. Genovese, *The Paradoxes of the American Presidency* (New York: Oxford University Press, 1998); and Michael A. Genovese, *The Presidential Dilemma* (New York: HarperCollins, 1995).

2. Theodore Draper, *A Very Thin Line: The Iran-Contra Affairs* (New York: Touchstone Books, 1991); and Jane Mayer and Doyle McManus, *Landslide: The Unmaking of the President, 1984–1988* (Boston: Houghton Mifflin, 1988).

3. Nancy V. Baker, *Conflicting Loyalties: Law and Politics in the Attorney General's Office, 1789–1990* (Lawrence: University Press of Kansas, 1992); Katy J. Harriger, *Independent Justice: The Federal Special Prosecutor in American Politics* (Lawrence: University Press of Kansas, 1992); and Rebecca Mae Salokar, *The Solicitor General: The Politics of Law* (Philadelphia: Temple University Press, 1992).

4. Harold Hongju Koh, *The National Security Constitution* (New Haven: Yale University Press, 1990).

5. Daniel P. Franklin, *Extraordinary Measure: The Exercise of Prerogative Powers in the United States* (Pittsburgh: University of Pittsburgh Press, 1991).

6. Michael A. Genovese, "Presidential Leadership and Crisis Management," *Presidential Studies Quarterly* (Spring 1986), pp. 300–309; and Genovese, "Presidents and Crisis: Developing a Crisis Management System in the Executive Branch," *International Journal on World Peace* (Spring 1987), pp. 101–19.

7. Michael A. Genovese, "Democratic Theory and the Emergency Powers of the President," *Presidential Studies Quarterly* (Summer 1979), pp. 283–89.

8. *New York Times*, September 8, 1942, p. 1.

9. Richard Longaker, "Introduction" to Clinton Rossiter, *The Supreme Court and the Commander in Chief*, expanded ed. (Ithaca, NY: Cornell University Press, 1976), xii.

10. Michael A. Genovese, *The Supreme Court, the Constitution, and Presidential Power* (Lanham, MD: University Press of America, 1980), chap. 3.

11. See Cronin and Genovese, *The Paradoxes of the American Presidency*, chap. 4 and 5.

4

Presidential Corruption in Historical Perspective

"Politics have no relation to morals."

—Niccoló Machiavelli

INTRODUCTION

American politics—like politics everywhere—has always had its seamy side. Was Watergate similar to or different from past examples of presidential corruption? And what effects has it had on efforts to curb, and root out, corruption thereafter? How did Watergate affect the character and morality of American political life and public expectations of it, if at all?

Chester Barnard reminds us that the chief role of the executive is to manage the values of the organization.[1] Presidents, no less than corporate executives, set the moral tone for their administrations, give clues as to acceptable or unacceptable behavior, and establish norms and limits. Presidents demonstrate by word and deed the kind of behavior that will be tolerated, and the standards applicable to the entire administration.

Presidents also may have an impact on the moral climate beyond their administrative apparati. They can use the "bully pulpit" to speak to the values of society.

For this reason, presidential corruption is an important if understudied issue. A great deal of scholarly attention has been devoted to the problem of governmental corruption.[2] Likewise, attention has focused on individual cases of presidential corruption.[3] But nowhere in the literature is there a work that brings these two areas of inquiry together in the hope of developing a framework for understanding presidential corruption.

In this chapter I attempt to define government corruption; examine the understanding of the framers of the U.S. Constitution regarding the causes and prevention of political corruption; briefly examine the administrations considered the most corrupt in U.S. history (Grant, Harding, Nixon, Reagan); develop a framework for understanding presidential corruption; and examine how well or poorly the framers' model dealt with political corruption at the presidential level. This should allow us to see how the Watergate crisis compares to other instances of presidential corruption.

DEFINING CORRUPTION

Political corruption is a difficult subject to research because so much remains hidden from view. Additionally, there is no commonly accepted definition of what constitutes corruption.

Several elements seem relevant when thinking about political corruption. First, political corruption relates to the conduct of a *public official* in his or her *public capacity*. This removes private or personal forms of scandal such as one's private sex life, unless such behavior has public consequences. Second, it involves behavior that *violates law* or accepted social norms. Third, it involves *gain* of some sort (e.g., money, power, position). Fourth, it thus involves a violation of the public trust.

PRESIDENTIAL CORRUPTION: THE FRAMERS' VIEW

"The world has always been inhabited by human beings who have always had the same passions."

—Machiavelli

Regardless of time, type of political system, culture, or legal/moral environment, the problem of *political corruption* is persistent and vexing. Where there is power, where there are resources of value, where the temptations seem worth the risk, the threat of corruption exists. No system has mastered the problem of eliminating corruption, and it is safe to say, none will. But some systems seem more prone to corruption than others. Why?

The framers of the U.S. Constitution were well aware of the persistence of political corruption, and knew that systematic corruption, or "a long train of abuses," could undermine stability or even lead to revolution. They were suspicious of (or dismissed as unattainable) the central tenets of classical republicanism (virtue and community). They embraced a new liberal (individualism and self-interest) basis for government, yet were still influenced somewhat by republicanism as a subordinate philosophy. How were they to reconcile these two competing and contradictory foundations of politics? The answer was found in the "new science of politics." Because virtue was not enough, and democracy somewhat dangerous, but embracing an autocratic model unacceptable, the framers were forced to conceptualize a new science that would govern politics. This dramatic break with the past reflected a new, even radical reformulation of the foundations of government.

The framers premised their political system, embodied in the Constitution, on the belief that *interest and virtue would guide*, though not in equal proportions. Interest, at least in the minds of the framers, preceded virtue. Historians such as Gordon Wood, John Diggins, and J.G.A. Pocock argue that by 1787, "the decline of virtue" meant that the new republic created a system "which did not require a virtuous people for its sustenance," but they overstate the case. The framers did not totally reject virtue; rather, they thought that one could not rely on virtue alone to triumph over interests. Therefore, interest became, in their minds, the dominant force that animated human behavior, and virtue was a secondary, though not unimportant force. The new science of politics would not rest on the hope that virtue would triumph.

The framers were less concerned with the way men (and at that time they meant males) *ought* to live, but with how they *did* live. They were concerned less with shaping character than with dealing with man "as he actually is."

This "new science of politics," grounded in an empiricism based in a "realistic" and not a utopian conception of human nature, assumed that humans were motivated not by ethics or virtue but by self-interest. To form a government with such baggage, the framers drew, not on the language of ethics but on the language of *natural science*. A balance or equilibrium kept order, not appeals to justice or virtue. Thus, interest must counterbalance interest, ambition must check ambition, faction must counteract faction, and power must meet power. This was a mechanical, architectural, or structural method.

In the new science of politics, the framers saw a rational ordering in the universe that could be transferred to the world of politics. As John Adams noted, governments could be "erected on the simple principles of nature." Madison wrote in similar Newtonian terms of constructing a government so "that its several constituent parts may, by their mutual relations, be the means of keeping each other in their proper places."[4]

If the people were not expected to be virtuous, neither were their rulers. If the ruler could not be trained in virtue, what prevented abuse of power and corruption? To answer this question, the framers relied on the mechanical devices of Newtonian physics, their new science of politics, given political life in the *separation of powers*.

INVENTING THE PRESIDENCY, PREVENTING CORRUPTION

When the framers of the Constitution met in Philadelphia to invent, among other things, a presidency,[5] they harbored no illusions about changing human nature so as to produce a virtuous ruler. Between the time of revolutionary fervor and the late 1780s, a shift in outlook had occurred. In the words of historian John P. Diggins, "The 'spirit of '76,' the pure flame of freedom and independence, had been replaced by the structures of political control."[6]

As the "Founders" became the "Framers," as concerns for revolutionary freedom gave way to the needs of governing, as class conflict began to threaten a unified republican society, the concern of the creators of the new constitution shifted to order, power, and control. How could one grant the government power, yet control power? Assuming that "a human being was an atom of self-interest," how can a government be formed that both takes power to order events yet does not threaten individual liberty? How could one energize the executive yet, in the absence of virtue, hold the executive in check?

Following the logic of the new science of politics, the framers embraced an essentially *structural* or *architectural* model that recognized greed or self-interest as "normal" among mortals, and so, sought to unleash man's material proclivities and allow self-interest to prevail, indeed even demand that it do so. In this way, a rough balance of powers could be achieved, an equilibrium, which, as Alexander Hamilton notes in *The Federalist*, would prevent "the extremes of tyranny and anarchy" that had plagued republics of the past. The framers knew that, as Madison would warn, "enlightened statesmen will not always be at the helm," and in the absence of virtuous rulers, only a properly constructed state could control the ambitions of power-hungry rulers. Though elections were to serve as one control, Madison knew that "experience has taught mankind the necessity of auxiliary precautions." For the framers, the primary precaution was that found in the way the three political offices were arranged so as to allow ambition to emerge, but set ambition against ambition. "The great security against a gradual concentration of the several powers in the same department, consists in giving to those who administer each department the necessary constitutional means and personal motives to resist encroachments of the others."[7]

Realizing that enlightened statesmen would not always rule, the framers set up a *Separation-of-Powers, Checks and Balances*, a system that encouraged the emergence of *institutional self-interest*, where ambition was made to counteract ambition, and law was the basis of action. This institutional equilibrium was built into the very structure of the government and was thus a mechanical means of controlling power.

By setting up institution against institution (but ironically also requiring institutions to cooperate and/or work with other institutions), the framers gave in to their jaundiced view of human nature and decided to check vice with vice, not with virtue. It therefore could create "energy" in the executive as a means of checking legislative energy.

Madison acknowledged that "there is a degree of depravity in mankind which requires a certain degree of circumspection and distrust." But he insisted that "there are other qualities in human nature, which justify a certain portion of esteem and confidence," and he wrote that "republican government presupposes the existence of these qualities in a higher degree than any other form." "Were the picture," he noted, "which have been drawn by the political jealousy of some among us, faithful likenesses of the human character, the inference would be that there is not sufficient virtue among men for self-government, and that nothing less than the chains of despotism can restrain them from destroying and devouring one another."[8]

How well, or poorly, has the framers' model served the nation? To answer that question, let us turn to the most prominent cases of presidential corruption in American history.

ULYSSES S. GRANT

After the assassination of Abraham Lincoln and after the failed presidency of Andrew Johnson, the nation turned to the popular Civil War general Ulysses S. Grant for leadership. On the surface, Grant seemed the right man for the job—strong, forceful, a leader proven under fire. But the hero who showed strength in war proved weak in politics, and his administration was victimized by widespread corruption. In the end, members of his Cabinet, his vice president, personal secretary, members of his staff, and even members of his family were implicated in wrongdoing.

At 45 years old, Grant was the youngest president elected up to that point in history. A political novice, Grant had numerous shortcomings: no political experience, only a superficial understanding of the workings of government, a blind trust in his appointees, a poor judge of character, and a conception of the presidency as primarily an *administrative* office where "except on rare occasions he was, as President, disposed to accept without question the work of Congress as the authoritative expression of the will of the American people."9

Grant was a weak president who largely abdicated power to an assertive Congress. He was a weak executive as well, granting his Cabinet substantial control of policy. Thus, within the administration, Grant was dependent on his Cabinet to guide him. The problem was that Grant was a poor judge of character. To staff his administration, Grant chose business and political figures whose ethical compasses were out of kilter. Many of these men took advantage of the president, resulting in what Jack Mitchell called "a story book of scandal, a veritable tomb of venality, a catalog of corruption."10

Though his administration was rife with corruption, Grant himself was incorruptible. He was victimized by those around him, trusted appointees who dragged his name through the mud. The undistinguished men he gathered around him tore his presidency apart. On December 5, 1876, the Congress heard a clerk read the president's final annual message to the Congress. Grant's words were a ringing confession, and admission of a man who, in the end, realized he was not big enough for the job of president. "It was my fortune or misfortune," he began, "to be called to the office of the Chief Executive without any previous political training. . . . Under such circumstances, it is but reasonable to suppose that errors of judgment must have occurred." He added, "Mistakes have been made, as all can see and I admit." It was, he insisted, not his own acts but those of his assistants who were "in nearly every case selected without a personal acquaintance with the appointee." He concluded that "Failures have been errors of judgment, not of intent."11

Why was the Grant administration so prone to corruption? Several factors stand out. First, Grant's inexperience; second, his poor choices to staff his presidency; third, and related, is his poor assessment of people; fourth, almost unfettered access to the administration by businessmen out to make a profit; fifth, his lack of insistence on high ethical standards; sixth, and perhaps most importantly, was Grant's lax management style. He simply was not in command of his own administration. Grant was detached and aloof from much of the business of government and simply was not minding the store. Finally, the temper of the times. Corruption in government and business was rife, and profiting from public service was seen as yet another means of gaining wealth.

Grant's friends, not his enemies, undermined his presidency. Towards the end of his life, Grant admitted, "I have made it a rule of my life to trust a man long after other people gave him up."12 Grant stood by his friends and family when they were accused of profiting from corruption in hoarding U.S. gold reserves, distributing goods to Indians, making contracts with railroads, and other deals. The cost of such "loyalty" was not only an administration that seemingly endorsed the brass-knuckle capitalism of the Gilded Age, but the loss of Grant's "moral authority" as president.

WARREN G. HARDING

"I am not fit for this office and never should have been here."
—Warren G. Harding

Until Watergate, historians regarded the presidency of Warren G. Harding (1921–1923) as the most corrupt of the twentieth century, if not all of U.S. history. When the corruption of the Harding administration was first exposed, American humorist Will Rogers called it the "great morality panic of 1924." It would, in the end, be much more than that. Indeed, during and immediately after Harding's brief presidential tenure, a trail of fraud, bribery, criminal conspiracy, cover-up, and suicide became ever more visible.

In the course of the Harding corruption, Interior Secretary Albert Fall gained the distinction of being the first Cabinet official in history to go to jail for acts committed while in office. Charles R. Forbes, head of the Veterans' Bureau, was caught skimming profits on war surplus supplies and taking kickbacks. Forbes's assistant, Charles Cramer, committed suicide (he left a suicide note addressed to President Harding, but the president never opened it); the personal aide to Attorney General Harry M. Daugherty, Jess Smith, also committed suicide; and a slew of other officials were involved in crimes and cover-ups.

Harding was a man of limited political talent but a handsome presence. He rose to national prominence in the aftermath of World War I with an exciting promise to "return to normalcy." An impressive speaker with a resonant voice and an excessively florid phraseology, Harding appealed to a wide range of people fed up with the demands and constraints of war, and tired of the moral preachments of President Woodrow Wilson and the Progressives. America, Harding understood, wanted to return to the security of simpler, less taxing times. Harding served this purpose, but his was a victory of style over substance. Harding was a poor judge of friends and associates. A college classmate joked: "The difference between you and George Washington is he couldn't tell a lie, and you can't tell a liar!"[13] This character flaw would prove Harding's undoing, as he became the victim of predatory "friends" who used the president to enhance their personal fortunes. Though Harding was not a participant in the acts of corruption committed during his watch, he did create an atmosphere in which his subordinates believed that they could get away with graft, and he failed to exercise control and discipline over his subordinates.

Of the many scandals of the Harding administration, three stand out as especially vexing: The Veterans' Bureau graft, the Attorney General fiasco, and Teapot Dome.

Charles Forbes was Harding's director of the Veterans' Bureau. Forbes, the president's friend and poker partner, controlled a budget of nearly a half billion dollars, the largest budget in the federal government at the time. While telling the president he was building hospitals for World War I veterans, Forbes proceeded to enrich himself at the veterans' expense. He began selling government medical supplies to private contractors at scandalously low prices, took kickbacks, and accepted bribes from hospital building contractors. When his activities came to light, Forbes was forced to resign. But a Senate investigating committee began digging into the affair. Charles Cramer, a suspect in the case, locked himself in his bathroom and shot himself. Later, a federal court jury found Forbes guilty of conspiracy to defraud the government, and he was sentenced to two years in Leavenworth Penitentiary and fined $10,000 (it is believed he accumulated over $2 million in graft in his short time in government service).

The mess at the Veterans' Bureau was soon followed by a scandal in the Attorney General's office. Attorney General Harry Daugherty's Justice Department became known as the "Department of Easy Virtue," as Daugherty was seen as the central figure in a web of graft and corruption, which spread throughout the Harding administration. Daugherty was suspected of all sorts of nefarious operations, but his accusers were having trouble nailing the Attorney General. Finally, in 1923, the House of Representatives took up an impeachment resolution against Daugherty. The Attorney General quickly set out to investigate the investigators, using burglaries and wiretaps. But the investigations into Daugherty's activities uncovered a series of shady deals, one of which led a coconspirator, Jess Smith, to commit suicide. Beside himself at the level of corruption in his own administration, President Harding confided to a journalist: "My God, this is a hell of a job! I have no trouble with my enemies. I can take care of my enemies all right. But my damn friends, my God damn friends, they're the ones that keep me walking the floor nights."[14]

The most famous scandal of the Harding administration was Teapot Dome.[15] The case involved the leasing of oil rights on government-owned land. Harding's Secretary of the Interior, Albert Fall, granted leasing rights without competitive bidding to Edward L. Doheny to drill in Elk Hills, California, and to Harry F. Sinclair for rights to Teapot Dome in Wyoming. After an exhaustive investigation, it was revealed that Fall had received $100,000 from both Doheny and Sinclair, and Fall was eventually convicted of bribery and sentenced to prison.

Historians generally portray Harding as lazy, insecure, and inadequate to the demands of office, consumed by a sexual appetite and derelict in his official duties. The historiography on Harding has reduced him to the position of presidential "failure." Despite the chorus of disapproval over his presidential tenure, Harding's faults were of skill and management style not of commission. Nothing has surfaced that suggested Harding was involved in or profited from the graft and corruption so prevalent in his administration. His biggest faults were trusting his "friends" too much, of being a poor judge of character, and of maintaining loyalty to people who clearly did not merit his trust. He did allow opportunities for graft to emerge; he failed to set and insist upon a high ethical standard; and due to lax management, was victimized by people selected to serve the president. But Harding did not lead those in his administration to break the laws.

In the end, the damage to the presidency due to the Harding-era corruption was minimal. His successor, Calvin Coolidge, brought a reputation for honesty to the office and urged investigations into and prosecution of any crimes or abuses of office. The integrity of other Cabinet members—especially Secretary of State Charles Evans Hughes, Secretary of Treasury Andrew Mellon, and Secretary of Commerce Herbert Hoover— counterbalanced the corruption of Fall, Daugherty, and others. And the public retained an essential "trust" in the Republicans during an age of unprecedented prosperity by dismissing the Harding corrupters as the venality of men while giving Republicans huge electoral wins in the presidential races of 1924 and 1928. The Harding scandals led to neither significant structural reform of government nor distrust of public officials. The presidency as an institution survived the scandals, and would grow in public respect and moral authority over the years, especially under Franklin Roosevelt's administration, which took pains to bring people into its confidence with "fireside chats" and broad-based appeals for public support.

RONALD W. REAGAN

> Most people fancy themselves innocent
> Those crimes of which they cannot be convicted.
>
> —Seneca

The Reagan presidency was unusual in the annals of presidential corruption in that the administration was deeply involved in two types of corruption: greed for money *and* greed for power, with the president involved in the latter. How, in the post-Watergate era could such levels of corruption occur?

Clearly the post-Vietnam/post-Watergate era posed different challenges to presidential leadership. The public, the press, and the Congress were all more suspicious and less willing to follow presidential leadership. And yet, presidents still governed in a Cold War context that seemed to require a brand of secrecy and even occasional duplicitousness, all but made criminal in the new rules of politics. Vietnam and Watergate changed the rules. Numerous laws were passed that called for more-open government, greater congressional involvement, and diminished presidential prerogatives. But if the rules in Washington had changed, the rules of the Cold War had not. In the Cold War context, presidents felt justified in engaging in secrecy, lying, and covert operations—when directed at an external enemy. But in Watergate, Nixon used some of those "foreign policy tools" at home, thereby undermining their use abroad, even when directed at a foreign adversary. Ronald Reagan, a determined cold warrior, faced these new challenges. It was not always a comfortable fit.

The Sleaze Factor

Ronald Reagan made a habit of railing against government. "Government," Reagan often said, "isn't the solution. Government is the problem." But during the Reagan years one of the problems clearly *was* the government and the illegal uses to which government power was sometimes used.

The quality of character of many of Ronald Reagan's appointees was sufficiently low, and the number of people caught with their hands in the governmental cookie jar so high, that commentators routinely spoke of "the sleaze factor." So frequent were charges of ethical violations leveled against Reagan administration officials that the House Subcommittee on Civil Service reported that over 225 Reagan appointees faced allegations of criminal or ethical wrongdoing,[16] in total number, the greatest volume of reported presidential corruption in history.[17] Although Reagan was not implicated in the goings on of the sleaze factor, he did engage in acts of questionable ethics and dubious legality in other areas (Iran-Contra).

It should be noted that part of the reason why so many Reagan officials had problems stems from the heightened prosecutorial style of post-Watergate politics. The press probed deeper, the public was more suspicious and cynical, the Congress was more prone to investigate the executive, and independent counsels gained authority to look into a wide range of allegations of executive branch wrongdoing.

The list of administration luminaries who were in ethical trouble is quite long. Richard Allen, Reagan's first appointment as National Security Adviser, was forced to resign for accepting gratuities. Labor Secretary Raymond Donovan was indicted (but not convicted) of defrauding the government. The Environmental Protection Agency (EPA) crimes of 1982 led to the head of the Superfund, Rita Lavalle's, conviction for perjury, and forced others to resign in disgrace. Investigations into Attorney General Ed Meese's behavior involved wide-ranging and complex charges, and a series of bizarre twists and turns, linking his office to scandals such as corporate profiteering in Webtech, conflict of interest investigations, and other charges, all of which led to the appointment of a special prosecutor to examine the charges. Top presidential aide Michael Deaver was convicted on three counts of perjury. Lyn Nofziger, Reagan's White House political director, was convicted of influence peddling. The HUD (Housing and Urban Development) scandal implicated HUD secretary Samuel Pierce and numerous other officials accused of approving HUD grants for political, financial, and personal favors, of influence peddling on a massive scale.

Why so many ethical lapses during the Reagan years? Several factors stand out: the ethical climate of the times in which "a culture of greed" emerged; the president's celebration of self-interest; Reagan's lax attitude about ethical violations; the president's failure to set a high ethical standard (he even vetoed an ethics bill in 1988); and the president's lax management style. All these facts contributed to an atmosphere in which those who wished to violate ethical and legal standards had opportunities to accumulate wealth with little reason for them to suspect that "the boss" would catch and punish them.

The Iran-Contra Crisis

What Suzanne Garment called "the Scandal Olympics"[18] escalated in the Iran-Contra scandal. It was a double scandal: Iran *and* Contra, together in one giant-size crisis, and the president was deeply involved. The Iran Crisis involved a scheme to trade arms to a terrorist nation in exchange for U.S. hostages. The Contra Crisis involved the illegal financing of a war in Nicaragua. Each of these two foreign policy ventures deserves criticism, but together they comprise a convoluted scandal that nearly brought down the Reagan presidency. This, however, was a different type of scandal, more of zealotry than venality.

The Iran Crisis. The Iran part of the crisis began with an effort to free a dozen American hostages being held in the Middle East by terrorists, primarily to embarrass the United States. After extensive discussions within the administration, the president authorized government officials to trade arms for hostages, using Israel as the go-between. This policy—to sell arms to a terrorist nation—contradicted stated policy as well as common sense.

In December 1983, Secretary of State George Shultz announced the creation of "Operation Staunch," a ban on selling arms to Iran, which the next month was officially listed by the United States as a sponsor of international terrorism. President Reagan even declared, in a speech before the American Bar Association on July 8, 1985, that Iran was an "outlaw state." He assured his audience that "America will never make concessions to terrorists," and added, "The American people are not going to tolerate. . . . These acts form outlaw states run by the strangest collection of misfits, Looney Tunes, and squalid criminals since the advent of the Third Reich."[19]

On August 6, 1985, President Reagan and Vice President George Bush, the Secretaries of State and Defense, the Chief of Staff, and the National Security Adviser met in the White House, in the president's private quarters. At that meeting a proposal to have Israel sell U.S. arms in Iran in exchange for the release of hostages was discussed. Using Israel ensured that, in National Security Adviser Robert McFarlane's words to the Congress, "all would be totally deniable." Secretary of State George Shultz and Secretary of Defense Caspar Weinberger came out strongly against the arms-for-hostages scheme.

Though no definitive decision emerged from this meeting, the arms-for-hostages deal proceeded. On August 20, 1985, the first plane, loaded with 96 TOW missiles, was sent from Israel to Iran. The government paid middleman arms merchant Manucher Ghorbanifar $1,217,410 to handle the transaction. But the Iranians did not keep their part of the deal: No hostages were released. The Iranians, believing quite correctly that they could blackmail the United States, demanded more. So, on September 15, 1985, the Israelis sent 408 more TOW missiles to Iran. One hostage, the Reverend Benjamin Weir was released. On September 18, a $5 million payment for the additional missiles was deposited in Ghorbanifar's Swiss bank account. Things degenerated from there: mysterious presidential "findings," failure to report to Congress covert acts as required by law, more arms-for-hostage trades, more money into Swiss bank accounts, more money to the Contras, more soliciting funds from foreign governments, and more.

The Contra Scandal. While the administration was busy trading arms for hostages, it was also struggling to find a way to fund a revolution in Nicaragua (in violation of the law) to assist the "Contra" forces trying to overthrow the Marxist-oriented Sandinista government. The United States was engaged in a series of covert operations, including the mining of Nicaraguan harbors (technically an act of war) but with mixed results. The Congress, frustrated with the acts of the administration, finally passed the Boland Amendment (tacked on to a defense appropriations bill) that prohibited aid to the Contras. The president signed the bill and almost immediately began to violate its provisions.

The administration thought it could kill two birds with one stone by linking efforts in Iran with the Contra aid scheme, and decided to use the profits from the Iranian arms deal to fund the Contras. The link between these two efforts was a Reagan security adviser, Oliver North.

In 1984 the president told Robert McFarlane to keep Contras together "body and soul," and diverting funds to the Contras served that purpose. As North wrote in the infamous "Diversion Memo":

$12 million will be used to purchase critically needed supplies for the Nicaraguan Democratic Resistance Forces. This material is essential to cover shortages in resistance inventories resulting from their current offensives and Sandanista counter-acts and to "bridge" the period between now and when Congressionally-approved lethal assistance (beyond the $25 million in "defensive" arms) can be delivered.[20]

Thus were two separate operations hitched together to form the Iran-Contra scandal.

In November 1986, reports began to circulate regarding the arms-for-hostages deal, and were soon followed by stories of the diversion of funds to the Contras. A mad scramble ensued in which Attorney General Ed Meese began an internal investigation noteworthy primarily for the incompetence with which it was conducted. After announcing that there would be an investigation, Meese failed to take custody of North's files, thereby giving North time to shred the evidence. So confident was North that he destroyed all the evidence that he assured National Security Adviser John Poindexter, "Don't worry. It is all taken care of." North later bragged that he was shredding documents while investigators were in the next room.

And what of Reagan's involvement? The president approved the secret arms-for-hostage trade with Iran. It is not certain whether he was aware of the diversion of funds to the Contras. When news of the scandal broke, the president went into a three-month cocoon,[21] and the administration appeared as if it might topple. But after the dismissals of North and Poindexter, a presidential inquiry (the Tower Commission), congressional hearings, and a special prosecutor's investigation, the president survived.

The cover-up of these crimes began at the early stages of both the Iran and Contra scandals. Secrecy was of the utmost importance, as the truth had to be kept from Congress and the American people. False chronologies were submitted to Congress, lies were told, perjury committed, evidence shredded (even a presidential finding authorizing a covert arms-for-hostage trade, dated December 5, 1985, was destroyed by Admiral Poindexter). The cover-up intensified after the broad dimensions of the scandal were revealed because, as Attorney General Meese testified at the North trial, he feared impeachment of the president.

There was a comic-opera quality to Iran-Contra that defies believability. The operations were run by Oliver North, a Marine lieutenant colonel, a bumbler who made fictional TV "superagent" Maxwell Smart look effective. North was regarded by some of his peers as "a hustler who had a habit of bending the truth to enhance his own reputation." And of North, presidential aide Mike Deaver once noted, "I used to keep Ollie out of Reagan's office because he was dangerous. He scared me."[22] North's actions involved "shredding parties" (which missed important documents); removing key documents from his office by having his secretary, Fawn Hall, hide them in her clothing; delivering gifts of pistols and chocolate cake to the Iranians; depositing $10 million in arms sale profits into the *wrong* Swiss bank account; being hoodwinked and blackmailed time after time by both the Iranians and his own business associates; and the list goes on. Pundits clucked that North's operation made it seem as if the Keystone Cops were running U.S. foreign policy. *New York Times* correspondent R. W. Apple, in his introduction to the Tower report summing up the congressional investigation into Iran-Contra, wrote that the report "pictures a National Security Council led by reckless cowboys, off on their own on a wild ride, taking direct operational control of matters that are the customary province of more sober agencies such as the CIA, the State Department and the Defense Department."[23] The congressional report on the Iran-Contra scandal noted:

The common ingredients of the Iran and Contra policies were secrecy, deception, and disdain for the law. A small group of senior officials believed that they alone knew what was right. They viewed knowledge of their actions by others in the Government as a threat to their objectives. They told neither the Secretary of State, the Congress nor the American people of their actions. When exposure was threatened, they destroyed official documents and lied to Cabinet officials, to the public, and to elected representatives in Congress. They testified that they even withheld key facts from the President [Ronald Reagan].

The report concluded:

Nevertheless, the ultimate responsibility for the events in the Iran-Contra Affair must rest with the President. If the President did not know what his National Security Advisers were doing, he should have. It is his responsibility to communicate unambiguously to his subordinates that they must keep him advised of important actions they take for the Administration. The Constitution requires the President to "take care that the laws be faithfully executed." This charge encompasses a responsibility to leave the members of his Administration in no doubt that the rule of law governs.

And the report further noted that the "cabal of the zealots" was in charge of decision-making in the Reagan White House.[24]

Lawrence Walsh, the independent counsel assigned to investigate the Iran-Contra scandal, issued a 700–page report very critical of the administration. Walsh, who claimed he was stymied by the administration in his investigation, argued that the president was far more deeply involved in the scandal than he claimed, concluding that the president "knowingly participated or at least acquiesced" in the cover-up of the scandal.[25] He also concluded that, statements notwithstanding, Vice President Bush knew about the scandal and withheld evidence. Walsh's investigation led to nearly a dozen convictions, including three counts against Oliver North (later overturned on technicalities).

What role did the president play in all this? Reagan was "obsessed" with the fate of the hostages. After Congress banned aid to the Contras, the president told McFarlane he "did not intend to break faith with the contras," and that they were to be kept together "body and soul." Beyond that, Reagan's role gets murky, if not contradictory.

Reagan insisted that government officials did not solicit private donations to support the Contras, yet, on May 15, 1987, the president claimed "It was my idea to begin with." Reagan asserted in November 1986 that "We did not, repeat, did not trade weapons or anything else for hostages." Yet, on December 5, 1985, the president signed an order (a presidential finding) that authorized a straight arms-for-hostages trade, which even included this strange mathematical formula for the trade:

H-hr: 1 707 w/300 TOWs = 1 AMCIT
H+10 Hrs: 1 707 (same A/C) w/300 TOWs = 1 AMCIT
H+16 Hrs: 1 747 w/50 HAWKS & 400 TOWs = 2 AMCITs
H+20 Hrs: 1 707 w/300 TOWs = 1 AMCIT[26]

Translated, this formula reads that upon the arrival of the first planeload of arms at H-Hour with 300 TOW weapons, one AMCIT (American citizen) would be freed.

When Secretary of State George Shultz and Secretary of Defense "Cap" Weinberger warned the president on December 7, 1985, that this would be unwise and illegal, the president dismissed their objections, declaring, "The American people will never forgive me if I fail to get these hostages out, over this legal question."[27] In the end, the Iranians received 2,000 TOW missiles, eighteen Hawk antiaircraft missiles, and spare parts valued at several million dollars. In exchange for the arms, three hostages were released. However, three other Americans were then taken captive, thereby "replenishing" the stock of U.S. hostages held by the captors.

Reagan's involvement in the Iran-Contra scandal, which became known as "Irangate," echoing the post-Watergate parlance for scandals, runs from claims that "Reagan knew everything,"[28] to Reagan's own "I don't recall,"[29] to "It was my idea to begin with."[30] The dilemma can be wrapped up in Reagan's three answers to one question. Asked by the Tower Commission whether he had approved, in advance, shipments of arms to Iran, the president first said that he had given oral approval to Bud McFarlane. Upon finding out from his Chief of Staff Donald Regan that this was illegal, the president went back and informed the Commission that he *did not* give prior approval. When these two responses raised questions about the president's mind and honesty, the president claimed ignorance: "I'm afraid that I let myself be influenced by other's recollections, not my own."

But the president did sign several presidential findings, which authorized arms sales to Iran and spelled out what was going on; he did participate in a number of discussions with key officials; and he did actively help solicit funds from third parties to support the Contras. The administration further lied to Congress and the American people, provided Congress with a false chronology of events, destroyed evidence, knew of crimes and failed to report them, profited from the arms sales, engaged in a criminal cover-up, violated several laws including the Boland Amendment, and withheld evidence. The administration further traded arms for hostages, illegally funded a revolutionary force in Central America, set up an illegal shadow government (known as the Enterprise), and diverted government money for private use.

Yet, the president survived. How? Some claim that there was an understanding in Congress that after the trauma of Watergate, the nation could not stand another president facing impeachment, and they thus agreed to go easy on the president, whose second term was winding down in any case.[31] Efforts to get to the bottom of the Iran-Contra scandal ended when, on December 24, 1992, President George Bush, Reagan's former vice president, issued pardons to Caspar Weinberger, Robert McFarlane, Elliott Abrams, and three CIA officials.

In spite of Lawrence Walsh's fourteen indictments, and eleven convictions, the Iran-Contra case remains unresolved. The destruction of evidence, the Attorney General's sloppy initial investigation, the pardons—all mean that we may never get to the bottom of this scandal.

A FRAMEWORK

In an effort to understand better the historical occurrence of presidential corruption, we can organize the four major cases (adding Nixon to this chapter's three other cases) into a framework (Table 4.1) which highlights some of the major variables. (At this writing, President Clinton has faced a series of corruption charges. It is premature, at this early date, to draw definitive conclusions regarding the level of corruption of his administration, though it is interesting, and perhaps significant, that Clinton's accusers use the Watergate scandal rather than the more recent Reagan ones as the framework for judging corruption, moral turpitude, and perjury.) One of the most important questions revolves around the level of presidential involvement in these cases of corruption.

What can we learn about presidential corruption from the four leading cases? As for the causes, the lure of money is strong, as evidenced by the Grant, Harding, and Reagan experiences. But it is not the presidents, but their underlings who fall to this temptation. Also, the drive for power is apparent in

Table 4.1
Presidential Corruption: A Framework

President	Grant	Harding	Nixon	Reagan
Terms	1869–1877	1921–1923	1969–1974	1981–1988
Party	Republican	Republican	Republican	Republican
Type of Corruption	Money	Money	Power	(A) Money (Sleaze) (B) Power (Iran–C)
Who was Involved	Cabinet +	Cabinet +	Pres; VP; Staff	(A) Cabinet & Staff (B) Pres; VP; Cabinet; Staff
Role of President	Minimal	Minimal	Deeply Involved	(A) Minimal (B) Deeply Involved
Management	Hands off Delegating	Hands off Delegating	Hierarchical	Hands off Delegating
Resolution	Served Two Full Terms	Died in Office	Forced to Resign as Impeachment Approached	Served Two Full Terms
Historical Reputation*	#36 Failure	#37 Failure	#35 Failure	#28 Below Average

Note: Murray/Blessing Poll; See Robert K. Murray and Tim H. Blessing, *Greatness in the White House* (University Park: The Pennsylvania State University Press, 1994).

two cases, Nixon and Reagan. Thus, both personal and institutional causes are evident.

An interesting pattern is associated with the degree of presidential involvement. In matters of money, presidents seem for the most part uninvolved, but in matters of power and ideology (Watergate and Iran-Contra), presidents have been highly involved. Also, in earlier periods, Cabinets were more involved in corruption rather than their presidential staffs. In the two recent cases of presidential corruption, however, the staffs (those closest to the president or inside the White House) were more involved. This reflects the shift in power from Cabinet to staff, which has taken place in the past few decades.

Presidential management style seems to have an impact in the level of corruption. When presidents adopt a hands-off style of management, the temptation and opportunity for corruption seems nearly irresistible though not inevitable. And when foreign policy and national security concerns loom large, as in the Cold War context, the "necessity" for secrecy contributes to potential abuses of power.

CONCLUSION

> With all its defects, delays and inconveniences, men have discovered no technique for long preserving free government except that the Executive be under the law.
>
> —U.S. Supreme Court
> *Youngstown Sheet and Tube Co. v. Sawyer*, 1952

As this book goes to press, President William Jefferson Clinton is embroiled in a series of scandals and accusations of wrongdoing. One thing is very clear: In a pre-Watergate era, most of the accusations against President Clinton would not have drawn very much press coverage, and hardly any would have led to judicial inquiries. In 1998 the U.S. House of Representatives voted to approve two articles of impeachment against President Clinton. On February 2, 1999, the Senate voted to acquit Clinton on both articles. But criticism and accusation continue to follow the president. It will be years before we can sort out the truth about "Zippergate" and related charges against President Clinton.

Charges of corruption against Presidents Truman and Eisenhower were handled within the political arena, not the courts. And stories of Presidents Kennedy and Johnson and their extramarital activities simply were not deemed appropriate for investigation and reporting. Today, nothing is off limits and seemingly everything requires the opportunity of special investigation.

While almost every president (or members of his administration) since the emergence of the modern presidency in the late ninteenth century has been accused of wrongdoing, the number of major scandals is relatively small. Indeed, going back to the beginning of the republic, in over two hundred years, only four presidents headed what might be called "corrupt administrations," though a rash of indictments of Clinton administration officials and questions about the president's and even the First Lady's financial dealings and the president's personal morality and fund-raising ethics make the Clinton administration a candidate for this dubious distinction. The Nixon defense that "everybody does it" is both cynical and historically incorrect. Everybody didn't do it.

A democracy cannot afford to be casual regarding corruption. If the public perceives corruption to be common and widespread, a general loss of trust in government is likely to follow. Leaders, institutions, even the law may be held up to ridicule. Cynicism and disaffection are likely to grow, and the people are more likely to drop out of the political process—all of which have occurred in the post-Watergate era.

In believing that self-interest rules over virtue as the animating force in human behavior, the founders structured politics to account for man's weakness, not to reflect his goodness. Were they correct? What overall impact has this view had in *shaping* behavior? Clearly, their actions had consequences in setting the ground rules of institutional conflict and interaction. In expecting rulers to be corrupt(ible) the framers set in motion institutional separation that made concerted action difficult and community building secondary. Setting power against power may reduce the chances of tyranny and corruption, but does constrict choices and discourage a positive community-based notion of public good.

When placed in comparative perspective, Watergate remains the most serious example of presidential corruption in U.S. history. Though other presidents have faltered, some by errors of commission, others by omission, no administration threatened the Constitution as did Richard Nixon and his cohorts. Congress noted that fact in its impeachment articles. More than anything else, it was Nixon's abuse of power and patterns of criminality that demanded impeachment—not only to bring Nixon before the bar of justice and restore balance in government, but also, perhaps more, to reaffirm the rule of law and regain the public's trust in government. In Watergate, presidential self-interest and ambition threatened to consume democracy itself.

NOTES

1. Chester Barnard, *Functions of the Executive* (Cambridge, MA: Harvard University Press, 1968).

2. James Madison, *The Federalist*, nos. 10 and 51.

3. Ibid., nos. 56 and 57.

4. Quoted in Richard Hofstadler, "The Founding Fathers," in Irving Horowitz, *The Moral Foundations of the American Republic* (Charlottesville: University Press of Virginia, 1987), 67.

5. Thomas E. Cronin, ed., *Inventing the American Presidency* (Lawrence: University Press of Kansas, 1989).

6. John P. Diggins, *The Lost Soul of American Politics* (New York: Basic, 1984), 48.

7. Madison, *The Federalist*, nos. 10 and 51.

8. Ibid., nos. 56 and 57.

9. W. E. Binkley, *The Powers of the President* (Garden City, NY: Doubleday, 1937), 159.

10. Jack Mitchell, *Executive Privilege: Two Centuries of White House Scandals* (New York: Hippocrene Books, 1992), chap. 4.

11. James E. Sefton, "Ulysses S. Grant," in Leonard W. Levy and Louis Fisher, eds., *Encyclopedia of the American Presidency* (New York: Simon and Schuster, 1994), vol. 2, p. 700.

12. Mitchell, *Executive Privilege*, 106.

13. Hope Ridings Miller, *Scandals in the Highest Office* (New York: Random House, 1973), 201–2.

14. Quoted in Michael Nelson and Sidney M. Milkis, *The American Presidency* (Washington, DC: CQ Press, 1990), 243.

15. Burl Noogle, *Teapot Dome* (Baton Rouge: Louisiana State University Press, 1982); J. Leonard Bates, *The Origins of Teapot Dome* (Urbana: University of Illinois Press, 1963).

16. Shelley Ross, *Fall from Grace* (New York: Ballantine, 1988), 269.

17. Robert Roberts, *White House Ethics* (Westport, CT: Greenwood Press, 1988), 175.

18. Suzanne Garment, *Scandal* (New York: Random House, 1991), 198.

19. Bob Schieffer and Gary Paul Gates, *The Acting President* (New York: E. P. Dutton, 1989), 230.

20. Theodore Draper, *A Very Thin Line* (New York: Touchstone, 1991), 33 and 302.

21. Jane Mayer and Doyle McManus, *Landslide* (Boston: Houghton Mifflin, 1998), "Introduction."

22. Schieffer and Gates, *The Acting President*, 249.

23. R. W. Apple, *The Tower Commission Report* (New York: Times Books, 1987), xv.

24. *Executive Summary of the Report of the Congressional Committees Investigating the Iran-Contra Affair; Senate Select Committee to Investigate Covert Arms Transactions with Iran* (Washington, DC: U.S. Government Printing Office, 1988).

25. David Johnston, "Reagan Had Role in Arms Scandal, Prosecutor Says," *New York Times*, January 19, 1994, p. 1.

26. Report of the President's Special Review Board, February 26, 1987, p. B36.

27. George Shultz, *Iran-Contra Hearings*, United States Congress, joint session, July 23, 1987.

28. Oliver L. North, *Under Fire* (New York: HarperCollins, 1991), excerpt in *Time*, October 28, 1991, p. 36.

29. Reagan to Tower commission, *Report of President's Special Review Board* issued February 26, 1987, and at Poindexter trial.

30. Reagan, May 15, 1987, to group of newspaper editors.

31. Seymour M. Hersh, "The Iran-Contra Committee: Did They Protect Reagan?" *New York Times Magazine*, April 29, 1990.

Richard Nixon at a news conference on April 30, 1971. © 1971, The *Washington Post*. Photo by Ellsworth Davis. Reprinted with permission

H. R. "Bob" Haldeman, Nixon's chief of staff, was considered the second most powerful man in the White House. He was convicted for Watergate-related crimes. National Archives

Charles "Chuck" Colson, one of the president's political operatives. Colson appealed to the "dark side" of President Nixon. He was convicted of Watergate-related crimes. National Archives

President Nixon at the swearing in of Elliot Richardson as attorney general. Richardson would resign that post when ordered to fire special prosecutor Archibald Cox. National Archives

John N. Mitchell after giving deposition in Watergate caper. © 1972, The *Washington Post*. Photo by Charles Del Vecchio. Reprinted with permission

John Ehrlichman was President Nixon's chief domestic policy advisor. He was convicted of Watergate-related crimes. © 1973, The *Washington Post*. Photo by Bob Burchette. Reprinted with permission

Former presidential aide John Dean III testifies for the second day before the Senate Water-gate Investigating Committee.© 1973, The *Washington Post*. Photo by James K. W. Atherton. Reprinted with permission

Chairman Sam Irvin (left) and counsel Samuel Dash face former White House chief of staff, H. R. Haldeman. © 1973, The *Washington Post*. Photo by Bob Burchette. Reprinted with permission

President Nixon surrounded by his family at the tearful farewell speech to the White House staff, August 9, 1974. National Archives

Among the mourners at the funeral of Richard M. Nixon are (left to right) G. Gordon Liddy and former Vice President Spiro T. Agnew. © 1994, The *Washington Post*. Photo by Bill O'Leary. Reprinted with permission

5

Nixon and the Media

"I don't mind a microscope, but when they use a proctoscope . . ."
—Richard Nixon

All presidents dislike the press at times. As an avenue to the public, the press reveals more than most presidents wish and usually exposes warts that presidents would prefer to keep concealed. (As one wag commented, "Presidents hate the press because they quote them.")

From the beginning of the republic, presidents have bemoaned what they saw as the irresponsibility or downright scandalousness of the press. George Washington once wrote that he was tired of being "buffeted in the public prints by a set of infamous scribblers," and John Adams complained of being "disgraced and degraded" in the press and was president while the Alien and Sedition Acts were used to arrest and prosecute opposition news editors. Thomas Jefferson, America's most eloquent advocate of press freedom ("Our liberty depends on the freedom of the press, and that cannot be limited without being lost," or "Where the press is free, and every man able to read, all is safe"), once wrote that "even the least informed of the people have learnt that nothing in a newspaper is to be believed."

In spite of the press's role as presidential critic, presidents need and use the press. Though it is a source of irritation, it is also a source of power. All presidents use, and most presidents dominate, the press. It is their vital link to the public and the best route to persuading the people and the Congress.

Thus the press can serve as an occasional check on presidential power as well as—and more often as—a tool for presidential power. Which of these it tends to be (and for all presidents it is at times both) depends on the issues (are trends and issues working for or against the president?), the personal skills of the president (is he persuasive?), and the management of the media (how well orchestrated is the president's public relations team?).

Whether the president is more or less skillful at manipulating and using the press to his advantage, one thing remains clear: The modern president is in a position to command the attention of the media and the nation as no other public figure can. As presidential power has grown in time of depression, world war, and the Cold War, so has the public's interest in presidential doings and personality. An elaborate press establishment now follows the president, attesting to the "celebrity status" of presidents and their families. From Franklin D. Roosevelt on, the president's every move, every action, every word is news that must be covered and reported. Presidents thus have the capacity to set the national agenda and focus the country's attention on issues as no one else can.

In general, presidents get fairly soft treatment in the press. Other than the final year of the Johnson, Nixon, and Carter presidencies, the Iran-Contra period for Reagan, and the Lewinsky scandal of the Clinton presidency, one would be hard pressed to find a year in which—overall—any president received a "bad" press. On balance, presidents receive fairly positive coverage at the hand of the national media. Of course, much of this positive coverage derives from careful presidential planning, manipulation, and the care and feeding of reporters.

In relations, adversarial or otherwise, between the president and the press, the president has a distinct advantage. While both sides have tools at their disposal, presidents hold the most powerful ones. Presidents have the capacity to reward friends through access, interviews, leaks, and so on, and to punish adversaries. A skillful president can use the media to exploit his office as a "bully pulpit," and the "communicator-in-chief" role gives presidents considerable power. The press is the president's conduit to the people, the primary link between president and public — a fact Franklin D. Roosevelt understood in inaugurating the presidential news conference and every president since FDR has used to get his message out, except Nixon and Reagan who found direct appeals in televised speeches rather than news conferences as a primary means of "communication" (see Table 5.1).

Richard Nixon always had a love-hate relationship with the press, although, in his early years in the House and Senate, Nixon had greater contact with reporters and often fed and received information from them. But later, each seemed to love hating the other. "Criticism from the press has been my

Table 5.1
Presidential News Conferences, 1949–1992

President	Total Conferences	Yearly Average	Monthly Average
Truman	160	40	3.3
Eisenhower, I	99	25	2.1
Eisenhower, II	94	24	2.0
Kennedy	65	22	1.9
Johnson	132	26	2.1
Nixon, I	30	8	0.6
Nixon, II	9	5	0.5
Ford	41	19	1.4
Carter	59	15	1.2
Reagan	23	6.6	0.6
Bush	64	16	1.3

Sources: Adapted from Gary King and Lyn Ragsdale, *The Elusive Executive: Discovering Statistical Patterns in the Presidency* (Washington, DC: CQ Press, 1988), 268.

lot throughout my political life," said Richard Nixon, and to an extent this was true. Former Nixon aide Bryce Harlow once went so far as to say that "the press was hooked on an anti-Nixon drug and could never break the addiction. It was terrible drag throughout Nixon's political career."

Washington Post reporter Lou Cannon said of the relationship, "Nixon hated us. It was reciprocated in some ways, but not as much as he thought." Nixon speechwriter William Safire has written that "when Nixon said, 'The press is the enemy,' . . . he was saying exactly what he meant: 'The press is the enemy, to be hated and beaten.' " To Safire, this attitude was Nixon's "greatest personal and political weakness and the cause of his downfall." Columnist Hugh Sidey went so far as to say that "Nixon's paranoia about the press was world class."

Nixon's problems with the press began in earnest during the 1960 presidential race. In his first campaign for president, Nixon blamed his loss—in part—on the media. Kennedy "looked" better than Nixon. The debates became, in Nixon's view, more a beauty contest than a genuine exchange of ideas, and Nixon felt victimized by the media. If style triumphed over substance, Nixon would blame the messenger. He vowed never to let the media—

especially television—do him in again. After losing the race for governor of California in 1962, Nixon finally blew up in public at the press. Apparently blaming the press for his defeat, Nixon held his infamous "last press conference," where an angry Nixon blasted the press for giving him "the shaft" and told the press that "you won't have Nixon to kick around any more."

But that was not the end of Richard Nixon's public life, and six years later, when he again ran for president, Nixon was determined not to let the press do him in again. This time Nixon would control, as much as possible, how the press saw, reported, and dealt with him. He would tightly manage access to himself and information about the campaign. Leaving almost nothing to chance, Nixon's 1968 campaign was the most tightly controlled presidential campaign to date.

The '68 campaign was chronicled by Joe McGinniss in *The Selling of the President 1968* as an exercise in media control and manipulation. It was an effort to "sell" Nixon as one would a product. A "new" Nixon was created and presented to the American voter. As McGinnis writes of the media control on behalf of Nixon's effort to reshape his public image: "Television was the only answer, despite its sins against him in the past, but not just any kind of television. An uncommitted camera could do irreparable harm. His television would have to be controlled. . . . This would be Richard Nixon, the leader, returning from exile. Perhaps not beloved, but respected. Firm but not harsh; just but compassionate. With flashes of warmth spaced evenly throughout."[1]

Determined not to expose himself to a hostile press, Nixon carefully orchestrated his public exposure so as to present the image he chose to have the public see. Although Nixon said a few days after his nomination that "I am not going to barricade myself into a television studio and make this an antiseptic campaign," that is precisely what was done. And it worked.

Roger Ailes, who choreographed Nixon's 1968 media image, knew why he had to produce shows that re-created Nixon. As Ailes said: "Now you put him on television, you've got a problem right away. He's a funny-looking guy. He looks like somebody hung him in a closet overnight and he jumps out in the morning with his suit all bunched up and starts running around saying, 'I want to be president.' I mean this is how he strikes some people. That's why these shows are important. To make them forget all that."[2]

There did seem to be a "new" Nixon: more relaxed, more controlled, mature, and strong. He would be a man of peace who would end the war in Vietnam. The new Nixon was ready to lead. Having been victimized by the press in the past, Nixon used the press and media in 1968. Television gave Nixon the means to re-create himself in the eyes of the American public. He would be television's master, not its victim.

In his bid for reelection in 1972, Nixon would control his image to an even greater degree than in the 1968 campaign.[3] Nixon could do this because he had (a) more than twice as much money as his opponent; (b) the advantage of incumbency; (c) a weak opponent; (d) a fairly submissive press; and (e) a fairly strong claim to success in his first term. Even the Watergate break-in received little adverse media attention, or notice, and Nixon was able to slide into his second term confident that he had indeed won the upper hand in dealing with the media.

How did Nixon deal with and attempt to control and manipulate the media during his presidency? How did he create, by 1972, an atmosphere in which he seemingly could dominate a sometimes-pliant press? Then, why did the press, in 1974, seemingly "gang up" on the president?

If one compares the treatment Nixon received from the press to that of other presidents, one finds that by a variety of measures, Nixon received fairly favorable treatment. One measure is the percentage of newspaper endorsements a candidate receives in the presidential election. By this standard, Nixon did quite well, receiving 54 percent of the newspaper endorsements over John Kennedy's 15 percent in 1960, a 60.8 to 14 percent margin over Hubert Humphrey in 1968, and an astronomical 71.4 to 5.3 percent margin over George McGovern in 1972.

Although the everyday news reporter is slightly more liberal than the average voter, it is still difficult to find many reporters who were consistently critical of Nixon. A study by John Orman of the valanced reporting in the periodical press found that Nixon received a demonstrably good press compared to other presidents (even though he took a beating in 1973 and 1974 from the press).[4] In short, other than during the Watergate period, Richard Nixon received fairly favorable press coverage.[5]

But Nixon, insecure and excessively sensitive to criticism, believed that the press was out to get him, and he classified them as an enemy. If an enemy was going to attack, it called for a counterattack. In fact, the Nixon administration developed the most complex and elaborate attack on the national press in our nation's modern history. It was an attack on the tone, content, and personnel of the news industry. What emanated from the Nixon White House was an attack aimed not at a single reporter deemed to be biased or unfair, but at the entire news industry, from news reporters to editors to publishers.

Richard Nixon's paranoia about the press teamed with his excessive desire for secrecy and found an outlet for his anger when leaks began to spring in the ship of state.[6] Troubled by what he saw as excessive leaking—especially relating to the duplicitous stance the United States was taking in the India-Pakistan war—and egged on by Henry Kissinger, the president ordered that the leaks be plugged. This led to the creation of the "Plumbers," who committed a variety of crimes that in the long run contributed to the president's downfall.

Part of the strategy of plugging leaks and punishing critical news reporters and columnists was the imposition of a wiretapping program—again at the insistence of Henry Kissinger—that targeted a number of media stars. Among those victimized by the wiretapping program were Hedrick Smith and William Beecher of the *New York Times*, Henry Brandon of the *London Sunday Times*, and Marvin Kalb of CBS News. Such invasions of privacy—which the courts judged to be illegal—were justified on national security grounds, but probably had more to do with Nixon's own feelings toward the press.

The goals in dealing with the press were: (a) discredit the media; (b) get the best coverage possible for the administration; and (c) go over the heads of the press—directly to the American public. Nixon wanted to turn public opinion against the news media, thus discrediting the source of criticism against the administration. If this could be done, if the press could be painted as part of the "radiclib" cabal out to get the president, then criticism of the administration could be discounted, or at least deflected.

President-elect Nixon decided in 1968 not to have a press secretary in the conventional sense. Instead of drawing his press secretary from the ranks of journalists, Nixon turned to private industry. Nixon was interested in the promotion of a product—the Nixon presidency—rather than a dialogue with reporters and the American people. Controlled news—public relations—was the watchword. Such a strategy reinforced the isolation of Nixon from the public mind. Nixon assigned Ron Ziegler to run the press office, and Herb Klein was appointed director of communications. At first, Klein was to serve as the communications powerhouse, but Klein quickly descended and press spokesman Ron Ziegler rose to become the administration's public voice.[7]

"Make the press look bad, make the President look good" was the overarching goal of the Nixon press machinery. To do this, an elaborate public relations effort was put into effect. John Ehrlichman notes that "Richard Nixon at times seemed to believe there was no national issue that was not susceptible to public relations treatment." Nixon organized the administration so as to maximize the opportunities afforded the president. As Ehrlichman notes, "Nixon came into the White House determined to exercise the fullest possible influence over what the press said about him and his administration." He and Bob Haldeman shared the view that no previous president had properly organized and staffed the White House to manage the news. They set about constructing an apparatus that would appear to serve the White House press corps, while, at the same time, sending volumes of information over their heads to small newspapers and television stations out in the hinterlands. The White House would try to systematically propagandize the general public. The "five o'clock group" met almost daily to discuss how to "play" stories in the media.

The president was rarely openly engaged in anti-press rhetoric or action. He would remain above the fray. But it is clear that the impetus and attitude of the anti-press campaign came from Nixon. Throughout H. R. Haldeman's notes are references about the president ordering his staff to "freeze out" this or that reporter; and telling them "no one to see press at all"; and "All NY Times reporters—all off list including K. punish the whole institution."

Nixon was especially sensitive to press criticism, took it personally, and sought revenge. H. R. Haldeman's notes taken in meetings with the president are full of critical references made by Nixon to news reporters. Nixon reserved a special contempt for the *New York Times*, the *Washington Post*, and *Newsweek* magazine. For example, on July 20, 1969, Nixon is quoted as saying, "Absolute order—complete cut off of *Times*"; or on July 18, 1969, "get *Time* in on Friday and *US News* give them the whole story. . . . Don't tell *Newsweek* anything."

The Nixon team's effort to manipulate the image presented of the president and manipulate the news media itself was not unique in kind, only in volume. All presidents try to influence or manage the news. But no previous president (and only Reagan and Clinton since) went to the lengths that Nixon did to manipulate the media.[8]

John Ehrlichman called Nixon "a talented media manipulator." But the most aggressive aspect of the Nixon press strategy was the "attack strategy" employed by the administration. Presidents have tended to use both the carrot and the stick when dealing with the press: Nixon emphasized the stick. He believed that the media represented "the greatest concentration of power in the United States"[9] and were part of the elite Eastern establishment out to get him. Newscaster Walter Cronkite once accused the Nixon administration of "a grand conspiracy to destroy the credibility of the press," of a "clear effort at intimidation of the press." This effort to discredit the press was carefully planned and elaborately orchestrated.

If the press was the enemy, Nixon would go over their heads, directly to the American people, "his" people. Nixon had a fear that if he gave his message to the press, the media would distort the message he was trying to get across. "My object," Nixon once said, "was to go over the heads of the columnists." The president often sought—and was granted—prime-time television access to make major policy and political speeches. This allowed the president to go directly to the voters without the filtering effect of TV and news reporters. Nixon, for example, gave more television addresses (32) than Kennedy (9), Johnson (15), and Ford (6) combined.

To Nixon, public speaking was "performance not communication."[10] His communication theory was to "(1) speak for the institution, not for oneself; (2) speak in controlled settings, not those permitting interlocutors; (3) speak for the ages, not for the tempestuous moment."[11]

In this sense, Nixon furthered his goal of appearing presidential. By using this method and speaking directly to the people, Nixon had almost total control of the medium and the message. He could surround himself with the symbols and paraphernalia that would help create the image he wanted. Nixon could speak to the people in words he chose. The press was effectively excluded from this process.

The overall control of the antipress strategy went through Haldeman's office, but Jeb Magruder and Charles Colson assumed day-to-day control. The initial strategy was laid out in a remarkable October 17, 1969, memorandum from Magruder to Haldeman entitled "The Shot-Gun Versus the Rifle." The memorandum advised dealing with press criticism not in a case-by-case way (Magruder cited twenty-one instances of the president, in a thirty-day period, requesting action against new stories), but in a broader, more general manner. The real problem, Magruder wrote, was "to get to this unfair coverage" in a way that "the networks, newspapers and Congress will react to and begin to look at things somewhat differently." To do this, Magruder suggested that the administration "begin an official monitoring system." He also proposed utilizing "the anti-trust division to investigate various media relating to anti-trust violations. Even the possible threat of anti-trust action I think would be effective in changing their views." He also suggested "utilizing the Internal Revenue Service as a method to look into the various organizations that we are most concerned about. Just a threat of an IRS investigation will probably turn their approach." Magruder also proposed that the administration "begin to show favorites in the media," and "utilize Republican National Committee for major letter writing efforts." Out of this memorandum sprang a series of actions designed to discredit the media, put it on the defensive, and, Magruder and the Nixon team hoped, to get more favorable coverage. This started an avalanche of activity directed against the press. The goal, as Haldeman aide Lawrence Higby noted in a memorandum to Magruder, was not to go after individual newsmen: "What we are trying to do here is to tear down the institution."

The president was very interested in a broad monitoring of television. In a March 11, 1969, memorandum to John Ehrlichman, Nixon notes that he wants to "monitor television programs—not only the political programs but the entertainment programs in which there are often deliberately negative comments which deserve some reaction on the part of our friends. One of the programs . . . was the 'Smothers Brothers.' In looking at it Sunday night . . . one said to the other that he found it difficult to find anything to laugh about—Vietnam, the cities, etc., but 'Richard Nixon solving these problems' and that's really funny.' " Nixon then added, "The line didn't get a particularly good reaction," but it was "the kind of line that should . . . receive some calls and letters strenuously objecting to that kind of attack."

The most visible arm of the attack on the news media was a series of speeches given by Vice President Spiro Agnew. The idea of using Agnew in this manner came, according to Haldeman, "right from the Oval Office." The first salvo was fired by Agnew in a November 13, 1969, speech written by Pat Buchanan and delivered in Des Moines, Iowa. In the speech, Agnew launched an all-out assault on the integrity of the three television networks. Noting that he was not proposing government censorship, Agnew asked "whether a form of censorship already exists" with the networks, "a small and unelected elite" determining what the people will see and hear. Later in the speech, the vice president reminded the networks that they enjoyed "a monopoly sanctioned and licensed " by the government (a warning of things to come) and called on the networks to be "made more responsive to the views of the nation." Agnew continued: "A small group of men, numbering perhaps no more than a dozen anchormen, commentators and executive producers, settle upon the twenty minutes or so of film and commentary that's to reach the public. . . . They decide what forty to fifty million Americans will learn of the day's events in the nation and in the world. . . . We do know that to a man these commentators and producers live and work in the geographical and intellectual confines of Washington, D.C., or New York City, the latter of which James Reston termed the most unrepresentative community in the entire United States. Both communities bask in their own provincialism, their own parochialism. We can deduce that these men read the same newspapers. They draw their political and social views from the same sources. Worse, they talk constantly to one another, thereby providing artificial reinforcement to their shared viewpoints."[12] A week later, in a speech in Montgomery, Alabama, Agnew again went on the attack, this time broadening his accusations to include the *New York Times* and the *Washington Post*.

Agnew's public attack on the honesty and integrity of the press was followed by a series of moves designed to put pressure on the media from a variety of fronts. Dean Burch, chairman of the Federal Communications Commission (FCC), called the heads of all three networks the day after President Nixon gave a major speech on Vietnam and requested transcripts of the news analyses the networks carried. He was doing so, he claimed, "at the request of the White House." Such thinly veiled efforts at intimidation were reinforced with other, more hard-hitting, actions.

By the summer of 1971 the White House pushed ahead even more forcefully: The enemies list was forwarded to John Dean, the Pentagon Papers case went ahead, the Plumbers broke into one of Daniel Ellsberg's psychiatrist's offices, and the FBI began investigating CBS correspondent Daniel Schorr. It was a full-court press. In addition, Attorney General John Mitchell contributed substantially to the antimedia effort with a legal assault on press freedom and the First Amendment by challenging the privacy of a reporter's sources. Mitchell also executed an attempt by the U.S. government at prior restraint of the press in the Pentagon Papers case.

Clay Whitehead, head of the White House Office of Telecommunications Policy, criticized news coverage of the president in forceful language and in 1972 announced that the administration would soon propose legislation that would hold local stations responsible at license-renewal time for the content of the network news and all the network-provided programming they broadcast. He also suggested that the FCC impose licensing-renewal requirements with "teeth." Whitehead wanted the local stations to pressure the networks to refrain from what he called "ideological plugola" and "elitist gossip in the guise of news analysis." By threatening the use of the licensing-renewal procedure, Whitehead hoped the local affiliates would pressure the networks into altering their news programs. He concluded his speech by saying, "Station managers and network officials who fail to act to correct imbalance or consistent bias from the networks—or who acquiesce by silence—can only be considered willing participants to be held fully accountable by the broadcaster's community at license-renewal time."

In connection with this, the administration orchestrated a letter-writing campaign that generated thousands of letter to the networks, supporting the administration. This letter-writing campaign—in which it was made to appear that thousands of ordinary citizens were spontaneously making their views known—was used throughout the Nixon presidency.

The two-pronged goal of discrediting the news media in the eyes of the public and frightening the press into submission continued as the administration pressed the networks on the fairness issue. Chuck Colson set up a series of off-the-record meetings with the network heads in which Colson introduced the possibility of government intervention in television news. In a memorandum to Haldeman describing the meetings, Colson wrote that "the networks are terribly nervous over the uncertain state of the law. . . . They are also apprehensive about us. Although they tried to hide this, it was obvious. The harder I pressed them (CBS and NBC) the more accommodating, cordial, and almost apologetic they became." He further wrote, "They were startled by how thoroughly we were doing our homework . . . the way in which we had so thoroughly monitored their coverage and our analysis of it. . . . They are terribly concerned with being able to work out their own policies with respect to balanced coverage and not to have policies imposed on them." Colson continued, "They are very much afraid of us and are trying hard to prove they are 'good guys.' " He concluded, "This all adds up to the fact that they are damned nervous and scared and we should continue to take a very tough line, face to face, and in other ways."[13]

The threat of license challenges became a reality when the administration discussed the future of two CBS affiliates, WJXT in Jacksonville and WPLG in Miami, both owned by the Washington Post; whose investigative reporting helped undo the Watergate cover-up. Part of a White House conversation between the president and Bob Haldeman deals with this matter.

The President: The main thing is the *Post* is going to have damnable, damnable problems out of this one. They have a television station and they're going to have it renewed.

Haldeman: They've got a radio station, too.

The President: Does that come up, too? . . . It's going to be goddam active here. . . . Well, the game has to be played awfully rough.

Soon thereafter, the federal licenses under which these two stations operated came up for renewal, and their licenses were challenged by people with known associations to the president. This challenge sent a chill throughout the industry. The *Post* was being made to pay for its reporting.

The administration also was displeased with the fledgling Corporation for Public Broadcasting (CPB). Annoyed at what they considered anti-administration reporting, the president vetoed the 1972 Public Broadcasting Bill and killed its funding for a two-year period.

The administration further turned up the heat in the spring of 1972 when Nixon speechwriter Patrick Buchanan, in an interview, complained about the bias on network news programs and cautioned that "a monopoly like this of a group of people with a single point of view and a single political ideology" was creating a situation in which they were "going to find something done in the area of anti-trust-type action." As a prelude to the 1972 presidential campaign, such a warning spoke volumes.

As the '72 campaign approached, and as the Democrats self-destructed and the McGovern candidacy declined, the Nixon administration eased up on the media. But the easing of pressure was short-lived. On October 29, 1972, Chuck Colson telephoned CBS president Frank Stanton to complain about the station's coverage of the Watergate break-in. Asked if the reporting was unfair, Colson responded, "Whether the report was fair or not, it should not have been broadcast at all." For the next few weeks, CBS seemed to back off on its Watergate coverage.

Just after the '72 campaign, Colson again called Stanton. According to an affidavit of Stanton's, Colson "said in substance that unless CBS substantially changed its news treatment of the Nixon Administration 'things will get much worse for CBS.' " Colson added that CBS "didn't play ball during the campaign" and that "we'll bring you to your knees in Wall Street and on Madison Avenue."

As the administration's attempts at media manipulation and intimidation increased, the president's contacts with the press decreased. The president's handlers jealously guarded Nixon, and he remained aloof and isolated from the press. After the 1972 election, the administration continued to heat up the media attack as FCC chair Dean Burch leaked word that he had proposed a rulemaking proceeding to determine whether the ownership of the major networks, was in the public interest. As Watergate became a bigger story, the president felt compelled to go public himself with the antipress line. In an October 26, 1973, press conference, Nixon said: "I have never heard or seen such outrageous, vicious, distorted reporting in twenty-seven years of public life. I'm not blaming anybody for that. Perhaps what happened is that what we did brought it about, and therefore the media decided that they would have to take that particular line. But when people are pounded night after night with that kind of frantic, hysterical reporting, it naturally shakes their confidence."

In 1973, in an effort to determine the extent of the administration's repeated accusations of media bias, the National News Council was formed. The council made numerous attempts to get the administration to document its charges against the media, but the administration could not or would not cooperate. Finally this effort was abandoned.

Because the administration was brought down, in part, due to the media's investigating and reporting about Watergate, one must ask, how successful was the Nixon attack on the media?

By the end of the 1972 campaign, it appeared as if the Nixon campaign against the press had indeed worked—for a time. The criticism against the president in the '72 campaign was very mild, and indeed, it was the McGovern campaign that received the harshest treatment. The networks and the major newspapers seemed to be on the defensive. As the Watergate story grew, the Nixon effort at media attack accelerated, but there was little the administration could do. The full weight of the charges against the president eventually overwhelmed the administration. The cumulative effect of revelation after revelation finally turned the public against the president, and all the attacks upon the press could not change the damaging impact of the facts of Watergate.

Many of the crimes and accusations of Watergate related to abuses of power concerned efforts to control or punish the press. Illegal wiretaps against newsmen, efforts to cover up crimes, the Ellsberg psychiatrist's break-in, excessive secrecy, the creation of the Plumbers to control news leaks, and a variety of other activities relating to the media contributed substantially to the decline and fall of Richard Nixon. His paranoia about the press proved to be a part of his own undoing.

Had Nixon a healthier, more balanced attitude about the press, he might not have been inclined to engage in the excesses that brought his presidency down. As Nixon speechwriter William Safire has written: "A hatred of the press . . . caused Nixon to go over the brink, to lose all sense of balance, to defend his privacy at the expense of everyone else's right to privacy, and to create the climate that led to Watergate."[14]

In the end, the press *did* help bring Richard Nixon down. The early investigative reporting by two young *Washington Post* reporters, Bob Woodward and Carl Bernstein, started a slow but steady diet of story after story, revelation after revelation, until the cover-up came unraveled, and the corruption of the Nixon administration was finally exposed.

The effect of Watergate on the media was astonishing. A "new" breed of investigative journalists took center stage, and the nature and style of reporting about presidents changed dramatically. In the post-Watergate era, the media has been more intrusive, more critical, less trusting, and always looking for the "gottcha" blockbuster exposé. And the media has ventured into once off-limit areas such as investigating a president's private life. Today, seemingly nothing is off limits, everything ripe for exposure—even the most private and personal aspects of a person's life. Watergate opened the floodgates of overly intrusive and highly personalized journalism, and, critics of the press now warn, has chilled interest in public service for fear of a too-intrusive press disrupting private lives, and has made politicians more insular and suspicious. Investigative news programs such as *60 Minutes* and *Hard Copy* fill the TV airwaves, and investigative reporting commands front-page space in newspapers. But the effect, say critics, has been ironic—less trust in government and even less knowledge about the inner workings of government while more news about public officials is being purveyed. In national opinion polls taken in the mid-1990s, the press ranked as low as Congress and the federal bureaucracy in public trust and esteem. Yet, at the same time, the public wanted an unfettered press to make sure that government officials did not abuse power. The public insisted on the "right to know"—a fact Nixon never fully understood or respected and, after

Watergate, a fact governing much of the way journalism and public business are publicly conducted.

NOTES

1. Joe McGinniss, *The Selling of the President, 1968* (New York: Trident, 1969), 34.

2. Ibid., 103.

3. Kathleen Hall Jamieson, *Packaging the Presidency: A History and Criticism of Presidential Campaign Advertising* (New York: Oxford University Press, 1984), chaps. 6 and 7.

4. John Orman, "Covering the American Presidency," *Presidential Studies Quarterly* 14 (Summer 1984), 381–90.

5. Several studies attempted to document media bias in the 1968 and 1972 presidential campaigns. For a study purporting bias against Nixon, see Edith Efron, *The News Twisters* (Los Angeles: Nash, 1971). For a study that found no anti-Nixon bias, see Richard Hofstetter, *Bias in the News* (Columbus: Ohio State University Press, 1976).

6. There are two types of leaks: controlled leaks (those that the president and his top advisers choose to give to the press to serve their own purposes); and uncontrolled leaks (when an individual gives information to the press that the president wishes to be keep secret).

7. Herbert Klein, *Making It Perfectly Clear* (Garden City, NY: Doubleday, 1980).

8. Joseph C. Spear, *Presidents and the Press: The Nixon Legacy* (Cambridge: MIT Press, 1984).

9. Nixon, fifth syndicated television interview with David Frost.

10. Redrick P. Hart, *The Sound of Leadership: Presidential Communication in the Modern Age* (Chicago: University of Chicago Press, 1987), 99. See also Michael Grossman and Martha Kumar, *Portraying the President: The White House and the News Media* (Baltimore: Johns Hopkins University Press, 1981).

11. Hart, *The Sound of Leadership*, 100. See also James Keogh, *President Nixon and the Press* (New York: Funk and Wagnall, 1972).

12. Gary Wills, *Nixon Agonistes* (New York: New American Library, 1970), 357–59.

13. William E. Porter, *Assault on the Media: The Nixon Years* (Ann Arbor: University of Michigan Press, 1976).

14. For Safire's analyses of Nixon and the press, see William Safire, *Before the Fall: An Inside View of the Pre-Watergate White House* (Garden City, NY: Doubleday, 1975), 341–65.

6

Conclusion: The Watergate Legacy

No man will ever bring out of the Presidency the reputation which carries him into it.

—Thomas Jefferson

Watergate has had a profound and largely negative impact on American politics in the twenty-five years since that scandal was uncovered. It has spawned a distrust in government among the American people (see Figure 6.1), led to a series of laws enacted to prevent future Watergates but that have made it more difficult to govern, unleashed a hostile and highly investigatory press, increased the partisan sniping in the political culture, and led to a more divisive relationship between the president and Congress. Further, the unintended consequences of the post-Watergate reforms have left presidents more vulnerable, or at least thinking they are so, and less able to function effectively as presidents.[1]

The presidency of Richard M. Nixon has left a scar on the body politic and undermined the fragile consensus that for decades characterized American politics. The delicate bonds of trust so necessary for a properly functioning democracy have degenerated into a slash-and-burn type of politics in which a "take no prisoners" attitude dominates. It is no wonder that voter apathy is high, voting turnout low, and trust in government down. Nixon and Watergate, by themselves, did not cause the degradation of American politics and erosion of public trust, though they contributed mightily to both, but Nixon and Watergate did recast the story of American public life from one of assumed good intentions to one of great suspicion.

Figure 6.1
Trust in Federal Government, 1958–1994

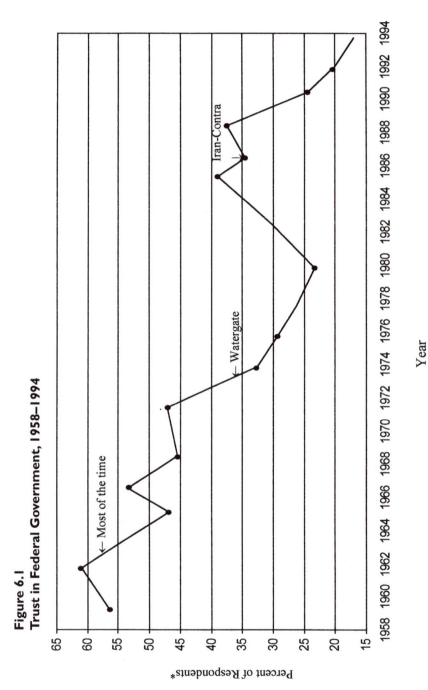

QUESTION: How much of the time do you think you can trust the government in Washington to do what is right? Just about always, most of the time, or only some of the time?

Source: Gallup Monthly, January 1994.

WHO IS RICHARD NIXON?

Much of the meaning of Watergate hinges on understanding Richard Nixon. In attempting to discover the "real" Nixon, one is struck with how many mysteries remain about the man and his appeal. Nixon has inspired more scholarly and popular writing than almost any other president, yet much remains hidden, shrouded in secrecy, obscured by shadows. In part, this is because the former president limited access to himself and fought to keep private many of his presidential papers. It is also because Nixon was such a complex, contradictory figure, defying simple analysis. He was more than, and different than, the sum of his many parts.

Friends, associates, critics, and commentators saw many different things in the man. Was he, as many of his former associates noted, a man with two very different, conflicting parts: the "good" and the "bad" Nixon, the light and dark sides? In this sense, was the battle for Nixon the battle of his better self against his worse self, a battle that was ultimately lost to the forces of darkness? Or was Nixon a paradox, a contradictory figure who could be so brilliant in foreign affairs, yet make so many needless mistakes in Watergate; lead an anticommunist movement, then embrace China and the Soviet Union; praise the free market, then impose wage and price controls; preach self-sufficiency, then propose the Family Assistance Plan? Nixon as paradox did all these things, embraced all these beliefs. Or was Nixon little more than a political chameleon, changing color and political stripes to advance his own political fortune without regard to ideology or national interest?

Nixon was all of the above. But the core of Nixon, the true Nixon, could be summed up in one phrase: He was a man obsessed with self-promotion. This self-promotion took form in his paranoid style of operation. That paranoid style poisoned his administration and led to his self-destruction.

Fundamentally, Nixon had no central philosophical beliefs, no deep ethical moorings. He was amoral, not immoral. His central pursuit was a rather narrow and short-term self-interest. This allowed him to shed what seemed to be deeply felt and long-held beliefs when it suited his career. Though his chameleon-like quality aided his rise to power, it did not guide him in the uses of power.

Nixon was in many ways a rootless wanderer, the product of a family that did not nourish his needs or give him stable roots; a man who was sensitive to the snubs of the "better sort," who never did accept Nixon; a man who got his first big break by upsetting incumbent Jerry Voorhis for a seat in Congress, and who learned early on in his career that attacking an opponent, as he did in his smear campaign against Helen Douglas in 1950, brought victory. Only one thing mattered: winning, showing "them" (his political *enemies* and all those who snubbed or criticized Nixon in the past).

There may have been, as so many of his former associates noted, a good and a bad Nixon, but in the end, it was the Nixon self-promotion that won out. Thus, his downfall is not a great tragedy in which a fatal flaw does in the good or innocent protagonist. No, Nixon's demise is the logical outcome of self-promotion gone mad, and insomuch as the "win by any means" attitude ruled (and rules) American culture and politics, it is a metaphor, and warning, about American values. Nixon was brilliant but amoral, experienced but insecure, capable but manipulative, obsessed with power but consumed by weakness, power seeking but paranoid. He was neither trusting nor trusted. He was the architect of some stunning successes in foreign policy and the author of a demeaning and destructive string of political misdeeds that culminated in Watergate. His mental elasticity, a sign of pragmatism to some, was really a reflection of his own opportunism. He was a polarizer, a divider. Nixon saw life as a battle against a hostile world, where enemies waited around every corner, and he acted accordingly.

He was a troubled man who governed in turbulent times. The toxic mixture of Nixon's personality with the events and forces of the political environment produced a poisoned outlook and a poisoned atmosphere. In different times, the negative aspects of Nixon's psyche might not have been challenged, pricked, activated to the extent they were, but Nixon came to power in 1968 amid a wrenching national self-doubt caused by an unpopular war, an uncompromising counterculture, and rising inflation. He promised to "bring us together," but instead let the cultural, social, and economic stresses tear him apart. Instead of coalition-building and political consensus, Nixon sought executive privilege and political revenge. In turbulent times, the challenge of leadership is to direct and manage change, to ease the transition. In this sense, Nixon failed to lead. Nixon did not create the conflicts and tensions of the 1960s, but he did little to manage them or channel the energies of change to constructive ends. Nixon was ill suited to rule in a time of turbulence.

THE NIXON PRESIDENCY

In a substantive sense, the Nixon presidency was filled with action: some grand accomplishments, and some tragic failures. In foreign affairs he inherited a war in Vietnam that could only have been won at the highest of costs, if at all. He extended, then ended that war, the first war America lost. He fathered détente with the Soviet Union and opened the door to China. He pursued a bold, creative strategy for developing a new international order, but failed to succeed in this daring initiative.

In domestic politics his agenda was very limited. After flirting with Disraeli-like reforms, Nixon retreated to a more conservative, then obstructionist approach. In the case of civil rights, for example, he refused to enforce court-ordered busing to promote racial integration of schools and catered to southern conservatives as part of his "southern strategy" to wean Democrats to the GOP. On the economic front, Nixon abdicated American international leadership, imposed wage and price controls at home, and artificially boosted the domestic economy shortly before the 1972 election. His economic policies were shortsighted, and though they aided his own reelection effort, they hurt the U.S. economy in the long run.

An examination of the Nixon presidency reinforces the view that personality is of importance in presidential politics. Because of Nixon's tendency toward paranoia, his administration took on a siege mentality. This infected his presidency. From the way Nixon organized and ran his administration, to the policy arenas, to Watergate, Nixon's personality stamped a distinctive paranoid style on his presidency.

One consequence was that, in process terms, Nixon often mishandled the major relationships of his presidency because he could not build trust. Be it the Congress, the public, the bureaucracy, or even his own staff, Nixon did not organize functionally, follow through on policy initiatives, or realistically articulate his goals. Nixon's must be judged a failed presidency in which Watergate was not the fatal cancer that destroyed an otherwise functional presidency but was the almost inevitable outgrowth of an over personalized, poorly organized, and overly politicized administration.

NIXON AND THE FUTURE OF THE PRESIDENCY

How can we avoid future Watergates and other forms of presidential corruption? The founders of the constitutional republic hoped to discourage corruption and the arbitrary use and abuse of power by separating power, dividing power, and sharing power among three semi-independent, semi-autonomous branches of government. By having ambition counteract ambition and power counteract power, no one could, for long, overwhelm the others. The rule of law embodied in the Constitution, not the will or whim of one person, was to be the guiding light. By instituting a system of checks and balances, the system had safeguards against tyranny. Overall, the system has worked well at preventing tyranny. Though many of today's critics bemoan the excessive checks built into the system, few would argue against the proposition that it has indeed been a viable safeguard against excessive arbitrary rule.

But this system of multiple checks frustrates presidents, especially in the modern age with its emphases on executive initiative and national security. The system was designed in many ways to frustrate leadership. Given the high level of public expectations and the limited amount of independent authority granted to the president, is it any wonder that presidents feel constrained and frustrated and sometimes turn to extraconstitutional means to make their case and effect their goals?

Strong presidents enhance executive power over the checks built into the system by a full use of the formal powers a president has to command, which have grown by usage over time, and a full use of the informal powers a president has to persuade. But because few presidents have the range of skills or the level of opportunity necessary to move on both these fronts, presidents will sometimes be tempted to move beyond the law, beyond the limits of their authority. When presidents take this step, as Nixon did during the Watergate period, how can they be checked?

Because the presidency has become the most powerful institution in America's government, only the combined efforts of an active Congress, an alert citizenry, an independent court system, a free press, and a professional bureaucracy can save the republic. In a way, these were all the things that Richard Nixon feared and perceived as enemies.

THE FATAL FLAW

Nixon, the most political of political men, was unable to make the important distinction between politics and governance. Politics is what one does to get elected; governance is what one does in attempting to lead or govern the nation. Nixon saw everything as politics—as the law of the jungle, as a tough, competitive world where you have to get them before they get you.

Governance is what is done for the good of the country. It is selfless, whereas politics tends to be selfish. Governance is high principle and vision put to the use of the state. Nixon—with the notable exception of certain parts of his foreign policy—seemed unable to move beyond politics to governance. As political columnist Hugh Sidey said, "He may have understood the world but he didn't understand the oath of office he took."[2]

To Nixon, politics was not about persuasion but about manipulation. Thus, his political character—his view of politics as war, of adversaries as enemies—did not embrace leadership as a persuasive force but as a means to manipulate the people and machinery of government. He saw politics as conflict management, not community building. In this sense, he limited himself to the narrowest interpretation of Harold Lasswell's definition of politics as "who gets what, when, and how."

Great presidents face difficult times by lifting the nation and elevating themselves. Their increase in political and personal power comes as a means to serve the national interest not an end in itself. Nixon, when faced with tough times, demeaned himself, his office, and the nation. He failed the most important test of leadership: character.

THE MEANING OF WATERGATE

Watergate, that generic word by which we refer to a range of crimes and improprieties, raised legal issues and moral issues. It spoke to who we are and what we believe. It tested our system and ourselves. Would the United States remain a limited government under the rule of law, or was it to become an imperial nation with an imperial presidency?

Watergate spawned a variety of legislative responses. In the aftermath of Nixon's abuses, the Congress went through a period of legislative activism that resulted in the passage of the Budget Control and Impoundment Act (1974), the War Powers Act (1973), the Case Act (1972), the Federal Election Campaign Act (1974), the Ethics in Government Act (1978), the Presidential Records Act (1978), the National Emergencies Act (1976), the Government in Sunshine Act (1976), the Federal Corrupt Practices Act (1977), the Foreign Intelligence Surveillance Act (1978), plus laws relating to privacy in banking and to setting up a vehicle for creating special prosecutors and the Freedom of Information Act (1974). These efforts were designed to limit and shrink imperial executive claims to republican proportions. Many think the reaction against presidential power went too far. Today, presidents often seem encumbered by too many checks, with too few balances.

One of the more obvious areas where "reform" may have gone too far is the case of the independent counsel law, which, critics charge, has been overused to the point of creating a potential for prosecutorial tyranny (e.g., Kenneth Starr's investigation of President Clinton). After Watergate, the independent counsel law, argue critics, has been used as part of a partisan game of "gotcha" wherein the party in control of Congress employed this device to harass, and in some cases, needlessly burden officials with investigations. In the Whitewater investigation of President Clinton's alleged real estate dealings in his native Arkansas, independent counsel Kenneth Starr spent over four years and over $40 million, as of 1998, investigating allegations against the president and First Lady, and a half dozen other independent counsels roamed the political landscape in search of official wrongdoing, with mixed results in terms of bringing indictments and getting convictions for crimes.

Most Democrats and Republicans now agree that some of these investigations have little merit and have been highly partisan. Pending the outcome of the highly visible Starr investigations into alleged Clinton wrongdoing in dismissing employees, raising money, subverting testimonies, and committing perjury, the Congress, the press, and the public are urging a thorough review of the uses of independent counsels. Still, one legacy of Watergate has been—and seems likely to be—the establishment of the independent counsel as an integral element of public life and governance.

"EVERYBODY DOES IT"

The defense of Nixon that says that it is "just politics," or "everybody does it," is both false and dangerous. It is false because even though other presidents did engage in immoral and illegal behavior, not one comes close to Nixon in volume, type, or degree of presidential involvement. Nixon's was a systematic abuse of power and subversion of law. It is dangerous because such an attitude breeds apathy, disrespect for the government, and contempt for American political institutions. Aside from that, the " everybody does it" excuse is no justification for misconduct.[3]

What John Mitchell called the "White House horrors" is without precedent in the United States. The United States is far from perfect, and past presidents are not without sin, but historian C. Vann Woodward sums up the difference between Nixon and his predecessors nicely:

Heretofore, no president has been proved to be the chief coordinator of the crime and misdemeanor charged against his own administration as a deliberate course of conduct or plan. Heretofore, no president has been held to be the chief personal beneficiary of misconduct in his administration or of measures taken to destroy or cover up evidence of it. Heretofore, the malfeasance and misdemeanor have had no confessed ideological purpose, no constitutionally subversive ends. Heretofore, no president has been accused of extensively subverting and secretly using established government agencies to defame or discredit political opponents and critics, to obstruct justice, to conceal misconduct and protect criminals, or to deprive citizens of their rights and liberties. Heretofore, no president has been accused of creating secret investigative units to engage in covert and unlawful activities against private citizens and their rights.[4]

One of the primary differences between Watergate and the scandals of most other administrations is that the scandals of the past almost always involved greed for private financial gain, and the president was the unwitting victim. The presidents of scandal-ridden administrations (with Ronald Reagan and perhaps Bill Clinton being the exception) were not knowingly a part of the corruption. In Watergate, the greed was for power, and the president was a direct participant in the corruption, even the author of it.

"THE SYSTEM WORKED!" (OR DID IT?)

After the fall of Nixon, one heard the popular refrain: "The system worked!" Existing structures and procedures protected liberty and reestablished the rule of law. After all, Nixon was caught and forced to leave office. But a haunting feeling remains. Did the system work, or did other forces bring about the revelations of abuses of power and criminal conduct by the president and his circle?

"The system" is the complex web of interrelated governmental and non-governmental actors who serve as a check on power. In Watergate the system included the media, Congress, the courts, the public, the CIA, the FBI, the Justice Department, the special prosecutor's office, and the grand jury. How well did the system perform its function?

The media began like a lamb but ended like a lion. Whereas they were manipulated by Nixon during the 1972 campaign and generally gave him very positive coverage, after the election, as the Watergate story got closer to the president, a herd mentality developed and they pounced on the story, pursuing it relentlessly. The Congress, especially in the Ervin and House Judiciary committees, played a very important role in the Watergate investigation. They moved slowly, methodically, but, as the evidence of abuse and crimes became known, they moved against the president. The courts, especially Judge Sirica and the Supreme Court at the end, were clearly a key in discovering the facts and pressing for compliance with the law. Again, they acted slowly, but effectively. The public, at first giving Nixon a landslide reelection victory and indifferent to the early reports on Watergate, eventually turned on the president like the media. The FBI and CIA were used and manipulated by Nixon, as was the Justice Department. The grand jury was essential in getting to the bottom of Watergate. Finally, the special prosecutor's office played an indispensable part in the process.

In the end, the system had to act in concert to expose the crimes of Watergate. For so many to act in concert is highly unusual. This speaks to the great difficulty of controlling a determined president. The system is indeed vulnerable when, even with all these institutions and interests working against the president, it was the "luck" of a taping system that finally strengthened the hands of the Congress, the special prosecutor, and the press in their efforts to bring out the truth. This suggests that the system may be a rather weak check on presidential abuses of power. "Watergate," wrote Water Lippmann, "shows how very vulnerable our constitutional system is. If the national government falls into the hands of sufficiently unprincipled and unscrupulous men, they can do terrible things before anyone can stop them."

The system worked more than anything else because of luck, accident, and ineptitude. After all, the first break-in of the Watergate was a botched job, as the bugs weren't properly installed. This necessitated a second break-in, at which time the burglars were caught. And they were caught because a piece of tape, used to keep the door's lock from catching, was placed across the lock in such a way that it could be seen. But even this did not alert the guard whom, on his rounds, simply removed the tape. When the burglars returned to the door, they taped it again, and again placed the tape across the lock so it could be seen on the outside. When security guard Frank Wills made his second round of the building and saw the tape across the same door for a second time, only then, was he alerted and called the police.

If Nixon had not taped himself, there would have been no "smoking gun" and Nixon might have survived. Certainly, the dimensions and depth of Nixon's abuses of power and crimes would not have been revealed without the tapes, which continue to suggest patterns of corruption in the Nixon White House as researchers review them. If the cover-up had been better managed, it might have held together. If Nixon had destroyed the tapes before their existence had become known, he would not have had do defy a subpoena—one of the acts on which an article of impeachment was based.

Nixon and Haldeman recognized the role luck played in the Watergate story, as evidenced by this March 20, 1973, taped exchange on how Watergate was "discovered":

Nixon: . . . a lot of bad breaks.

Haldeman: Yeah.

Nixon: We got a bad break with the judge, for example.

Haldeman: Monumental bad breaks and a string of 'em — one leading to another.

Nixon: This judge, that . . .

Haldeman: . . . one lousy part-time night guard at the Watergate who happened to notice the tape on the, on the locks on the doors. If he hadn't seem them—the thing probably would never have busted. If you hadn't had Watergate—you wouldn't have had Segretti. You wouldn't have had any of that stuff.

In another sense, "the system" refers to the two-hundred-year-old constitutional framework and the assumptions upon which it is based. This Madisonian system, described in *Federalist No. 51*, believed that "ambition must be made to counteract ambition," that by separating power, viable checks might protect the liberty of the citizen, and prevent one branch of government from overawing the others and undermining republican government altogether.

The framers of the Constitution saw human nature neither in excessively benign nor unmercifully harsh terms. Humans were capable of great good and great evil. The founders knew man's darker side, his darker impulses, and sought to control this while also empowering government. In a way, it was precisely for the Richard Nixons of the world that the separation of powers and checks and balances were created.

But one principal instrument the founders thought might check, or at least remedy, executive abuse was the impeachment process. Long before Watergate, impeachment had proved a cumbersome and often ineffectual means to prevent or punish political abuses of power. Party politics and press scrutiny—nonprescribed checks unanticipated by the framers—had assumed a primary role in identifying abuses. The electoral process became the great "check." The threat of impeachment in Watergate attested to the gravity of the charges against Nixon. It was part of a process of investigation leading to Nixon's possible removal.

In Watergate, the impeachment process itself was shown to have very limited utility. It can be used only in truly extraordinary circumstances. And although the United States does have periodic accountability (elections), and ultimate accountability (impeachment), the government and people do not have an effective formal system of daily accountability (routine and continuous). Informal means—public vigilance—must bear the burden of constant oversight of government.

Finally, it was "the system" that allowed Nixon to rise to the highest office in the land, in spite of the many clues from his career as to what "the real Nixon" was like. It was the system that Nixon used and manipulated for so long. Thus, the system both nourished and eventually revealed the crimes of Richard Nixon.

WHY WATERGATE?

Throughout the complex web of crimes and dirty tricks, wiretaps and obstruction of justice, one keeps coming back to the gnawing question: Why Watergate? What caused the administration to engage in the volume and type of corruption that it did?

Theories abound. The most frequently mentioned cause of Watergate is Nixon himself. His personality, past experiences, operating style, and worldview in many ways infected those around him and led to the abuses of Watergate. Some go so far as to say that Nixon's personality made Watergate inevitable; others suggest more cautiously that he made Watergate possible or probable. Watergate can best be understood as the interplay of Nixon's distrust, insecurities, obsessions, fears, and hatreds creating an infectious atmosphere that warped those who served him and set Watergate in motion. A series of intersecting "wars" collided to cause Watergate. The *war in Vietnam*, which Nixon inherited and had such a difficult time ending, added to the pressures that, when combined with the Nixon personality, led to wiretaps, break-ins, attempts to suppress dissent and muzzle the press, and more. Next, the *war at home*, with its antiwar demonstrations and social upheaval, put added strain on the Nixon White House. Finally, there was the *partisan war*. Nixon saw democratic elections as war and adversaries as enemies. Besieged everywhere, Nixon and his White House inner circle resorted to extraordinary means to win the various "wars."

Nixon left the *presidency* battered and bruised. After Watergate, the imperial presidency was reduced to an imperiled presidency. For a time, deadlock, gridlock, and paralysis characterized president-Congress relations in the post-Watergate era of divided and divisive government. Indeed, not until Ronald Reagan's presidency would a president get his major legislative packages passed by Congress. Over a quarter-century later, the presidency still has not recovered its pre-1960s luster.

Watergate also created a "special prosecutor" mentality, where seemingly all offenses, real or imagined, by presidents and their underlings lead to the appointment of a special counsel to investigate executive-branch behavior. Presidents Reagan, Bush, and Clinton were forced to fend off a wide variety of charges of misconduct. Such a prosecutorial zeal greatly distracted all of the presidents and forced them to spend much time on legal matters, though admittedly, special prosecutors successfully prosecuted some officials in the Reagan and Clinton administrations.

The *Congress* has become more divided, divisive, and deadlocked. A hyperpartisanship has swept our politics, which sees adversaries as enemies. The level of political debate and dialogue has sunk to petty name-calling, rumor spreading, and personal attack. Congress replaces debate over the merits of issues with investigations designed to replicate a Watergate exposé. Nearly every difference of opinion has a "gate" suffix: Koreangate, Iran-Contra-gate, Travelgate, Zippergate, etc. One would be hard pressed to find the silver lining in this dark cloud of abrasiveness.

The *political parties* also have become hyperpartisan and often have fought their political battles not so much on the basis of ideas but on personal grounds. Policy differences are converted into "I got ya" contests of who can dig up the most embarrassing personal foible on whom.

The fragile *consensus* that animated government in the post–World War II era has been shattered by Watergate and other events. We have become a more divisive, smaller people, atomized and divided by our differences, not unified in pursuit of the common good. Thus we have become a more individualistic, harder people. The public discourse hardly includes concern for the poor, the disabled, the weak, the sick, and the oppressed.

The role of *money* in the political process has, after a brief decline, risen in importance. Our political parties and candidates are awash in money—the source of some of it quite questionable. The impression of having a "government for sale" is not new, but the costs have risen dramatically, and public trust has declined accordingly.

Finally, the *presidency* itself is a greatly diminished office. Vietnam, Watergate, and the end of the Cold War have led to a shrinking of the power and prestige of the office, and left the nation seemingly rudderless.

It is unfair to put all the blame for these troubles on the shoulders of Watergate and Richard Nixon. Many factors coalesced to bring about these problems. But the major step down the road to a more divisive and diminished democracy stems from the corruption of Watergate—corruption from which, over twenty-five years later, we have not yet recovered.

CONCLUSION

The abuses known as Watergate were the most pervasive and systematic subversion of the political rights of American citizens and sabotage of the democratic electoral process in the history of the United States. Never before had so many done so much to so many at so high a level in violation of laws and norms of this nation. Watergate went beyond the presidential corruptions of the past, for while most previous corruption involved isolated crimes or greed for money, Watergate was systematic and comprehensive and aimed at the rights of citizens and the democratic electoral process. And the president was right in the middle of the corruption.

Among the casualties of Watergate are a president who was named as an *unindicted co-conspirator* by a grand jury and who was eventually forced to resign (he was also disbarred), a vice president who pleaded no contest to income tax evasion and who was forced to resign (he too was disbarred), an attorney general who went to jail, a former secretary of commerce who went to jail, a chief of staff who went to jail, a president's counsel who went to jail, a president's chief domestic adviser who went to jail, a president's appointments secretary who went to jail, a president's personal attorney who went to jail, and the list goes on. Over two dozen-administration figures went to jail because of Watergate.

Thomas Paine once said that in America, the Constitution is king. The downfall of Richard Nixon struck a blow for the concept that no man is above the law, not even the president. Though Nixon could attempt to justify his actions in a 1977 interview with David Frost by saying, "When the President does it, that means that it is not illegal," this view was rejected by nearly all segments of the American system. The words of Supreme Court Justice Louis Brandeis remained operative: "If Government becomes the law-breaker, it breeds contempt for law." Reverence for the laws, Abraham Lincoln once said, should "become the political religion of the nation."

What responsibility do "the people" bear for Watergate? If Watergate was due in large part to the personality and politics of Nixon, were the people who elected him accomplices in the ensuing abuses of power? After all, Nixon the politician had been on the political scene since 1948; his slashing campaign style, his character flaws, his ethical lapses were a part of the public record. All the elements in Nixon that led to the abuses of Watergate were operative and observable in embryonic form in his previous political behavior. There is a saying, "In a democracy, people tend to get the government they deserve." Did the American people "deserve" Watergate? This sobering possibility is brought home forcefully by historian Henry Steele Commager, who, in 1976, chillingly observed:

The basic problem posed by Watergate and all its attendant horrors is neither constitutional nor political; it is moral. It is not a problem posed by an Administration in Washington; it is one posed by the American people. After all, we can never get away from the most elementary fact: The American people reelected Mr. Nixon by a majority of nearly eighteen million votes. Either they did not know what kind of man he was, in which case they were inexcusably negligent or inexcusably naive, or they did know what kind of man he was and did not care or perhaps liked him as he was—as some Americans still like him the way he is. The latter explanation is probably nearer to the truth. Did he not—indeed, does he not—represent qualities in the American character that are widespread and even taken for granted? In himself and in the curious collection of associates he gathered around him, he represents the acquisitive society, the exploitative society, and the aggrandizing society. He represents what is artificial, meretricious, and manipulative. He represents the American preference for the synthetic over the real, for advertising over the product, for public relations over character, for spectator sports over active games, and for spectator politics over participatory democracy. He represents, too, the widespread American conviction that anything can be bought: culture, education, happiness, a winning football team or the Presidency.[5]

After Watergate, the Congress passed a variety of laws designed to discourage future Watergates and abuses of power. As important as these laws may be, they are not sufficient to the task. Laws are not self-executing. A nation of laws depends upon the people to enliven the law. A dedicated citizenry is the only hope against tyranny. As Judge Learned Hand said, "Liberty lies in the hearts of men and women; when it dies there, no constitution, no law, no court can save it; no constitution, no law, no court can even do much to help it." Of all the checks that are to balance the American political system none is more powerful than alert and aroused public opinion. A thoughtful, responsible, aware public is the best defense against tyranny. There is no substitute for an aroused citizenry, no hope unless there is a rebirth of what Thomas Cronin calls "citizen politics." Richard Nixon exposed one of the vulnerabilities of the American political system. "The system" will not protect us; we must be ever vigilant.

The era of cynicism that Watergate spawned ushered in a period of deep political apathy. Democracy cannot long endure the contempt of the people. Rather than recapture their democracy, many people dropped out. Rather than right wrongs, many threw stones (verbal and otherwise) at what was supposed to be "their" government. Swept up in a culture of mistrust, democracy almost became the chief casualty of an age of cynicism.

Prosperity and the "feel-good" politics of the Reagan years seemingly restored American's faith in the regenerative powers of American capitalism and democracy, at least for the middle and upper classes. The collapse of communism in the Soviet Union and eastern Europe, the "victory" in the Persian Gulf War, and the seeming global expansion of American power all promised a new world order with America at the helm. Democracy seemed triumphant. In such a world, Watergate became a relic of another age in the public mind. The question remains, though, How much of what Americans learned about the abuses of power from Watergate will remind them that democracy always stands in danger of being corrupted?

NOTES

1. Thomas E. Cronin and Michael A. Genovese, *The Paradoxes of the American Presidency* (New York: Oxford University Press, 1998).

2. Quoted in Kenneth Thompson, ed., *The Nixon Presidency* (Lanham: University Press of America, 1987), 307.

3. C. Vann Woodward, ed., *Responses of the Presidents to Charges of Misconduct* (New York: Dell, 1974), and Shelly Ross, *Fall from Grace* (New York: Ballantine, 1988).

4. Woodward, *Responses*, xxvi.

5. Henry Steele Commager, "Watergate and the Schools," in David C. Saffell, ed., *American Government: Reform in the Post-Watergate Era* (Cambridge, MA: Winthrop, 1976), 6.

Biographies: The Personalities Behind the Watergate Crisis

Agnew, Spiro T. (1918–1996)

The 39th Vice President of the United States, Spiro T. Agnew made history in 1973 when he became only the second vice president in history to resign (John C. Calhoun in 1832 was the first, but did so for political reasons) and the first to do so under duress. On August 10, 1973, Agnew entered a *nolo contendere* (no contest) plea in the U.S. District Court in Baltimore, Md., to a single charge of failure to report $29,500 income to the IRS. Judge Walter E. Hoffman declared Agnew's plea "the full equivalent to a plea of guilty," fined him $10,000, and sentenced him to three years of unsupervised probation. Hoffman told the now former vice president that he would have sentenced him to prison had it not been for a personal appeal by the Attorney General. In 1974 a Maryland Court of Appeals declared Agnew's disbarment on the grounds of moral turpitude.

Agnew's *nolo contendere* plea was the tip of an investigative iceberg that included accusations of extortion, bribery, and income tax evasion. In a 1981 Maryland taxpayer's suit, a civil court found that Agnew had solicited $147,500 in bribes while he served as Baltimore county executive and later as Maryland governor. Agnew's final bribe payment of $17,500 in cash was delivered while Agnew was serving as vice president.

Born in Baltimore, Maryland, on November 9, 1918, the only son of Theodore Anagnostopoulus, a Greek immigrant who shortened his name after coming to the United States, Agnew studied chemistry at the Johns Hopkins University, and received a law degree from the University of Baltimore. He served in the Army during WWII and the Korean War.

In 1996 Agnew was elected Governor of Maryland. Two years later, he was Richard Nixon's surprise pick ("Spiro Who?" people asked) for vice president. Agnew quickly became the administration's top partisan spokesman, attacking the press and student demonstrators and calling for "law and order." In 1969 he said "a spirit of national masochism prevails, encouraged by an effete corps of impudent snobs who characterize themselves as intellectuals." In 1970 he remarked "we have more than our share of the nattering nabobs of negativism," and he criticized "pusillanimous pussyfooters," "vicars of vacillation," and the "hopeless, hysterical hypochondriacs of history." After Agnew's resignation, Nixon appointed Gerald Ford as vice president. This opened the door to Nixon's impeachment because Ford's reputation for honesty better suited the needs of the nation.

Colson, Charles W. (1931–   )

Charles Colson was Nixon's partisan troubleshooter and one of the street fighters who appealed to Nixon's "dark side." Colson, who formally served as special counsel to the president, was Nixon's partner in concocting paranoid responses to political events. He brought out and fed the worst parts of Nixon's personality. Colson once said, "I would walk over my grandmother if necessary to get Nixon reelected." Responsible for developing Nixon's "enemies list," and deeply involved in several aspects of the Watergate cover-up effort, Colson became one of the first of Nixon's insiders to crack under pressure.

Colson was the main contact between E. Howard Hunt, one of the Watergate burglars, and the White House. It was through Hunt that demands for hush money and clemency were conveyed from the defendants to the White House.

Born on October 16, 1931, in Boston, Colson graduated from Brown University and received his law degree from George Washington University. Colson was a Republican activist who became Nixon's political operative and "dark side" ally. In a plea bargain with prosecutors, Colson pled guilty to obstructure of justice. After serving a Watergate-related prison sentence, Colson became a "born-again Christian" active in several religious causes, especially in American prison outreach programs.

Cox, Archibald (1912–   )

In 1973 Archibald Cox became the first of two special prosecutors appointed to investigate allegations of wrongdoing in the Nixon administration. Nixon ordered Cox fired in what became known as the "Saturday night massacre" for attempting to force Nixon to release tape recordings of conversations between the president and former members of his administration who were facing criminal charges.

Cox was a Democrat, with ties to the Kennedy administration. He was appointed special prosecutor by a former student, Elliott Richardson. Cox later became head of the citizen lobbying group Common Cause.

Born on May 17, 1912, in Plainfield, New Jersey, Cox graduated from Harvard University and Harvard Law School. He was law clerk for Judge Learned Hand. Cox began teaching at the Harvard law school at the age of thirty-four. He served as Solicitor General in the Kennedy administration.

Dean, John W. (1938–   )

John W. Dean was the man who blew the lid off the Nixon administration's criminal cover-up. Born on October 14, 1938, in Akron, Ohio, Dean graduated from Georgetown University law school in 1965. Dean was appointed the president's counsel (his lawyer) in 1970, only five years after graduating law school. Dean was a participant in the cover-up, but when prosecutors began to build a criminal case against Dean, and when Dean feared Nixon was about to make him the "fall guy" in Watergate, he turned star witness for the government and implicated the president in criminal acts.

Dean was the chief witness in the Senate hearings that investigated Nixon and was the president's primary accuser. At first, it was Dean's word against the president's, but when it was revealed that Nixon had been taping his conversations, proof of whose word was true became available. From that point on, the focus of Watergate shifted to a battle over the tapes.

In October 1973, Dean pleaded guilty to conspiracy to obstruct justice and defraud the United States. He served a four-month prison sentence. Dean's book *Blind Ambition* (1976) remains one of the most insightful of the Watergate books. He lives in Southern California where, among other activities, he produces radio programs.

Ehrlichman, John D. (1925–1999)

The former director of White House domestic policy, John D. Ehrlichman became one of Nixon's closest advisors. Born in Tacoma, Washington, on March 20, 1925, Ehrlichman was a classmate of Bob Haldeman at UCLA. Before joining the Nixon administration, Ehrlichman practiced law in Seattle, Washington. Appointed counsel to the president in 1969, later that year he rose to become Assistant to the President for Domestic Affairs.

Ehrlichman was involved in a variety of Watergate-related crimes, including illegal wiretaps, domestic intelligence, the break-in of Daniel Ellsburg's psychiatrist's office, the Plumbers, and the cover-up. He was convicted on a number of criminal counts, including having ordered the break-in of Ellsburg's psychiatrist's office. He served eighteen months in prison.

After Watergate, Ehrlichman became an author of several fiction and non-fiction books. He settled in Santa Fe, New Mexico, then moved to Atlanta. He died on February 14, 1999.

Ervin, Sam J. (1896–1985)

Senator Sam J. Ervin was a conservative Democrat and an expert on the Constitution who headed the Senate Select committee to investigate the 1972 Presidential Campaign Activities, known as the Ervin Committee. Born on September 27, 1896, in Morgantown, North Carolina, Ervin received his BA in 1917 from the University of North Carolina and his law degree from Harvard in 1922. He served in World War I. Ervin spent six years as associate justice of the North Carolina Supreme Court. In 1954 he was appointed to fill an U.S. Senate seat to replace Clyde R. Hoey who had died. He was reelected thereafter until his retirement.

Known for his homespun style and conservative politics, Ervin's down-home veneer and winning personality masked a deep, insightful intellect and a hard-nosed, tough-minded politician. His deft touch as chair of the "Ervin Committee" proved damaging to the president as the general public—though initially suspicious of the investigation into Watergate—soon found the hearings both dramatic and entertaining.

His autobiography, *Preserving the Constitution*, was published in 1985. He died on April 23, 1985.

Ford, Gerald R. (1913–   )

Gerald Ford became the 38th President of the United States, on August 9, 1974, following Richard Nixon's resignation. Born Leslie King on July 14, 1913 in Omaha, Nebraska, his parents divorced and his mother remarried. Adopted by his new father, he took the name Ford. A star athlete, Ford played football for the University of Michigan. He graduated from Yale University Law School and served in the Navy during World War II. After a long career in the House of Representatives, representing Michigan, he rose to minority leader and developed a reputation for honesty. He also served as a member of the Warren Commission. Ford was appointed vice president by Richard Nixon following the resignation of Spiro T. Agnew in 1973. He served as vice president for only eight months before becoming president.

Ford was the first appointed vice president and, therefore, the nation's first unelected president. His first public words after assuming the presidency were: "My fellow Americans, our long national nightmare is over."

One month later, Ford granted Nixon a full pardon for all offenses he "may have committed" as president. In the aftermath of Watergate, Ford, while a decent and honest man, suffered from a public and congressional backlash against presidents. His presidency was short (2 years) and of limited effectiveness. He followed the Nixon–Kissinger program in American foreign policy but introduced no significant domestic policy initiatives. He lost in his bid for election to the presidency in 1976 to Jimmy Carter. In his retirement, Ford has largely stayed away from politics.

Haig, Alexander M. (1924–)

Alexander M. Haig was Nixon's chief of staff at the time of the president's resignation. Born on December 2, 1924, in Philadelphia, Pennsylvania, Haig attended Notre Dame but graduated from West Point in 1947. In 1962 he earned his master's degree in international relations from Georgetown University. He served in Korea and Vietnam. Haig was a career military man who, in 1969, worked for Henry Kissinger, becoming his deputy. Made a four-star general in 1972, Haig, it was said, ran the White House in the tense final days of Watergate.

In 1982 he became Ronald Reagan's secretary of state, but was removed from that post, as he proved too controversial and too independent for the Reagan team. In 1988 he sought the Republican party nomination for president.

Haldeman, H. R. "Bob" (1926–1994)

Harry Robbins Haldeman, an advertising executive and Nixon loyalist, served as the president's chief of staff until his resignation in 1973. Born in Los Angeles, California, on October 27, 1926, he graduated form UCLA and became an advertising executive and Nixon follower. Considered the second most powerful man in the White House (after the president), Haldeman was a tough, "no nonsense," "zero-defect" taskmaster. His crew-cut hair in an age of long hair served as a graphic reminder of the cultural differences between the administration and its adversaries.

Haldeman was Nixon's gatekeeper. He spent more time with the president than anyone else did, and his handwritten notes of these meetings—now available for examination at the National Archives—are a valuable source of information on the workings of the Nixon administration.

As Nixon's right-hand man, Haldeman was involved in a variety of Watergate crimes. He, along with Mitchell, Ehrlichman, and others, was convicted of a series of crimes including obstruction of justice. After his release from jail, Haldeman avoided the glare of publicity. In 1994 his book and

CD-ROM *The Haldeman Diaries* attempted to give an inside the White House account of the Nixon administration.

Hunt, E. Howard (1918–   )

E. Howard Hunt was one of the James Bond-type figures in the Nixon White House. A former CIA operative engaged in covert activities, and a prolific spy novelist, Hunt volunteered for service in the Navy during World War II, where he served in the Pacific. He later joined the Office of Strategic Services, the precursor to the CIA. Soon thereafter he worked for the CIA in Vienna, Mexico City, Tokyo, Uruguay, and Madrid. He served on the CIA planning staff during the Bay of Pigs fiasco. John Ehrlichman hired Hunt to work on secret White House projects, and he was involved with the Plumbers, the Fielding break-in, as well as the Watergate break-in.

Hunt was convicted in the Watergate break-in and served time in federal prison. He used Charles Colson as his White House go-between while in prison, and from prison his demands for clemency and money led to complications in the cover-up attempt, as Hunt was able to extract "hush money" from the Nixon White House.

Jaworski, Leon (1905–1982)

The man who replaced Archibald Cox as special prosecutor, Leon Jaworski won the conviction of many of Nixon's top advisers. Jaworski made the decision—against the advice of most of his staff—"not" to indict Richard Nixon. Instead, Nixon was named an "unindicted co-conspirator" by the grand jury.

Born in Waco, Texas, on September 19, 1905, Jaworski graduated from Baylor University. At the age of nineteen, he graduated from Baylor University Law School, and made his courtroom debut at the age of twenty. Following World War II, he served as a colonel in the war crimes section of the Judge Advocate General's department of the Army, prosecuting war criminals in Nuremberg. Jaworski served as president of the American Bar Association in 1971–1972, and was Special Assistant Attorney General from 1962–1965. His appointment as special prosecutor in 1973 was seen by many as a way to avoid any hint of political partisanship in the investigation of Nixon and his administration.

Jaworski, a conservative Democrat, charted a middle course in his dealings with Nixon. He was not certain that a president could be indicted so decided not to cross that bridge, instead leaving it to the Congress to pursue the case via the possibility of impeachment.

Liddy, G. Gordon (1930–   )

The flamboyant G. Gordon Liddy, who was involved in the Watergate break-in, is a former FBI agent turned Plumber. Liddy planned and executed the hapless break-in, along with a variety of other crimes and dirty tricks. He was convicted of conspiracy, burglary, and illegal wiretapping and served time in a minimum security prison.

Born on November 30, 1930, in New York City, he graduated from Fordham University and Fordham Law School. Liddy worked on the staff of the Domestic Council and in 1971 became general counsel to the Committee for the Re-election of the President, then served as counsel to the Nixon finance committee.

After serving time in prison for his Watergate crimes, Liddy became a notorious "shock jock" radio talk show host, frequent guest on cable TV public affairs programs, and lecturer on college campuses. His book, *Will* (1980), celebrated his macho style of spying and was unrepentant in its description of Watergate.

Magruder, Jeb Stuart (1934–   )

Jeb Magruder was the first of many Nixon administration officials to resign under duress. He worked for Bob Haldeman and Herbert Klein in the White House, and in 1971 became deputy director of the Committee for the Re-election of the President.

Magruder was involved in the Watergate cover-up from the beginning. He entered a plea bargain with prosecutors in which he pled guilty to a felony charge of unlawful conspiracy to intercept wire and oral communications, to obstruct justice, and defraud the United States and spent time in a federal minimum security prison.

Born in New York City on November 5, 1934, Magruder graduated from Williams College, and attended the University of Chicago's business school. After the Watergate affair, Magruder, like Charles Colson, sought atonement for his crimes and became a minister.

McCord, James (1919–   )

One of the first cracks in the Watergate cover-up came when James McCord sent Judge John Sirica a letter informing the judge that there was much more to Watergate than had come out in court. A retired senior CIA officer, McCord had his own small security firm when the White House tapped him for covert operation projects. He was officially employed by the Committee to Reelect the President as its chief of security. McCord was one of the

Watergate burglars and was convicted of the break-in. He served time in federal prison.

When he was arrested in the Democratic headquarters in the Watergate Hotel, McCord gave his name as Edward Martin. When the FBI learned of McCord's real identity, a clear link was drawn from the burglars to the White House.

Mitchell, John N. (1913–1988)

John Mitchell was head of Nixon's 1972 reelection effort and was involved in many of the illegal activities of the campaign. Indicted in 1974 on charges that he approved the Watergate break-in and assisted in the cover-up, Mitchell was found guilty in 1975 of conspiracy, obstruction of justice, and perjury. He was sentenced to two and one half to eight years in prison.

After working with Nixon in a New York law firm, Mitchell went on to chair Nixon's 1968 campaign, serve as his attorney general, and chair the 1972 reelection effort. While reluctant to engage in many of G. Gordon Liddy's illegal schemes, Mitchell eventually gave in and approved several illegal campaign activities.

Nixon, Richard M. (1913–1994)

The 37th President of the United States, Richard Nixon resigned the office in August 1974 as his impeachment and conviction seemed a certainty. He was the first president in history to resign.

Born on January 9, 1913, in Yorba Linda, California, Nixon graduated from Whittier College and Duke University Law school. He served in the Navy during World War II. Nixon served in the House of Representatives, the Senate, and as vice president. He narrowly lost a bid for the presidency in 1960 to John F. Kennedy, was defeated in an effort to become governor of California in 1962, but made a comeback in 1968 to win the presidency. In 1972 he won reelection in a landslide. Best known for his achievements in foreign policy, Nixon opened doors to China, developed détente with the Soviet Union, and extended and then ended the war in Vietnam. Richard Nixon was a complex man, driven by fear and insecurity to overcompensate. This led to political overkill, as adversaries were seen as enemies and politics as war. Nixon orchestrated some of the crimes of Watergate, was deeply involved in the cover-up, and ultimately was forced to leave office in disgrace.

In the twenty-two years from his resignation to his death in 1994, Nixon engaged in a tireless effort to revive his reputation. The author of numerous books on politics, Nixon could never fully shake Watergate. Still, his writings and his knowledge of foreign policy earned him grudging respect in many public circles, even as the memory of Watergate haunted him and reminded America of the danger of an "imperial presidency." He died on April 22, 1994, in New York City.

Richardson, Elliott L. (1920–)

The only person in U.S. history to hold four Cabinet posts, Elliott L. Richardson was appointed Secretary of Health, Education and Welfare in 1970, Secretary of Defense in 1973, Attorney General in 1973, and Secretary of Commerce in 1976. He resigned from his post as Attorney General when Nixon ordered him to fire Special Prosecutor Archibald Cox. Richardson and his successor refused. This "Saturday Night Massacre" outraged the public and forced Nixon to accept another special prosecutor, Leon Jaworski, who proved as tenacious in seeking evidence as Cox.

Richardson, a moderate Republican of patrician bearing and manner, refused to cave in to administration pressure and independently pursued the charges against Nixon by appointing tough special prosecutors and giving them the authority to do their jobs.

Born in Boston, Massachusetts on July 20, 1920, he graduated from Harvard College and Harvard Law School. He served in the Army during World War II. Richardson was law clerk to Judge Learned Hand and later to Supreme Court Justice Felix Frankfurter. In 1975 he served as U.S. Ambassador to Great Britain.

Rodino, Peter (1909–)

The longtime Congressman from Newark, New Jersey, who headed the House Judiciary Committee, many thought that Peter Rodino was not up to the task of heading the impeachment inquiry. But Rodino performed his task fairly and very capably, rising to the demands of the occasion. His obvious fairness during the televised impeachment hearings gave a national audience reassurance that the hearings were bipartisan and fair.

First elected to Congress in 1948, his primary achievement was to establish Columbus Day a national holiday. Though not regarded as a legislative heavyweight, Rodino's natural caution proved a valuable resource in the heated drama and pressures of the impeachment hearings.

Sirica, John (1904–1992)

John Sirica was the federal judge who presided over the trial of the Watergate burglars. Convinced that the whole story had not been revealed, he pressed the burglars to reveal which higher ups in the Nixon administration ordered the break-in. When one of the defendants, James McCord, broke, the Watergate cover-up began to crumble. Sirica was a tough, no-nonsense judge. He would not rest with guilty pleas from the original Watergate defendants, and eventually helped get to the bottom of the Watergate story.

Born in Waterbury, Connecticut, on March 19, 1904, the son of Italian immigrants, Sirica rose from poverty to earn his law degree from Georgetown University in 1926. He supported himself through school as a boxer. In 1957 Eisenhower appointed Sirica, a Republican, to the U.S. District Court for the District of Columbia. He was Chief Judge of that court from 1971 to 1974.

Woodward and Bernstein

The famous by-line of "Woodward and Bernstein" was Robert "Bob" Woodward and Carl Bernstein. This team of *Washington Post* reporters was unrelenting in its efforts to uncover the Watergate cover-up.

Woodward was born in Geneva, Illinois, on March 26, 1943. His father was a Republican county judge. Woodward graduated from Yale University in 1965. He served in the Navy for five years. Bernstein was born on February 14, 1944, in Washington, D.C. He dropped out of the University of Maryland after three years.

Their pursuit of the Watergate story—when very few reporters were interested in their story—eventually led to revelation after revelation against the administration. In a cinematic dramatization of their book, *All The President's Men*, they were portrayed on screen by Robert Redford and Dustin Hoffman.

Currently Bob Woodward is an editor at the *Washington Post*. Carl Bernstein is an editor for *Vanity Fair* magazine.

Ziegler, Ronald L. (1939–)

From 1969 until the end of the administration, Ron Zeigler served as President Nixon's press secretary. A former Bob Haldeman protégé at the J. Walter Thompson ad agency, Ziegler, a graduate of the University of Southern California, had worked on several of Nixon's campaigns.

Ziegler conducted the daily press briefings and towards the end they were often quite confrontational. After the arrests at the Watergate complex, Ziegler dismissed the incident as merely "a third-rate burglary attempt." On Nixon's last night in the White House, Ziegler said to the president of Nixon's decision to resign, "It's the right decision. You've had a great presidency, sir."

Primary Documents of the Watergate Crisis

Document 1
JOHN DEAN'S "ENEMIES LIST" MEMO

The following are excerpts from the August 16, 1971, memo dealing with White House Counsel John Dean's creation of an "enemies list" in the Nixon White House. Dean attempted to pressure the IRS to audit those on the enemies list. Also, he planned to use this list after the 1972 election to "*screw*" the administration's political opponents.

This memorandum addresses the matter of how we can maximize the fact of our incumbency in dealing with persons known to be active in their opposition to our administration. Stated a bit more bluntly—how we can use the available federal machinery to screw our political enemies.

After reviewing this matter with a number of persons possessed of expertise in the field, I have concluded that we *do not* need an elaborate mechanism or game plan, rather we need a good project coordinator and full support for the project. In brief, the system would work as follows:

! Key members of the staff [e.g., Colson, (Harry) Dent, (Peter) Flanigan, (Patrick) Buchanan] should be requested to inform us as to who they feel we should be giving a hard time.

! The project coordinator should then determine what sorts of dealings these individuals have with the federal government and how we can best screw them (e.g., grant availability, federal contracts, litigation, prosecution, etc.).

! The project coordinator then should have access to and the full support of the top officials of the agency or department in proceeding to deal with the individual.

I have learned that there have been many efforts in the past to take such actions, but they have ultimately failed—in most cases—because of lack of support at the top. Of all those I have discussed this matter with, Lyn Nofziger appears the most knowledgeable and most interested. If Lyn had support he would enjoy undertaking the activity as the project coordinator. You are aware of some of Lyn's successes in the field, but he feels that he can only employ limited efforts because there is a lack of support.

Document 2
THE ENEMIES "PRIORITY LIST"

The following is Charles Colson's response to the Dean memorandum dated September 9, 1971. This is the enemies "priority list." Colson was instrumental in pressuring governmental agencies to go after Nixon's "enemies."

1. Picker, Arnold M., United Artists Corporation: Top Muskie fundraiser. Success here could be both debilitating and very embarrassing to the Muskie machine. If effort looks promising, both Ruth and David Picker should be programmed and then a follow-through with United Artists.

2. Barkan, Alexander E., National Director of AFL-CIO's Committee on Political Education: Without a doubt the most powerful political force programmed against us in 1968. ($10 million dollars, 4.6 million votes, 115 million pamphlets, 176,000 workers—all programmed by Barkan's C.O.P.E.—So says Teddy White in The Making of the President '68). We can expect the same effort this time.

3. Guthman, Ed, Managing Editor LA Times: Guthman, former Kennedy side, was a highly sophisticated hatchetman against us in '68. It is obvious he is the prime mover behind the current Key Biscayne effort. It is time to give him the message.

4. Dane, Maxwell, Doyle, Dane and Bernbach: The top Democratic advertising firm—They destroyed Goldwater in '64. They should be hit hard starting with Dane.

5. Dyson, Charles, Dyson-Kissner Corporation: Dyson and Larry O'Brien were close business associates after '68. Dyson has huge business holdings and is presently deeply involved in the Businessmen's Educational

Fund, which bankrolls a national radio network of 5 minute programs—Anti-Nixon in character.

6. Stein, Howard, Dreyfus Corporation: Heaviest contributor to McCarthy in '68. If McCarthy goes will do the same in '72. If not, Lindsay or
McGovern will receive the funds.

7. Lowenstein, Allard: Guiding force behind the 18-year-old "dump
Nixon" vote drive.

8. Halperin, Morton, leading executive at Common Cause: A scandal
would be most helpful here.

9. Woodcock, Leonard, UAW: No comments necessary.

Document 3
THE "SMOKING GUN" TAPE

Transcript of a recording of a meeting between the President and H. R.
Haldeman, the Oval Office, one week after the arrests at the DNC headquarters of the Watergate Hotel, June 23, 1972, from 10:04 A.M. to
11:39 A.M. In this conversation, dubbed the "smoking gun" tape, the
president agrees to an obstruction of justice.

HALDEMAN: O.K.—that's fine. Now, on the investigation, you know, the
Democratic break-in things, we're back to the—in the, the problem area because the FBI is not under control, because Gray doesn't exactly know how
to control them, and they have, their investigation is now leading into some
problem areas, because they've been able to trace the money, not through the
money itself, but through the bank, you know, sources—the banker himself.
And, and it goes in some directions we don't want it to go. Ah, also there
have been some things, like an informant came in off the street to the FBI in
Miami, who was a photographer or has a friend who is a photographer who
developed some films through this guy, Barker, and the films had pictures of
Democratic National Committee letterhead documents and things. So I
guess, so it's things like that that are gonna, that are filtering in. Mitchell
came up with yesterday, and John Dean analyzed very carefully last night
and concludes, concurs now with Mitchell's recommendation that the only
way to solve this, and we're set up beautifully to do it, ah, in that and that . . .
the only network that paid any attention to it last night was NBC . . . they did
a massive story on the Cuban . . .

PRESIDENT: That's right.

HALDEMAN: . . . thing.

PRESIDENT: Right.

HALDEMAN: That the way to handle this now is for us to have Walters call Pat Gray and just say, "Stay the hell out of this. . . . This is, ah, business here we don't want you to go any further on it." That's not an unusual development . . .

PRESIDENT: Um huh.

HALDEMAN: . . . and, uh, that would take care of it.

PRESIDENT: What about Pat Gray, ah, you mean he doesn't want to?

HALDEMAN: Pat does want to. He doesn't know how to, and he doesn't have, he doesn't have any basis for doing it. Given this, he will then have the basis. He'll call Mark Felt in, and the two of them . . . and Mark Felt wants to cooperate because . . .

PRESIDENT: Yeah.

HALDEMAN: . . . he's ambitious.

PRESIDENT: Yeah.

HALDEMAN: Ah, he'll call him in and say, "We've got the signal from across the river to, to put the hold on this." And that will fit rather well because the FBI agents who are working the case, at this point, feel that's what it is. This is CIA.

PRESIDENT: But they've traced the money to 'em.

HALDEMAN: Well, they have, they've traced to a name, but they haven't gotten to the guy yet.

PRESIDENT: Would it be somebody here?

HALDEMAN: Kent Dahlberg.

PRESIDENT: Who the hell is Kent Dahlberg?

HALDEMAN: He's, ah, he gave $25,000 in Minnesota and, ah, the check went directly in to this, to this guy Barker.

PRESIDENT: Maybe he's a . . . bum . . . He didn't get this from the committee though, from Stans.

HALDEMAN: Yeah. It is. It is. It's directly traceable and there's some more through some Texas people in—that went to the Mexican bank which they can also trace to the Mexican bank . . . they'll get their names today. And (pause)

PRESIDENT: Well, I mean, ah, there's no way . . . I'm just thinking if they don't cooperate, what do they say? They, they, they were approached by the Cubans. That's what Dahlberg has to say, the Texans too. Is that the idea?

HALDEMAN: Well, if they will. But then we're relying on more and more people all the time. That's the problem. And, ah, they'll stop if we could, if we take this other step.

PRESIDENT: All right. Fine.

HALDEMAN: And, and they seem to feel the thing to do is get them to stop?

PRESIDENT: Right, fine.

HALDEMAN: They say the only way to do that is from White House instructions. And it's got to be to Helms and, ah, what's his name? . . . Walters.

PRESIDENT: Walters.

HALDEMAN: And the proposal would be that Ehrlichman (coughs) and I call them in . . .

PRESIDENT: All right, fine.

HALDEMAN: . . . and say, ah . .

PRESIDENT: How do you call him in, I mean you just, well, we protected Helms from one hell of a lot of things.

HALDEMAN: That's what Ehrlichman says.

PRESIDENT: Of course, this is a, this is a hunt, you will—that will uncover a lot of things. You open that scab, there's a hell of a lot of things and that we just feel that it would be very detrimental to have this thing go any further. This involves these Cubans, Hunt, and a lot of hanky-panky that we have nothing to do with ourselves. Well, what the hell, did Mitchell know about this thing to any much of a degree?

HALDEMAN: I think so. I don't think he knew the details, but I think he knew.

PRESIDENT: He didn't know how it was going to be handled though, with Dahlberg and the Texans and so forth? Well, who was the asshole that did? (Unintelligible) Is it Liddy? Is that the fellow? He must be a little nuts.

HALDEMAN: He is.

PRESIDENT: I mean he just isn't well screwed on, is he? Isn't that the problem?

HALDEMAN: No, but he was under pressure, apparently, to get more information, and as he got more pressure, he pushed the people harder to move harder on—

PRESIDENT: Pressure from Mitchell?

HALDEMAN: Apparently.

PRESIDENT: Oh, Mitchell, Mitchell was at the point that you made on this, that exactly what I need from you is on the—

HALDEMAN: Gemstone, yeah.

PRESIDENT: All right, fine, I understand it all. We won't second-guess Mitchell and the rest. Thank God it wasn't Colson.

HALDEMAN: The FBI interviewed Colson yesterday. They determined that would be a good thing to do.

PRESIDENT: Um hum.

HALDEMAN: Ah, to have him take a . . .

PRESIDENT: Um hum.

HALDEMAN: An interrogation, which he did, and that, the FBI guys working the case had concluded that there were one or two possibilities, on, that this was a White House, they don't think that there is anything at the Election Committee, they think it was either a White House operation and they had some obscure reasons for it, nonpolitical . . .

PRESIDENT: Uh huh.

HALDEMAN: Or it was a . . .

PRESIDENT: Cuban thing—

HALDEMAN: Cubans and the CIA. And after their interrogation of, of . . .

PRESIDENT: Colson.

HALDEMAN: . . . Colson, yesterday, they concluded it was not the White House, but are now convinced it is a CIA thing, so the CIA turnoff would . . .

PRESIDENT: Well, not sure of their analysis, I'm not going to get that involved. I'm (unintelligible).

HALDEMAN: No, sir. We don't want you to.

PRESIDENT: You call them in . . . Good. Good deal. Play it tough. That's the way they play it and that's the way we are going to play it.

HALDEMAN: O.K. We'll do it.

PRESIDENT: Yeah, when I saw that news summary item, I of course knew it was a bunch of crap, but I thought, ah, well, it's good to have them off on this wild hare things because when they start bugging us, which they have, we'll know our little boys will not know how to handle it. I hope they will though. You never know. Maybe, you think about it. Good!

After a time, Nixon and Haldeman return to a discussion of Watergate and conspire to obstruct an FBI investigation by telling the FBI that the break-in was a CIA activity.

PRESIDENT: When you get in these people . . . when you get these people in, say: "Look, the problem is that this will open the whole, the whole Bay of Pigs thing, and the President just feels that" . . . ah, without going into the details . . . don't, don't lie to them to the extent to say there is no involvement, but just say this is sort of a comedy of errors, bizarre? Without getting into it, "the President believes that it is going to open the whole Bay of Pigs thing up again. And, ah, because these people are plugging for, for keeps and that they should call the FBI in and say that we wish for the country, don't go any further into this case," period.

HALDEMAN: O.K.

PRESIDENT: That's the way to put it, do it straight (unintelligible).

HALDEMAN: Get more done for our cause by the opposition than by us at this point.

PRESIDENT: You think so?

HALDEMAN: I think so, yeah.

PRESIDENT: Still (unintelligible) moves (unintelligible) very close election (unintelligible) he keeps saying if he moves a little—

HALDEMAN: They're all . . . that's the whole thing. The *Washington Post* said it in its lead editorial today. Another "McGovern's got to change his position," and that that would be a good thing, that's constructive. Ah, the whitewash for change.

PRESIDENT: *Post* prints the news so they'll say that is perfectly all right.

HALDEMAN: 'Cause then they are saying . . . on the other hand . . . that maybe we're not so smart. We have to admire the progress he's made on the basis of the position he's taken and maybe he's right and we're wrong.

PRESIDENT: To be very (unintelligible) (laughs).

HALDEMAN: Sitting in Miami played into our hand a little bit.

PRESIDENT: No.

HALDEMAN: They, ah, eliminated their law prohibiting male homosexuals from wearing female clothing, now the boys can all put on their dresses . . . so the gay lib is going to turn out 6,000 has to (laughs). I hope they (unintelligible) them . . .

PRESIDENT: How did they (unintelligible)?

Document 4
SECOND NIXON-HALDEMAN MEETING, JUNE 23, 1972
(OVAL OFFICE)

Transcript of a recording of a meeting between the president and H. R. Haldeman, the Oval Office, June 23, 1972, from 1:04 P.M. to 1:13 P.M. This is a follow-up to the previous taped conversation.

PRESIDENT: O.K. (unintelligible) and, ah, just, just postpone the (unintelligible, with noises) hearings (15 seconds unintelligible, with noises) and all that garbage. Just say that I have to take a look at the primaries (unintelligible) recover (unintelligible) I just don't (unintelligible) very bad, to have this fellow Hunt, ah, you know, ah, it's, he, he knows too damn much and he was involved, we happen to know that. And that it gets out that the President (unintelligible) He said . . . whole, this is all involved in the Cuban thing, that it's a fiasco, and it's going to make the FBI—ah, CIA look bad, it's going to make Hunt look bad, and it's likely to blow the whole, ah, Bay of Pigs thing which we think would be very unfortunate for CIA and for the country at this time, and for American foreign policy, and he just better tough it and lay it on them.—Isn't that what you . . .

HALDEMAN: Yeah, that's, that's the basis we'll do it on and just leave it at that.

PRESIDENT: I don't want them to get any ideas we're doing it because our concern is political.

HALDEMAN: Right.

PRESIDENT: And at the same time, I wouldn't tell them it is not political.

HALDEMAN: Right.

PRESIDENT: I would just say, "Look, it's because of the Hunt involvement," just say (unintelligible, with noise) sort of thing, the whole cover Ha, uh, basically this (unintelligible).

Document 5
THIRD NIXON-HALDEMAN MEETING, JUNE 23, 1972
(EOB OFFICE)

Transcript of a recording of a meeting between the president and H. R. Haldeman in the EOB office on June 23, 1972, from 2:20 P.M. to 2:45 P.M., after Haldeman met with FBI and CIA officials. In this tape, Bob Haldeman confirms to the president that their obstruction of justice has succeeded.

HALDEMAN: Well, it's no problem. Had the . . . two of them in, uh, state to health (unintelligible) but it's kind of interesting. Walters said that, uh, make a point. I didn't mention Hunt at the opening. I just said that, that, uh, this thing which we give direction to we're gonna create some very major potential problems because they were exploring leads that led back into, to, uh, areas it will be harmful to the CIA, harmful to the government (telephone rings). But, didn't have anything to with, with, with (unintelligible) kind of thing.

PRESIDENT: (Answers telephone) Hello? Chuck, I wondered if you would, ah, give John Connaly a call. He's on his trip. I don't want him to read it in the papers before Monday about this quota thing and say, "Look, uh, he met, uh, we're gonna to this, but, but, I checked, uh, I asked you about the situation, and you personally checked your calendar and made, have an understanding. It's only temporary (unintelligible). It won't affect (unintelligible) people (unintelligible)." O.K.? I didn't want him to read it the papers. Good. Bye. (Hangs up telephone.)

HALDEMAN: I think Helms did, too. Helms said well, uh, I've had no contact (unintelligible) and, uh—

PRESIDENT: God (unintelligible).

HALDEMAN: (Unintelligible.) Gray called and said, uh, yesterday, and said uh, that he thought—

PRESIDENT: Who did, Gray?

HALDEMAN: Gray had called Helms, which we knew, and said, ah, uh, I think we've run right into the middle of a CIA covert operation.

PRESIDENT: Gray said that?

HALDEMAN: Yeah. And (unintelligible) said nothing we've done at this point and ah (unintelligible) says well it sure looks to me like it is (unintelligible) and ah, that was the end of that conversation (unintelligible) the problem is it tracks back to the Bay of Pigs and it tracks back to some other—if their leads run out to people who had no involvement in this, except by contacts and connection, but it gets to areas that are at the (unintelligible) to be raised? The whole problem of this, this Hunt fellow, uh . . . So at that point Helms kind of got the picture (unintelligible). He said, he said, "We'll be very happy to be helpful to, ah, you know, and we'll handle everything you want. I would like to know the reason for being helpful." And it may have appeared when he wasn't going to get it explicitly but was gonna get it through generally. So he said fine. And Walters (unintelligible). Walters is going to make a call to Gray. That's the way we put it and that's the way it was left.

PRESIDENT: How would that work though? How would — for example, if they're desperate (unintelligible) got somebody from Miami bank to be here to count the inventory.

HALDEMAN: (Unintelligible) they can to that (unintelligible). Somebody (unintelligible). But, the point John made was the Bureau doesn't, the Bureau is going on, on this because they don't know what they're uncovering.

(Unintelligible) say should continue to pursue it, uh, they don't need to because they've already got their case as far as the, uh, charges against these men, (unintelligible) and, oh, as they pursue it because they're uncovering some (unintelligible). Sure enough, that's exactly what—but we didn't in any way say we had any political . . . interest or concern or anything like that, ah, (unintelligible). One thing Helms did raise is he said that, that Gray, he asked Gray why he felt they're going into a CIA thing and Gray said, "Well, because of the characters involved and the amount of money involved." Said there's a lot of dough in this someone and, oh, (unintelligible) there is the possibility that one of our guys—that probably has some significance to the question (unintelligible).

PRESIDENT: (Unintelligible) Well, we'll cross that bridge.

HALDEMAN: Well, I think they will 'cause our, see, there isn't any question.

PRESIDENT: If it runs back to the bank—so, what the hell, they, who knows, maybe Dahlberg's contributed to the CIA (unintelligible).

HALDEMAN: CIA gets money as we know 'cause, I mean their money moves in a lot of different ways, too.

PRESIDENT: Yeah. However we thought that it did a lot of good. (Unintelligible.)

HALDEMAN: Right.

PRESIDENT: Can you imagine what Kennedy would have done with that?

Document 6
WHITE HOUSE TAPES, MARCH 21, 1973

Discussion of the need to pay "hush money" to criminal defendants, commit perjury, and continue the cover-up. This tape was a key piece of evidence in the trial of Haldeman and the other coconspirators.

Dean: Now, where, where are the soft spots on this? Well, first of all, there's the, there's the problem of the continued blackmail.

President: Right.

Dean: Which will not only go on now, it'll go on when these people are in prison, and it will compound the obstruction of justice situation. It'll cost money. It's dangerous. Nobody, nothing—people around here are not pros at this sort of thing. This is the sort of thing Mafia people can do: washing money, getting clean money, and things like that, uh—we're we just don't know about those things, because we're not used to, you know we are not criminals and not used to dealing in that business. It's, uh, it's, uh—

President: That's right.

Dean: It's a tough thing to know how to do.

President: Maybe we can't even do that.

Dean: That's right. It's a real problem as to whether we could even do it. Plus there's a real problem in raising money. Uh, Mitchell has been working on raising some money. Uh, feeling he's got, you know, he's got one, he's one of the ones with the most to lose. Uh, but there's no denying the fact that the White House, and, uh, Ehrlichman, Haldeman, Dean are involved in some of the early money decisions.

President: How much money do you need?

Dean: I would say these people are going to cost, uh, a million dollars over the next, uh, two years.

President: We could get that.

Dean: Uh huh.

President: You, on the money, if you need the money, I mean, uh, you could get the money. Let's say—

Dean: Well, I think that we're going.

President: What I meant is, you could, you could get a million dollars. And you could get it in cash. I, I know where it could be gotten.

Dean: Uh huh.

President: I mean it's not easy, but it could be done. But, uh, the question is who the hell would handle it?

Dean: That's right. Uh . . .

President: Yeah. Well, what do you need, then? You need, uh, you don't need a million right away, but you need a million. Is that right?

Dean: That's right.

President: You need a million in cash, don't you? If you want to put that through, would you put that through, uh, this is thinking out loud here for a moment—would you put that through the Cuban Committee?
You need it in cash, don't you? If you want to put—

Dean: All right. Let, let me, uh—

President: Go ahead.

Dean: Continue a little bit here now. The, uh, I, when I say this is a, a growing cancer, uh, I say it for reasons like this. Bud Krogh, in his testimony before the grand jury, was forced to perjure himself. Uh, he is haunted by it. Uh, Bud said, "I haven't had a pleasant day on the job."

President: Huh? Said what?

Dean: He said, "I have not had a pleasant day on my job." Uh, he talked, apparently, he said to me, "I told my wife all about this," he said. "The, uh, the curtain may ring down one of these days, and, uh I may have to face the music, which I'm perfectly willing to do." Uh.

President: What did he perjure himself on, John?

Dean: His, did uh, did he know the Cubans? He did. Uh.

President: He said he didn't?

Dean: That's right. They didn't press him hard, or that he . . .

President: He might be able to—I am just trying to think. Perjury is an awful hard rap to prove. He could say that I—Well, go ahead.

Dean: [Coughs] Well, so that's, that's the first, that's one perjury. Now, Mitchell and, and, uh, Magruder are potential perjuries. There is always the possibility of any one of these individuals blowing. Hunt, Liddy. Liddy is in jail right now; he's serving his—trying to get good time right now. I think Liddy is probably, in his, in his own bizarre way, the strongest of all of them. Uh, so there's—there is that possibility.

President: Well, you, your major, your major guy to keep under control is Hunt.

Dean: That's right.

President: I think because he knows . . .

Dean: He knows so much.

President: About a lot of other things.

Dean: He knows so much. Right. Uh, he could sink Chuck Colson. Apparently, apparently he is quite distressed with Colson. He thinks Colson has abandoned him. Uh. Colson was to meet with him when he was out there, after, now he had left the White House. He met with him through his lawyer. Hunt raised the question; he wanted money. Colson's lawyer told him that Colson wasn't doing anything with money, and Hunt took offense with that immediately, that, uh, uh, that Colson had abandoned him. Uh.

President: Don't you, just looking at the immediate problem, don't you have to have—handle Hunt's financial situation—

Dean: I, I think that's . . .

President: Damn soon?

Dean: That is, uh, I talked to Mitchell about that last night.

President: Mitchell.

Dean: And, and, uh, I told—

President: Might as well. May have the rule you've got to keep the cap on the bottle that much.

Dean: That's right; that's right.

President: In order to have any options.

Dean: That's right.

President: Either that or let it all blow right now.

Dean continued to go over other possible legal problems. He told the president of the need for continued perjury in the future to protect the cover-up. After Haldeman joined the meeting, they continued to explore ways of containing the mess.

President: Coming back, though, to this. So you got that; the, uh, hanging over. Now. If, uh—you, you see, if you let it hang there, the point is you could let all or only part. The point is, your feeling is that we just can't continue to, to pay the blackmail of these guys?

Dean: I think that's our greatest jeopardy.

Haldeman: Yeah.

President: Now, let me tell you, it's—

Dean: 'Cause that is—

President: No problem, we could, we could get the money. There is no problem in that. We can't provide the clemency. The money can be provided. Mitchell could provide the way to deliver it. That could be done. See what I mean?

In a continuation of this conversation, the maintenance of the cover-up continued to depend on perjury from several of the participants. But how to guarantee continued perjury? The president instructed:

Dean: You can't have a lawyer before a grand jury.

Haldeman: Okay, but you, but you, you do have rules of evidence. You can refuse to, to talk.

Dean: You can take the Fifth Amendment.

President: That's right. That's right.

Haldeman: You can say you forgot, too, can't you?

Dean: Sure.

President: That's right.

Dean: But you can't—you're—very high risk in perjury situation.

President: That's right. Just be damned sure you say I don't—

Haldeman: Yeah.

Dean: Remember, I can't recall, I can't give any honest, an answer to that that I can recall. But that's it.

Finally, they return to Hunt's demand for hush money, and realize that it is a problem that must be met.

Dean: This is Hunt's opportunity.

*President:*That's why, that's why—

Haldeman: God, if he can lay this—

President: That's why your, for your immediate thing you've got no choice with Hunt but the hundred and twenty or whatever it is. Right?

Dean: That's right.

President: Would you agree that that's a buy time thing, you better damn well get that done, but fast!

Dean: I think he ought to be given some signal, anyway, to, to—

President: Yes.

Dean: Yeah-you know.

President: Well for Christ's sakes get it in a, in a way that, uh. Who's, who's going to talk to him? Colson? He's the one who's supposed to know him.

Dean's original goal was to get the president somehow to end the cover-up. But by the close of the meeting the cover-up expanded. Exasperated, Dean told the president the administration was not in a position to maintain the cover-up. The meeting concluded with an agreement to expand the cover-up.

President: All right. Fine. And, uh, my point is that, uh we can, uh, you may well some—I think it is good, frankly, to consider these various options. And then, once you, once you decide on the plan—John and you had the right plan, let me say, I have no doubts about the right plan before the election. And you handled it just right. You contained it. Now after the election we've got to have another plan, because we can't have, for four years, we can't have this thing—you're going to be eaten away. We can't do it.

Dean: Well, there's been a change in the mood—

Haldeman: John's point is exactly right, that the erosion here now is going to you, and that is the thing that we've got to turn off, at whatever the cost. We've got to figure out where to turn it off at the lowest cost we can, but at whatever cost it takes.

Dean: That's what, that's what we have to do.

President: Well, the erosion is inevitably going to come here, apart from anything, you know, people saying that, uh, well, the Watergate isn't a major concern. It isn't. But it would, but it will be. It's bound to be.

Dean: We cannot let you be tarnished by that situation.

Document 7
SUPREME COURT RULING ON THE WHITE HOUSE TAPE CONTROVERSY

The tape controversy reached the Supreme Court. In these excerpts of the Court's ruling, the Justices order, 8–0, that the president must turn over the White House tapes to the Court.

UNITED STATES v. RICHARD M. NIXON
SUPREME COURT OF THE UNITED STATES

Nos. 73–1766 and 73–1834

United States, Petitioner,
73–1766   v.
Richard M. Nixon, President
    Of the United States,
          et al.

On Writs of Certiorari to the United States
Court of Appeals for the District of
Columbia Circuit before Judgment.

Richard M. Nixon, President
    of the United States,
          Petitioner,
73–1834   *v*
          United States.

[July 24, 1974]

MR. CHIEF JUSTICE BURGER delivered the opinion of the Court.

This case presents for review the denial of a motion, filed on behalf of the president of the United States, in the case of *United States v. Mitchell*, to quash a third-party subpoena *duces tecum* issued by the United States District Court for the District of Columbia pursuant to Fed. Rule Crim. Proc. 17 (c). The subpoena directed the President to produce certain tape recordings and documents relating to his conversations with aides and advisers. The court rejected the President's claims of absolute executive privilege, of lack of jurisdiction, and of failure to satisfy the requirements of Rule 17 (c). The President appealed to the Court of Appeals. We granted the United States' petition for certiorari before judgment, and also the President's responsive cross-petition for certiorari before judgment, because of the public importance of the issues presented and the need for their prompt resolution.

The District Court held that the judiciary, not the President, was the final arbiter of a claim of executive privilege. The court concluded that, under the circumstances of this case, the presumptive privilege was overcome by the Special Prosecutor's prima facie "demonstration of need sufficiently compelling to warrant judicial examination in chambers . . ." The court held, finally, that the Special Prosecutor had satisfied the requirements of Rule 17 (c). The District Court stayed its order pending appellate review on condition that review was sought before 4 p.m., May 24. The court further provided that matters filed under seal remain under seal when transmitted as part of the record.

On May 24, 1974, the President filed a timely notice of appeal from the District Court order, and the certified record from the District Court was docketed in the United States Court of Appeals for the District of Columbia Circuit. On the same day, the President also filed a petition for writ of mandamus in the Court of Appeals seeking review of the District Court order.

Later on May 24, the Special Prosecutor also filed, in this Court, a petition for writ of certiorari before judgment. On May 31, the petition was granted with an expedited briefing schedule. On June 6, the President filed, under seal, a cross-petition for writ of certiorari before judgment. This cross-petition was granted June 15, 1974 and the case was set for argument on July 8, 1974.

THE CLAIM OF PRIVILEGE

A

Having determined that the requirements of Rule 17 (c) were satisfied, we turn to the claim that the subpoena should be quashed because it demands "confidential conversations between a President and his close advisors that it would be inconsistent with the public interest to produce." The first contention is a broad claim that the separation of power doctrine precludes judicial review of a President's claim of privilege. The second contention is that if he does not prevail on the claim of absolute privilege, the court should hold as a matter of constitutional law that the privilege prevails over the subpoena *duces tecum.*

In the performance of assigned constitutional duties each branch of the Government must initially interpret the Constitution, and the interpretation of its powers by any branch is due great respect from the others. The President's counsel, as we have noted, reads the Constitution as providing an absolute privilege of confidentiality for all presidential communications. Many decisions of this Court, however, have unequivocally reaffirmed the holding of *Marbury v. Madison*, 1 Cranch 137 (1803), that "it is emphatically the province and duty of the judicial department to say what the law is."

No holding of the Court has defined the scope of judicial power specifically relating to the enforcement of a subpoena for confidential presidential communications for use in a criminal prosecution, but other exercises of powers by the Executive Branch and the Legislative Branch have been found invalid as in conflict with the Constitution. *Powell v. McCormack, supra; Youngstown, supra.* In a series of cases, the Court interpreted the explicit immunity conferred by express provisions of the Constitution on Members of the House and Senate by the Speech or Debate Clause. U.S. Const. Art. I '6. *Doe v. McMillan*, 412 U.S. 306 (1973); *Gravel v. United States*, 408 U.S. 606 (1973); *United States v. Brewster*, 408 U.S. 501 (1972); *United States v. Johnson*, 383 U.S. 169 (1966). Since this Court has consistently exercised the power to construe and delineate claims arising under express powers, it must follow that the Court has authority to interpret claims with respect to powers alleged to derive from enumerated powers.

Ours system of government "requires that federal courts on occasion interpret the Constitution in a manner at variance with the construction given the document by another branch." And in *Baker v. Carr*, 369 U.S., at 211, the Court stated:

Deciding whether a matter has in any measure been committed by the Constitution to another branch of government, or whether the action of that branch exceeds whatever authority has been committed, is itself a delicate exercise in constitutional interpretation, and is a responsibility of this Court as ultimate interpreter of the Constitution.

Notwithstanding the deference each branch must accord the others, the "judicial power of the United States" vested in the federal courts by Art. III, ~ 1 of the Constitution can no more be shared with the Executive Branch than the Chief Executive, for example, can share with the Judiciary the veto power, or the Congress share with the Judiciary the power to override a presidential veto. Any other conclusion would be contrary to the basic concept of separation of powers and the checks and balances that flow from the scheme of a tripartite government.

We therefore reaffirm that it is "emphatically the province and the duty" of this Court "to say what the law is" with respect to the claim of privilege presented in this case.

B

In support of his claim of absolute privilege, the President's counsel urges two grounds one of which is common to all government and one of which is peculiar to our system of separation of powers. The first ground is the valid need for protection of communications between high government officials and those who advise and assist them in the performance of their manifold duties; the importance of this confidentiality is too plain to require further discussion. Human experience teaches that those who expect public dissemination of their remarks may well temper candor with a concern for appearances and or their own interests to detriment of the decision making process. Whatever the nature of the privilege of confidentiality of presidential communications in the exercise of Art. II powers the privilege can be said to derive from the supremacy of each branch within its own assigned area of constitutional duties. Certain powers and privileges flow from the nature of enumerated powers. The protection of the confidentially of presidential communications has similar constitutional underpinnings.

The second ground asserted by the President's counsel in support of the claim of absolute privilege rests on the doctrine of separation of powers. Here it is argued that the independence of the Executive Branch within its own sphere insulates a president from a judicial subpoena in an ongoing criminal prosecution, and thereby protects confidential presidential communications.

However, neither the doctrine of separation of powers, nor the need for confidentiality of high level communications, without more, can sustain an absolute, unqualified presidential privilege of immunity from judicial process under all circumstances. The President's need for complete candor and objectivity from advisers calls for great deference from the courts. However, when the privilege depends solely on the broad, undifferentiated claim of public interest in the confidentiality of such conversations, a confrontation with other values arises. Absent a claim of need to protect military, diplomatic or sensitive national security secrets, we find it difficult to accept the argument that even the very important interest in confidentiality presidential communications is significantly diminished by production of such material for *in camera* inspection with all the protection that a district court will be obliged to provide.

The impediment that an absolute, unqualified privilege would place in the way of the primary constitutional duty of the Judicial Branch to do justice in criminal prosecutions would plainly conflict with the function of the courts under Art. III. In designing the structure of our Government and dividing and allocation the sovereign power among three coequal branches, the Framers of the Constitution sought to provide a comprehensive system, but the separate powers were not intended to operate with absolute independence. "While the Constitution diffuses power the better to secure liberty, it also contemplates that practice will integrate the dispersed powers into a workable government. It enjoins upon its branches separateness but interdependence, autonomy but reciprocity." To read the Art. II powers of the President as providing an absolute privilege as against a subpoena essential to enforcement of criminal statutes on no more than a generalized claim of the public interest in confidentiality of nonmilitary and nondiplomatic discussions would upset the constitutional balance of "a workable government" and gravely impair the role of the courts under Art. III.

C

Since we conclude that the legitimate needs of the judicial process may outweigh presidential privilege, it is necessary to resolve those competing interests in a manner that preserves the essential functions of each branch. The right and indeed the duty to resolve that question does not free the judiciary from according high respect to the representations made on behalf of the President.

The expectation of a President to the confidentiality of his conversations and correspondence, like the claim of confidentiality of judicial deliberations, for example, has all the values to which we accord deference for the privacy of all citizens and added to those values the necessity for protection of the public interest in candid, objective, and even blunt or harsh opinions in presidential decision-making. A President and those who assist him must be free to explore alternatives in the process of shaping policies and making decisions and to do so in a way many would be unwilling to express except privately. These are the considerations justifying a presumptive privilege for presidential communications. The privilege is fundamental to the operation of government and inextricably rooted in the separation of powers under the Constitution. In *Nixon v. Sirica* (1973), the Court of Appeals held that such presidential communications are "presumptively privileged," and this position is accepted by both parties in the present litigation. We agree with Mr.

Chief Justice Marshall's observation, therefore, that "in no case of this kind would a court be required to proceed against the President as against an ordinary individual."

But this presumptive privilege must be considered in light of our historic commitment to the rule of law. This is nowhere more profoundly manifest than in our view that "the twofold aim (of criminal justice) is that guilt shall not escape or innocence suffer." We have elected to employ an adversary system of criminal justice in which the parties contest all issues before a court of law. The need to develop all relevant facts in the adversary system is both fundamental and comprehensive. The ends of criminal justice would be defeated if judgments were to be founded on a partial or speculative presentation of facts. The very integrity of the judicial system and public confidence in the system depend on full disclosure of all the facts, within the framework of the rules of evidence. To ensure that justice is done, it is imperative to the function of courts that compulsory process be available for the production of evidence needed either by the prosecution or by the defense.

Only recently the Court restated the ancient proposition of law, albeit in the context of a grand jury inquiry rather than a trial, "that the public . . . has a right to every man's evidence' except for those persons protected by a constitutional, common law, or statutory privilege." The privileges referred to by the Court are designed to protect weighty and legitimate competing interests. Thus, the Fifth Amendment to the Constitution provides that no man "shall be compelled in any criminal case to be a witness against himself." And, generally, an attorney or a priest may not be required to disclose what has been revealed in professional confidence. These and other interests are recognized in law by privileges against forced disclosure, established in the Constitution, by statute, or at common law. Whatever their origins, these exceptions to the demand for every man's evidence are not lightly created nor expansively construed, for they are in derogation of the search for truth.

In this case the President challenges a subpoena served on him as a third party requiring the production of materials for use in a criminal prosecution on the claim that he has a privilege against disclosure of confidential communications. He does not place his claim of privilege on the ground they are military or diplomatic secrets. As to these areas of Art. II duties the courts have traditionally shown the utmost deference to presidential responsibilities. In *C. & S. Air Lines v. Waterman Steamship Corp.*, (1948), dealing with presidential authority involving foreign policy considerations, the Court said:

The President, both as Commander-in-Chief and as the Nation's organ for foreign affairs, has available intelligence services whose reports are not and ought not to be published to the world. It would be intolerable that courts, without the relevant information, should review and perhaps nullify actions of the Executive taken on information properly held secret.

In *United States v. Reynolds* (1952), dealing with a claimant's demand for evidence in a damage case against the Government the Court said:

It may be possible to satisfy the court, from all the circumstances of the case, that there is a reasonable danger that compulsion of the evidence will expose military matters which, in the interest of national security, should not be divulged. When this is the case, the occasion for the privilege is appropriate, and the court should not jeopardize the security which the privilege is meant to protect by insisting upon an examination of the evidence, even by the judge alone, in chambers.

No case of the Court, however, has extended this high degree of deference to a President's generalized interest in confidentiality. Nowhere in the Constitution, as we have noted earlier, is there any explicit reference to a privilege of confidentiality. Nowhere in the Constitution, as we have noted earlier, is there any explicit reference to a privilege of confidentiality, yet to the extent this interest relates to the effective discharge of a President's powers, it is constitutionally based.

The right to the production of all evidence at a criminal trial similarly has constitutional dimensions. The Sixth Amendment explicitly confers upon every defendant in a criminal trial the right "to be confronted with the witnesses against him" and "to have compulsory process for obtaining witnesses in his favor." Moreover, the Fifth Amendment also guarantees that no person shall be deprived of liberty without due process of law. It is the manifest duty of the courts to vindicate those guarantees and to accomplish that it is essential that all relevant and admissible evidence be produced.

In this case we must weigh the importance of the general privilege of confidentiality of presidential communications in performance of his responsibilities against the inroads of such a privilege on the fair administration of criminal justice. The interest in preserving confidentiality is weighty indeed and entitled to great respect. However we cannot conclude that advisers will be moved to temper the candor of their remarks by the infrequent occasions of disclosure because of the possibility that such conversations will be called for in the context of a criminal prosecution.

On the other hand, the allowance of the privilege to withhold evidence that is demonstrably relevant in a criminal trial would cut deeply into the guarantee of due process of law and gravely impair the basic function for the courts. A President's acknowledged need for confidentiality in the communications of his office is general in nature, whereas the constitutional need for production of relevant evidence in a criminal proceeding is specific and central to the fair adjudication of a particular criminal case in the administration of justice. Without access to specific facts a criminal prosecution may be totally frustrated. The President's broad interest in confidentiality of communications will not be vitiated by disclosure of a limited number of conversations preliminarily shown to have some bearing on the pending criminal cases.

We conclude that when the ground for asserting privilege as to subpoenaed materials sought for use in a criminal trial is based only on the generalized interest in confidentiality, it cannot prevail over the fundamental demands of due process of law in the fair administration of criminal justice. The generalized assertion of privilege must yield to the demonstrated, specific need for evidence in a pending criminal trial.

D

We have earlier determined that the District Court did not err in authorizing the issuance of the subpoena. If a President concludes that compliance with a subpoena would be injurious to the public interest he may properly, as was done here, invoke a claim of privilege on the return of the subpoena. Upon receiving a claim of privilege from the Chief Executive, it became the further duty of the District Court to treat the subpoenaed material as presumptively privileged and to require the Special Prosecutor to demonstrate that the presidential material was "essential to the justice of the (pending criminal) case." Here the District Court treated the material as presumptively privileged, proceeded to find that the Special Prosecutor had made a sufficient showing to rebut the presumption and ordered an *in camera* examination of the subpoenaed material. On the basis of our examination of the record we are unable to conclude that the District Court erred in ordering the inspection. Accordingly we affirm the order of the District Court that subpoenaed materials be transmitted to that court. We now turn to the important question of District Court's responsibilities in conducting the *in camera* examination of presidential materials or communications delivered under the compulsion of the subpoena *duces tecum*.

Since this matter came before the Court during the presidency of a criminal prosecution, and on representations that time is of the essence, the mandate shall issue forthwith.

Affirmed.

MR. JUSTICE REHNQUIST took no part in the consideration or decision of these cases.

Document 8
THE HOUSE JUDICIARY COMMITTEE RESOLUTION
TO IMPEACH RICHARD NIXON

The following is the report of the House Judiciary Committee and the resolution to impeach Richard M. Nixon, issued after Mr. Nixon's resignation. The report details the charges against the former president.

House Calendar No. 426

93D CONGRESS   HOUSE OF REPRESENTATIVES   REPORT

2d Session   No. 93—1305

IMPEACHMENT OF RICHARD M. NIXON, PRESIDENT
OF THE UNITED STATES

AUGUST 20, 1974—Referred to the House Calendar and ordered
to be printed

Mr. RODINO, from the Committee on the Judiciary, submitted
the following

R E P O R T
together with
SUPPLEMENTAL, ADDITIONAL, SEPARATE, DISSENTING, MI-
NORITY, INDIVIDUAL AND CONCURRING VIEWS

The committee on the Judiciary, to whom was referred the consideration of recommendations concerning the exercise of the constitutional power to impeach Richard M. Nixon, President of the United States, having considered the same, reports thereon pursuant to II. Re. 803 as follows and recommends that the House exercise its constitutional power to impeach Richard M. Nixon, President of the United States, and that articles of impeachment be exhibited to the Senate as follows:

RESOLUTION

Impeaching Richard M. Nixon, President of the United States, of high crimes and misdemeanors.

Resolved, That Richard M. Nixon, President of the United States, is impeached for high crimes and misdemeanors, and that the following articles of impeachment be exhibited to the Senate:

Articles of impeachment exhibited by the House of Representatives of the United States of America in the name of itself and of all of the people of the United States of America, against Richard M. Nixon, President of the United

States of America, in maintenance and support of its impeachment against him for high crimes and misdemeanors.

ARTICLE I

In his conduct of the office of President of the United States, Richard M. Nixon, in violation of his constitutional oath faithfully to execute the office of President of the United States and, to the best of his ability, preserve, protect, and defend the Constitution of the United States, and in violation of his constitutional duty to take care that the laws be faithfully executed, has prevented, obstructed, and impeded the administration of justice, in that:

On June 17, 1972, and prior thereto, agents of the Committee for the Re-election of the President committed unlawful entry of the headquarters of the Democratic National Committee in Washington, District of Columbia, for the purpose of securing political intelligence. Subsequent thereto, Richard M. Nixon, using the powers of his high office, engaged personally and through his subordinates and agents, in a course of conduct or plan designed to delay, impede, and obstruct the investigation of such unlawful entry; to cover up, conceal and protect those responsible; and to conceal the existence and scope of other unlawful covert activities.

The means used to implement this course of conduct or plan included one or more of the following:

1. making or causing to be made false or misleading statements to lawfully authorized investigative officers and employees of the United States;

2. withholding relevant and material evidence or information from lawfully authorized investigative officers and employees of the United States;

3. approving, condoning, acquiescing in, and counseling witnesses with respect to the giving of false or misleading statements to lawfully authorized investigative officers and employees of the United States and false or misleading testimony in duly instituted judicial and congressional proceedings;

4. interfering or endeavoring to interfere with the conduct of investigations by the Department of Justice of the United States, the Federal Bureau of Investigation, the Office of Watergate Special Prosecution Force, and Congressional Committees;

5. approving, condoning, and acquiescing in, the surreptitious payment of substantial sums of money for the purpose of obtaining the silence or influencing the testimony of witnesses, potential witnesses or individuals who participated in such unlawful entry and other illegal activities;

6. endeavoring to misuse the Central Intelligence Agency, an agency of the United States.

7. disseminating information received from officers of the Department of Justice of the United States to subjects of investigations conducted by law-

fully authorized investigative officers and employees of the United States, for the purpose of aiding and assisting such subjects in their attempts to avoid criminal liability;

8. making false or misleading public statements for the purpose of deceiving the people of the United States into believing that a thorough and complete investigation has been conducted with respect to allegations of misconduct on the parts of personnel of the executive branch of the United States and personnel of the Committee for the Re-election of the President and that there was no involvement of such personnel in such misconduct; or

9. endeavoring to cause prospective defendants, and individuals duly tried and convicted, to expect favored treatment and considerations in return for their silence or false testimony, or rewarding individuals for their silence or false testimony.

In all of this, Richard M. Nixon has acted in a manner contrary to his trust as President and subversive of constitutional government, to the great prejudice of the cause of law and justice and to the manifest injury of the people of the United States.

Wherefore Richard M. Nixon, by such conduct, warrants impeachment and trial, and, removal from office.

ARTICLE II

Using the powers of the office of President of the United States, Richard M. Nixon, in violation of his constitutional oath faithfully to execute the office of President of the United States and to the best of his ability, preserve, protect, and defend the Constitution of the United States, and in disregard of his constitutional duty to take care that the laws be faithfully executed, has repeatedly engaged in conduct violating the constitutional rights of citizens, impairing the due and proper administration of justice and the conduct of lawful inquiries, or contravening the laws governing agencies of the executive branch and the purposes of these agencies.

This conduct has included one or more of the following:

1. He has, acting personally and through his subordinates and agents, endeavored to obtain from the Internal Revenue Service, in violation of the constitutional rights of citizens, confidential information contained in income tax returns for purposes not authorized by law, and to cause, in violation of the constitutional rights of citizens, income tax audits or other income tax investigations to be initiated or conducted in a discriminatory manner.

2. He misused the Federal Bureau of Investigation, the Secret Service, and other executive personnel, in violation or disregard of the constitutional rights of citizens, by directing or authorizing such agencies or personnel to conduct or continue electronic surveillance or other investigations for pur-

poses unrelated to national security, the enforcement of laws, or any other lawful function of his office; and he did direct the concealment of certain records made by the Federal Bureau of Investigation of electronic surveillance.

3. He has, acting personally and through his subordinates and agents, in violation or disregard of the constitutional rights of citizens, authorized and permitted to be maintained a secret investigative unit within the office of the President, financed in part with money derived from campaign contributions, which unlawfully utilized resources of the Central Intelligence Agency, engaged in covert and unlawful activities, and attempted to prejudice the constitutional right of an accused to a fair trail.

4. He has failed to take care that the laws were faithfully executed by failing to act when he knew or had reason to know that his close subordinates endeavored to impede and frustrate lawful inquiries by duly constituted executive, judicial, and legislative entities concerning the unlawful entry into the headquarters of the Democratic National Committee, and the cover up thereof, and concerning other unlawful activities, including those relating to the confirmation of Richard Kleindienst as Attorney General of the United States, the electronic surveillance of private citizens, the break-in into the offices of Dr. Lewis Fielding, and the campaign financing practices of the Committee to Re-elect the President.

5. In disregard of the rule of law, he knowingly misused the executive power by interfering with agencies of the executive branch, including the Federal Bureau of Investigation, the Criminal Division, and the Office of Watergate Special Prosecution Force, of the Department of Justice, and the Central Intelligence Agency, in violation of his duty to take care that the laws be faithfully executed.

In all of this, Richard M. Nixon has acted in a manner contrary to his trust as President and subversive of constitutional government, to the great prejudice of the cause of law and justice and to the manifest injury of the people of the United States.

Wherefore Richard M. Nixon, by such conduct, warrants impeachment and removal from office.

ARTICLE III

In his conduct of the office of President of the United States, Richard M. Nixon, contrary to his oath faithfully to execute the office of President of the United States and, to the best of his ability, preserve, protect, and defend the Constitution of the United States, and in violation of his constitutional duty to take care that the laws be faithfully executed, has failed without lawful cause or excuse to produce papers and things as directed by duly authorized subpoenas issued by the Committee on the Judiciary of the House of Representatives on April 11, 1974, May 30, 1974, and June 24, 1974, and willfully disobeyed such subpoenas. The subpoenaed papers and things were deemed necessary by the committee in order to resolve by direct evidence fundamental, factual questions relating to Presidential direction, knowledge, or approval of actions demonstrated by other evidence to be substantial grounds for impeachment of the President. In refusing to produce these papers and things, Richard M. Nixon, substituting his judgment as to what materials were necessary for the inquiry, interposed the powers of the Presidency against the lawful subpoenas of the House of Representatives, thereby assuming to himself functions and judgments necessary to the exercise of the sole power of impeachment vested by the Constitution in the House of Representatives.

In all of this, Richard M. Nixon has acted in a manner contrary to his trust as President and subversive of constitutional government, to the great prejudice of the cause of law and justice, and to the manifest injury of the people of the United States.

Wherefore Richard M. Nixon, by such conduct, warrants impeachment and trial and removal from office.

Document 9
THE NIXON STATEMENT UPON RELEASING
THE NEW TAPES

Following is the statement by President Nixon, August 5, 1974, upon release of the White House tapes as ordered by the Supreme Court. Release of these tapes caused support of Nixon to evaporate in Congress and led to his resignation.

I have today instructed my attorneys to make available to the House Judiciary Committee, and I am making public, the transcripts of three conversations with H. R. Haldeman on June 23, 1972. I have also turned over the tapes of these conversations to Judge Sirica, as part of the process of my compliance with the Supreme Court ruling.

On April 29, in announcing my decision to make public the original set of White House transcripts, I stated that "as far as what the President personally knew and did with regard to Watergate and the cover-up is concerned, these materials—together with those already made available—will tell it all."

Shortly after that, in May, I made a preliminary review of some of the 64 taped conversations subpoenaed by the special prosecutor.

Among the conversations I listened to at that time were two of those of June 23. Although I recognized that these presented potential problems, I did not inform my staff or my counsel of it, or those arguing my case, nor did I amend my submission to the Judiciary Committee in order to include and reflect it. At the time, I did not realize the extent of the implications, which these conversations might now appear to have. As a result, those arguing my case, as well as those passing judgment on the case did so with information that was incomplete and in some respects erroneous. This was a serious act of omission for which I take full responsibility and which I deeply regret.

Since the Supreme Court's decision 12 days ago, I have ordered my counsel to analyze the 64 tapes, and I have listened to a number of them myself. This process has made it clear that portions of the tapes of these June 23 conversations are at variance which certain of my previous statements. Therefore, I have ordered the transcripts made available immediately to the Judiciary Committee so that they can be reflected in the committee's report, and included in the record to be considered by the House and Senate.

In a formal written statement on May 22 of last year, I said that shortly after the Watergate break-in I became concerned about the possibility that the FBI investigation might lead to the exposure either of unrelated covert activities of the CIA, or of sensitive national security matters that the so-called "plumbers" unit at the White House had been working on, because of the CIA and plumbers connections of some of those involved. I said that I therefore gave instructions that the FBI should be alerted to coordinate with the CIA, and to ensure that the investigation not expose these sensitive national security matters.

That statement was based on my recollections at the time—some 11 months later—plus documentary materials and relevant public testimony of those involved.

The June 23 tapes clearly show, however, that at the time I gave those instructions I also discussed the political aspects of the situation, and that I was aware of the advantages this course of action would have with respect to limiting possible public exposure of involvement by persons connected with the re-election committee.

My review of the additional tapes has, so far, shown no other major inconsistencies with what I have previously submitted. While I have no way at this stage of being certain that there will not be others, I have no reason to believe that there will be. In any case, the tapes in their entirety are now in the process of being furnished to Judge Sirica. He has begun what may be a rather lengthy process of reviewing the tapes, passing on specific claims of executive privilege on portions of them, and forwarding to the special prosecutor those tapes or those portions that are relevant to the Watergate investigation.

It is highly unlikely that his review will be completed in time for the House debate. It appears at this stage, however, that a House vote on impeachment is, as a practical matter, virtually a foregone conclusion, and that the issue will therefore go to trial in the Senate. In order to insure that no other significant relevant materials are withheld, I shall voluntarily furnish to the Senate everything from these tapes that Judge Sirica rules should go to the special prosecutor.

I recognize that this additional material I am now furnishing may further damage my case, especially because attention will be drawn separately to it rather than to the evidence in its entirety. In considering its implications, therefore, I urge that two points be borne in mind.

The first of these points is to remember what actually happened as a result of the instructions I gave on June 23. Acting Director Gray of the FBI did coordinate with Director Helms and Deputy Director Waters of the CIA. The CIA did undertake an extensive check to see whether any of its covert activities would be compromised by a full FBI investigation of Watergate. Deputy Director Walters then reported back to Mr. Gray that they would not be compromised. On July 6, when I called Mr. Gray, and when he expressed concern about improper attempts to limit his investigation, as the record shows, I told him to press ahead vigorously with his investigation—which he did.

The second point I would urge is that the evidence be looked at in its entirely, and the events be looked at in perspective. Whatever mistakes I made in the handling of Watergate, the basic truth remains that when all the facts were brought to my attention, I insisted on a full investigation and prosecution of those guilty. I am firmly convinced that the record, in its entirety, does not justify the extreme step of impeachment and removal of a President. I trust that as the constitutional process goes forward, this perspective will prevail.

Document 10
PRESIDENT NIXON'S STATEMENT OF RESIGNATION

Speech given over national television announcing his plan to leave office, August 8, 1974.

Good evening.

This is the 37th time I have spoken to you from this office in which so many decisions have been made that shape the history of this nation.

Each time I have done so to discuss with you some matters that I believe affected the national interest. And all the decisions I have made in my public life I have always tried to do what was best for the nation.

Throughout the long and difficult period of Watergate, I have felt it was my duty to persevere; to make every possible effort to complete the term of office to which you elected me.

In the past few days, however, it has become evident to me that I no longer have a strong enough political base, I felt strongly that it was necessary to see the constitutional process through to its conclusion; that to do otherwise would be unfaithful to the spirit of that deliberately difficult process, and a dangerously destabilizing precedent for the future.

But with the disappearance of that base, I now believe that the constitutional purpose has been served. And there is no longer a need for the process to be prolonged.

I would have preferred to carry through to the finish whatever the personal agony it would have involved, and my family unanimously urged me to do so.

But the interests of the nation must always come before any personal considerations. From the discussions I have had with Congressional and other leaders I have concluded that because of the Watergate matter I might not have the support of the Congress that I would consider necessary to back the very difficult decisions and carry out the duties of this office in the way the interests of the nation will require.

I have never been a quitter.

To leave office before my term is completed is opposed to every instinct in my body. But as President I must put the interests of America first.

America needs a full-time President and a full-time Congress, particularly at this time with problems we face at home and abroad.

To continue to fight through the months ahead for my personal vindication would almost totally absorb the time and attention of both the President and the Congress in a period when our entire focus should be on the great issues of peace abroad and prosperity without inflation at home.

Therefore, I shall resign the Presidency effective at noon tomorrow. Vice President Ford will be sworn in as President at that hour in this office.

As I recall the high hopes for America with which we began this second term, I feel a great sadness that I will not be here in this office working on your behalf to achieve those hopes in the next two and a half years.

But in turning over direction of the Government to Vice President Ford I know, as I told the nation when I nominated him for that office 10 months ago, that the leadership of America will be in good hands.

In passing this office to the Vice President I also do so with the profound sense of the weight of responsibility that will fall on his shoulders tomorrow, and therefore of the understanding, the patience, the cooperation he will need from all Americans.

As he assumes that responsibility he will deserve the help and the support of all of us. As we look to the future, the first essential is to begin healing the wounds of this nation. To put the bitterness and division of the recent past behind us and to rediscover those shared ideals that lie at the heart of our strength and unity as a great nation and as a free people.

By taking this action, I hope that I will have hastened the start of that process of healing which is so desperately needed in America.

I regret deeply any injuries that may have been done in the course of the events that led to this decision. I would say only that if some of my judgments were wrong—and some were wrong—they were made in what I believed at the time to be the best interests of the nation.

To those who have stood with me during these past difficult months, to my family, my friends, the many others who've joined in supporting my cause because they believed it was right, I will be eternally grateful for your support.

And to those who have not felt able to give me your support, let me say I leave with no bitterness toward those who have opposed me, because all of us in the final analysis have been concerned with the good of the country however our judgments might differ.

So let us all now join together in affirming that common commitment and in helping our new President succeed for the benefit of all Americans.

I shall leave this office with regret at not completing my term but with gratitude for the privilege of serving as your President for the past five and a half years.

These years have been a momentous time in the history of our nation and the world. They have been a time of achievement in which we can all be proud—achievements that represent that shared efforts of the Administration, the Congress and the people. But the challenges ahead are equally great.

And they, too, will require the support and the efforts of a Congress and the people, working in cooperation with the new Administration.

We have ended America's longest war. But in the work of securing a lasting peace in the world, the goals ahead are even more far-reaching and more difficult. We must complete a structure of peace, so that it will be said of this generation—our generation of Americans—by the people of all nations, not only that we ended one war but that we prevented future wars.

We have unlocked the doors that for a quarter of a century stood between the United States and the People's Republic of China. We must now insure that the one-quarter of the world's people who live in the People's Republic of China will be and remain, not our enemies, but our friends.

In the Middle East, 100 million people in the Arab countries, many of whom have considered us their enemies for nearly 20 years, now look on us as their friends. We must continue to build on that friendship so that peace can settle at last over the Middle East and so that the cradle of civilization will not become its grave.

Together with the Soviet Union we have made the crucial breakthroughs that have begun the process of limiting nuclear arms. But, we must set as our goal, not just limiting, but reducing and finally destroying these terrible weapons so that they cannot destroy civilization.

And so that the threat of nuclear war will no longer hang over the world and the people, we have opened a new relationship with the Soviet Union. We must continue to develop and expand that new relationship so that the two strongest nations of the world will live together in cooperation rather than confrontation.

Around the world—in Asia, in Africa, in Latin America, in the Middle East—there are millions of people who live in terrible poverty, even starvation. We must keep as our goal turning away from production for war and expanding production for peace so that people everywhere on this earth can at last look forward, in their children's time if not in our time, to having the necessities for a decent life.

Here in America we are fortunate that most of our people have not only the blessing of liberty but also the means to live full and good, and by the world's standards even abundant, lives.

We must press on, however, toward a goal not only of more and better jobs but of full opportunity for every man, and of what we are striving so hard right now to a achieve—prosperity without inflation.

For more than a quarter of a century in public life, I have shared in the turbulent history of this evening.

I have fought for what I believe in. I have tried, to the best of my ability, to discharge those duties and meet those responsibilities that were entrusted to me.

Sometimes I have succeeded. and sometimes I have failed. But always I have taken heart from what Theodore Roosevelt said about the man in the arena whose face is marred by dust and sweat and blood, who strives valiantly, who errs and comes short again and again because there is no effort without error and shortcoming, but who does actually strive to do the deed, who knows the great enthusiasm, the great devotion, who spends himself in a worthy cause, who at the best knows in the end the triumphs of high achievements and with the worst if he fail, at least fails while daring greatly.

I pledge to you tonight that as long as I have a breath of life in my body I shall continue in that spirit. I shall continue to work for the great causes to which I have been dedicated throughout my years as a Congressman, a Senator, Vice President and President, the cause of peace—not just for

America but among all nations—prosperity, justice and opportunity for all of our people.

There is one cause above all, to which I have been devoted and to which I shall always be devoted for as long as I live.

When I first took the oath of office as President five and half years ago, I made this sacred commitment: to consecrate my office, my energies and all the wisdom I can summon to the cause of peace among nations.

I've done my very best in all the days since to be true to that pledge.

As a result of these efforts, I am confident that the world is a safer place today, not only for the people of America but for the people of all nations, and that all of our children have a better chance than before of living in peace rather than dying in war.

This, more than anything, is what I hoped to achieve when I sought the Presidency. This, more than anything, is what I hope will be my legacy to you, to our country, as I leave the Presidency.

To have served in this office is to have felt a very personal sense of kinship with each and every American. In leaving it, I do so with this prayer: May God's grace be with you in all the days ahead.

Document 11
PRESIDENT FORD'S SPEECH PARDONING
RICHARD NIXON

On September 8, 1974, President Gerald Ford issued a pardon to Richard Nixon for all crimes he "may have" committed while in office. This pardon led to suspicions that Ford had struck a deal with Nixon prior to Nixon leaving office. No proof of such a deal has ever turned up.

Ladies and gentlemen, I have come to a decision which I felt I should tell you, and all my fellow citizens, as soon as I was certain in my own mind and conscience that it is the right thing to do.

I have learned already in this office that only the difficult decisions come to this desk. I must admit that many of them do not look at all the same as the hypothetical questions that I have answered freely and perhaps too fast on previous occasions. My customary policy is to try and get all the facts and to consider the opinions of my countrymen and to take counsel with my most valued friends. But these seldom agree, and in the end the decision is mine.

To procrastinate, to agonize, to wait for a more favorable turn of events that may never come, or more compelling external pressures that may as well be wrong as right, is itself a decision of sorts and a weak and potentially dangerous course for a President to follow.

I have promised to uphold the Constitution, to do what is right as God gives me to see the right, and to do the very best I can for America. I have asked your help and your prayers, not only when I became President, but many times since.

The Constitution is the supreme law of our land and it governs our actions as citizens. Only the laws of God, which govern our consciences, are superior to it. As we are a Nation under God, so I am sworn to uphold our laws with the help of God. And I have sought such guidance and searched my own conscience with special diligence to determine the right thing for me to do with respect to my predecessor in this place, Richard Nixon and his loyal wife and family.

Theirs is an American tragedy in which we all have played a part. It can go on and on and on or someone must write "the end" to it.

I have concluded that only I can do that. And if I can, I must.

There are no historic or legal precedents to which I can turn in this matter, none that precisely fit the circumstances of a private citizen who has resigned the Presidency of the United States. But it is common knowledge that serious allegations and accusations hang like a sword over our former President's head as he tries to reshape his life, a great part of which was spent in the service of this country and by the mandate of its people.

After years of bitter controversy and divisive national debate, I have been advised and am compelled to conclude that many months and perhaps more years will have to pass before Richard Nixon could hope to obtain a fair trial by jury in any jurisdiction of the United States under governing decisions of the Supreme Court.

I deeply believe in equal justice for all Americans, whatever their station or former station. The law, whether human or divine, is no respecter of persons but the law is a respecter of reality. The facts as I see them are that a former President of the United States, instead of enjoying equal treatment with any other citizen accused of violating the law, would be cruelly and excessively penalized either in preserving the presumption of his innocence or in obtaining a speedy determination of his guilt in order to repay a legal debt to society.

During this long period of delay and potential litigation, ugly passions would again be aroused, our people would again be polarized in their opinions, and the credibility of our free institutions of government would again be challenged at home and abroad. In the end, the courts might well hold that Richard Nixon had been denied due process and the verdict of history would be even more inconclusive with respect to those charges arising out of the period of his Presidency of which I am presently aware.

But it is not the ultimate fate of Richard Nixon that most concerns me—though surely it deeply troubles every decent and compassionate person. Rather my concern is the immediate future of this great country. In this I dare not depend upon my personal sympathy as a longtime friend of the Former President nor my professional judgment as a lawyer. And I do not.

As President, my primary concern must always be the greatest good of all the people of the United States, whose servant I am.

As a man, my first consideration is to be true to my own convictions and my own conscience.

My conscience tells me clearly and certainly that I cannot prolong the bad dreams that continue to reopen a chapter that is closed. My conscience tells me that only I, as President, have the Constitutional power to firmly shut and seal this book. My conscience says it is my duty, not merely to proclaim domestic tranquility, but to use every means I have to ensure it.

I do believe that the buck stops here and that I cannot rely upon public opinion polls to tell me what is right. I do believe that right makes might, and that if I am wrong ten angels swearing I was right would make no difference. I do believe with all my heart and mind and spirit that I, not as President but as a humble servant of God, will receive justice without mercy if I fail to show mercy.

Finally, I feel that Richard Nixon and his loved ones have suffered enough, and will continue to suffer no matter what I do, no matter what we as a great and good Nation can do together to make his goal of peace come true.

Now, therefore, I, Gerald R. Ford, President of the United States, pursuant to the pardon power conferred upon me by Article II, Section 2, of the Constitution, have granted and by these presents do grant a full, free, and absolute pardon unto Richard Nixon for all offenses against the United States which he, Richard Nixon, has committed or may have committed or taken part in during the period from January 20, 1969 through August 9, 1974.

Document 12
1997 RELEASE OF TAPES

"I ordered that they use any means necessary, including illegal means to accomplish this goal. . . . The president of the United States can never admit that." These words, spoken by President Nixon in 1973, are part of a series of tapes released in late 1997. These newly released White House tapes demonstrate an even deeper involvement by Nixon in the crimes of Watergate than had been previously known.

Ever since the existence of audiotapes of Nixon administration conversations was revealed, a heated battle has taken place over their control. Nixon, and later his heirs, fought to prevent release of the recordings.

Recently, historian Stanley Kutler won a suit ordering release of the tapes. Kutler, author of the book *The Wars of Watergate* (1990), has published transcriptions of some of the recently released tapes. His book, entitled *Abuse of Power: The New Nixon Tapes* (1997), reveals sordid details of the secret, inner workings of the Nixon mind. These tapes show conclusively Nixon's sale of ambassadorships, criminal cover-up, use of hush money, obstruction of justice, and paranoid personality. What follows are excerpts from the tapes released in 1997.

EXCERPTS FROM TRANSCRIPTS OF 201 HOURS OF TAPES

Participants in the recording are designated by the following initials:

N: President Richard M. Nixon

H: H. R. Haldeman, White House chief of staff

K: Henry A. Kissinger, national security adviser

Z: Ronald L. Ziegler, White House spokesman

AH: Gen. Alexander M. Haig, Jr.

COVER-UP

June 21, 1972: The cover-up began almost immediately after the Watergate break-in. Nixon knew that an investigation of the break-in could quickly lead directly to the White House.

N: What's the dope on the Watergate incident? Anything break on that?

H: . . . Mitchell's concern is the FBI, the question of how far they're going in the process. He's concerned that be turned off . . .

The problem is that there are all kinds of other involvements and if they started a fishing expedition on this they're going to start picking up tracks. . . . The only tie they've got to the White House is that this guy's name was in their books, Howard Hunt, and that Hunt used to be a consultant—

N: To the White House?

H: —to Colson at the White House. . . . You've got to be careful of pushing that too hard, because he was working on a lot of stuff. . . . It lead to other things.

N: . . . My view is, and I still hold with this view, that in terms of the reaction of people, the reaction is going to be primarily Washington and not the country, because I think the country doesn't give much of a [expletive] about it, other than the ones we've already bugged. . . . Most people around the country think that this is routine, that everybody's trying to bug everybody else. . . . [The Watergate Story] is not one that's going to get people that goddamn excited . . . because they don't give a (expletive) about repression and bugging and all the rest. . . . Let's just look at wiretapping. The country's for it. The whole country.

THE FALL GUY

June 30, 1972: The president learns that Liddy will take the blame for Watergate. The campaign cash that financed the break-in will be tied to an "embezzlement."

H: We're going to write a scenario—in fact, we're going to have Liddy write it—which brings all of the loose ends that might lead anywhere at all to him . . .

N: What does he get out of it? What's his penalty?

H: Not too much. They don't think it'll be any big problem. Whatever it is, we'll take care of him . . .

N: And we'll give him—we'll take care of him, too. Well, it's good to have some people like that.

H: He may have to go to jail for a while or something, but he'll survive that.

N: What the hell. Worse than that, he's breaking into the Democratic Committee, Christ. That's no blot on a man's record.

H: Well, the embezzlement of those funds, too, and violation of the Campaign Spending Act.

N: That's probably a fine . . .

H: Wrapping it all up into this, it doesn't make much difference. We'll wait a discreet interval and pardon him.

N: You don't want to pardon him now?

H: After the election.

N: Sure . . . it's just such a ridiculous goddamn thing, it really is.

MONEY IN BOXES

July 25, 1972: The president asks Mr. Haldeman how much hidden campaign cash is on hand at the White House.

N: Incidentally, can I ask a question? Do we have any funds that (campaign treasurer Maurice) Stans doesn't know about that's not in cash?

H: Well, we have cash that Stans—yes, we have some cash that Stans—yes, we have some cash that Stans can't do anything about. He knows we have it.

N: We can handle it with a non-reporting (unintelligible), but we've got some and we may have to do something about that.

H: And Rose has got some cash (This was $100,000 from Dwayne Andreas, the agri-business magnate, in the safe of the president's secretary, Rose Mary Woods.).

N: O.K., good.

H: We don't have as much as we were going to have. We have about $300,000 but we can get anything we want. We got scared, everybody got scared, because of the (unintelligible) thing and the problem of getting ourselves tied into cash (unintelligible).

N: The $300,000 is left . . .

H: It's in our cash in boxes. . . . I think it's $300,000.

N: That isn't a hell of a lot . . .

H: We can tap—we also have cash that they have that we can tap. We don't have to use only our cash. There is unreported cash over there (at campaign headquarters) that they'll expend at our direction.

BUYING SILENCE

Aug. 1, 1972: The Watergate burglars are about to be indicted. Nixon asks Mr. Haldeman about the cost of buying their silence with hush money.

N: Let's be fatalistic about the goddamn thing.

H: If it blows, it blows.

N: If it blows, it blows, and so on. I'm not that worried about it, to be really candid with you.

H: It's worth a lot of work to try and keep it from blowing.

N: Oh, my, yes.

H: But if it blows, we'll survive it.

N: After all . . . nobody at a higher level was involved, the White House not being involved, and all that stuff. . . . Are the Cubans going to plead not guilty?

H: I don't know. But everybody's satisfied. They're all out of jail, they've all been taken care of. We've done a lot of discreet checking to make sure there's no discontent in the ranks, and there isn't any.

N: They're all out on bail.

H: Hunt's happy.

N: At considerable cost, I guess?

H: Yes.

N: It's worth it.

H: It's very expensive. It's a costly—

N: That's what the money is for. . . . They have to be paid. That's all there is to that. They have to be paid. . . . You say no cooperation from the Justice Department. I understand the FBI.

H: It's been very hard . . .

N: That is scary.

PARANOIA

April 27, 1973: The president talks seriously about impeachment. He is enraged, cursing Dean. Even his dog, King Timahoe, infuriates him.

N: That goddamn press. . . .

Z: They didn't call for impeachment. They referred to it, you know, the wording.

N: Christ, impeach the President on John Dean—on John Dean's word. . . . He came in, there's, there's a cancer in the heart of the White House, on the heart of the Presidency. (The dog barks) King! . . . goddamn, get off me! . . . But they can't want, frankly, to see Agnew be President.

Z: That's right.

N: No, really. You know—well, I don't think of impeachment, Good God Almighty, the point is they've got to want this country to succeed. The whole hopes of the whole goddamn world of peace, Ron, you know where they rest, they rest right here in this damn chair. . . . The press has got to realize that whatever they think of me, I'm the only one at the present time in this whole wide blinking world that can do a goddamn thing, you know. Keep it from blowing up. . . . Look, if we went in with sackcloth and ashes and fired the whole White House staff . . . that isn't going to satisfy these goddamn cannibals. They'd still be after us. Who are they after? Hell, they're not after Haldeman or Ehrlichman or Dean; *they're after me,* the President. They hate my guts.

"DESTROY HIM"

May 8, 1973: The president talks with his chief of staff, Alexander M. Haig, Jr.

N: Did you see the Harris poll, by any chance?

AH: No, I didn't see it.

N: By a vote of 59 to 31, they thought the President should be given the benefit of the doubt on this matter and should be allowed to finish his term. You know, the next three-and-a-half years. But the other interesting thing is by a vote of 77 to 13 they opposed suggestion that the President resign.

AH: Of course. My God. . . . It's unthinkable. It's unthinkable.

N: Oh, they may, but you see, only one person (is) trying to do that. You realize that. That's Dean. And goddamn him . . . one disloyal President's counsel, a lawyer, of all people, not just a—a Henry Kissinger walking out, you know, as a disgruntled person, people will understand it. But the President's lawyer? Jesus Christ. I mean, this is a—

AH: Well, he's a sniveling coward.

N: I think we can destroy him—we must destroy him.

AH: Have to.

N: We never can allow this to happen—even if I was guilty as hell, but I'm not (unintelligible). I was dragged into this, son of a bitch, because of stupid people. Well-intentioned stupid people.

AH: That's something entirely different. Here we've got a vicious little coward who's trying to protect his ass at any cost.

N: And therefore he's got to be destroyed.

IMPEACHMENT

May 10, 1973: The president talks with his former chief of staff, Haldeman.

N: Bob, I don't think people give a (expletive) about the CIA thing. I don't really think they care. I don't think they care about bugging Ellsberg—I mean, running into the psychiatrist—[or] bugging the goddamn Pentagon—I mean—

AH: Watergate.

N: Watergate. I think the cover-up deal was a problem and the obstruction of justice was a problem in the sense that it looks like we've tried to—what I mean—we were not carrying out *the law*, so-called.

AH: Yeah.

N: That is a problem. . . . But the main thing is that all this crap about the President should resign—

AH: Don't even listen.

N: Nobody should even raise such things. . . . If I walk out of this office, you know, on this (expletive) stuff, why it would leave a mark on the American political system. It's unbelievable. . . . But the other thing is—the other thing, if they ever want to get up to the impeachment thing, fine, fine. . . . My point is that if they get to that, the President of the United States, my view is then *fight like hell.*

Appendix: Legal Problems of the Nixon Administration

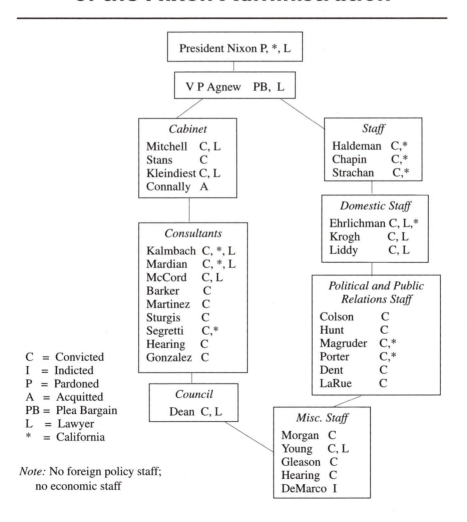

President Nixon P, *, L

V P Agnew   PB, L

Cabinet

Mitchell   C, L
Stans   C
Kleindiest C, L
Connally   A

Staff

Haldeman   C,*
Chapin   C,*
Strachan   C,*

Domestic Staff

Ehrlichman C, L,*
Krogh   C, L
Liddy   C, L

Consultants

Kalmbach C, *, L
Mardian   C, *, L
McCord   C, L
Barker   C
Martinez C
Sturgis   C
Segretti C,*
Hearing   C
Gonzalez C

Political and Public Relations Staff

Colson   C
Hunt   C
Magruder C,*
Porter   C,*
Dent   C
LaRue   C

C = Convicted
I = Indicted
P = Pardoned
A = Acquitted
PB = Plea Bargain
L = Lawyer
* = California

Council

Dean C, L

Misc. Staff

Morgan C
Young   C, L
Gleason C
Hearing C
DeMarco I

Note: No foreign policy staff;
    no economic staff

Glossary of Selected Terms

Cambodia: The country, bordering on Vietnam, which the Nixon administration ordered invaded in 1970 in an effort to cut off North Vietnamese sanctuaries. When word of the invasion crept out after months of secrecy, U.S. campuses erupted in demonstrations, leading to deaths of students at Kent State and Jackson State Universities.

Certiorari: A Latin term used in judicial proceedings, a writ of certiorari is an order from an appellate court to a lower court ordering that the records of a case be sent up to the higher court for review. Almost all cases that reach the Supreme Court do so via this route.

Clemency: Meaning forgiveness of punishment. The Watergate burglars demanded, and the Nixon administration offered, clemency for silence.

Cover-up: The effort to conceal and divert attention away from the crimes of Watergate.

Deep Throat: The mysterious source of information on Watergate for investigative journalists Woodward and Bernstein of the *Washington Post*, it is not known whether this source is real or fictitious, one person or a composite of several sources. Named after an infamous pornographic film of the period, Deep Throat repeatedly enjoined the reporters to "follow the money." Speculation as to the identity of Deep Throat has varied widely and wildly. Woodward and Bernstein have said they will not reveal the identity of Deep Throat until he or she passes away.

Dirty Tricks: Acts, often illegal, taken by Nixon subordinates to disrupt and sabotage the campaigns of political opponents.

Enemies List: A list assembled by members of the Nixon administration that included the names of people and groups thought to be "enemies" of the president. This list was used, in the words of White House Counsel John Dean, "to screw our political enemies."

Executive Privilege: The claim that the president may withhold information from Congress.

Huston Plan: A scheme of dirty tricks and illegal activities, approved by Nixon administration officials, but put to an end by FBI director J. Edgar Hoover.

Impeachment: The sole constitutional method for potentially removing a sitting president on grounds of "high crimes and misdemeanors." The House Judiciary Committee holds hearings and makes a recommendation to the full House, who then votes on impeachment. If Articles of Impeachment are approved, the president is tried in the Senate.

Imperial Presidency: A term coined by historian Arthur Schlesinger, Jr., to denote a presidency grown too large in power, and seemingly above the law.

In camera: A legal term from the Latin meaning "in secret" or "in private," this usually refers to a judge examining evidence, meeting with attorneys, or reviewing court-related material in private in his chambers, and not in open court.

Obstruction of Justice: Interfering with a governmental or law enforcement investigation.

Operation Gemstone: The plan, devised by G. Gordon Liddy, to burglarize, bug, and disrupt the Democrats' Watergate headquarters.

Pardon: An act of forgiveness to acts committed. The president has very broad, independent pardoning powers.

Pentagon Papers: The name of a government report on the origins of U.S. involvement in the Vietnam War. When these papers were released by Daniel Ellsberg, they caused an uproar in the Nixon administration.

Perjury: Lying under oath.

Plumbers: Organized within the Nixon administration to "plug leaks," the Plumbers, a secret private force, engaged in a variety of illegal activities, including breaking and entering.

Saturday Night Massacre: When special prosecutor Archibald Cox refused to cease efforts to obtain Nixon's tapes, he was fired. This led to the resignation of the Attorney General Richardson and assistant Attorney General Ruckelshau who refused to do the firing, and started a public outcry against the president.

Special Prosecutor: An independent counsel with broad investigative powers appointed to investigate alleged crimes in the Nixon administration.

Subpoena: Writ for summoning a witness or ordering the submission of evidence.

Unindicted Co-Conspirator: Not knowing if a sitting president could be indicted, the special prosecutor named Nixon an unindicted co-conspirator in the trials of Haldeman, Ehrlichman, and others.

Vietnam: Southeast Asian nation going through a civil war. In the 1960s and 1970s, the United States aided the South against the North in this lengthy and divisive war.

Watergate: The name of a Washington, D.C., hotel-office complex. The Democratic National Committee had its offices in this complex. Nixon associates broke into the headquarters but were arrested. Later the term Watergate became an umbrella term for the illegal acts of the Nixon administration.

Wiretap: Intercepting communications by "tapping" telephone wires or other forms of communication.

Annotated Bibliography

Abrahamsen, David. *Nixon vs. Nixon: An Emotional Tragedy*. New York: Farrar, Straus, and Giroux, 1977. This psychobiography of Nixon looks at the inner core of the man as a way of understanding and explaining Nixon's political behavior. The author sees Nixon as a tragic figure, destroyed from within by the self-doubt and insecurity of a psychopathic personality.

Agnew, Spiro T. *Go Quietly . . . or Else*. New York: Morrow, 1980. In this self-serving autobiography, the former vice president, who was forced out of office by a criminal investigation, and who pled *nolo contendere* to charges of tax evasion, attempts to tell his side of the story. Agnew was the front man for much of Nixon's political attack strategy.

Aitken, Jonathan. *Nixon: A Life*. London: Weidenfelt and Nicholson, 1993. A very sympathetic view of Nixon written by a conservative member of the British Parliament. Nixon granted Aitken access to material not available to all researchers, and the book provides some useful, if carefully screened, insights.

Ambrose, Stephen E. *Nixon, Volume II: The Triumph of a Politician 1962–1972*. New York: Simon and Schuster, 1989. Thorough and readable, this second of three volumes on Nixon deals with the rise and triumph of Richard Nixon. A good source for context of the times and key issues.

———. *Nixon, Volume III: Ruin and Recovery 1973–1990*. New York: Simon and Schuster, 1991. The final days of Nixon are covered in the third volume of this ambitious biography. Ambrose does a fine job in getting us inside the Nixon psyche.

Ben-Veniste, Richard, and George Frampton, Jr. *Stonewall: The Real Story of the Watergate Prosecution*. New York: Simon and Schuster, 1977. Two top officials of the special prosecutor's office give an insider's account of the legal case that developed against the president. The politics of the special prosecutor's office shows how some of the key legal issues were resolved.

Bernstein, Carl, and Bob Woodward. *All the President's Men*. New York: Simon and Schuster, 1974. When no one else was paying much attention to Watergate, *Washington Post* reporters Woodward and Bernstein laid the groundwork for the initial uncovering of the crimes committed by Nixon administration officials. This book reads more like a "whodunit" as the authors present a mystery story as much as a piece of investigative journalism.

Breslin, Jimmy. *How the Good Guys Finally Won: Notes from an Impeachment Summer*. New York: Viking, 1975. One of America's top writers turns his considerable talents to Watergate. Seen through the eyes of House Speaker Thomas P. "Tip" O'Neill, this book does an excellent job illuminating the politics of Watergate and the insiders' games of power.

Chesen, Eli S. *President Nixon's Psychiatric Profile*. New York: Wyden, 1973. A psychobiography of Nixon that—like many other such works—sees Nixon's self-defeating core personality as the root of his downfall. Chesen argues that Nixon was a compulsive-obsessive personality type.

Colodny, Len, and Robert Gettlin. *Silent Coup: The Removal of Richard Nixon*. New York: St. Martin's Press, 1991. A conspiracy theory look at the underside of Watergate in which the authors argue that a cabal of foreign policy officials hidden deep in the foreign affairs bureaucracy conspired to bring Nixon down because he "was too dovish." Relying on rumor and hearsay, the authors use virtually no scholarly sources for this peculiar but interesting work.

Colson, Charles W. *Born Again:* Old Tappan, NJ: Spire Books, Fleming H. Revell Co., 1977. One of Nixon's dirty tricksters, Colson played into the president's "dark side." Here, Colson as a born-again Christian does a public *mea culpa*, "confessing" some sins and excusing others.

Congressional Quarterly, Inc. *Watergate: Chronology of a Crisis*. Wayne Kelley, exec. ed., Washington, DC: Congressional Quarterly, 1975. Information based, unbiased, and clear, this product of the nonpartisan *Congressional Quarterly* provides invaluable material for understanding Watergate.

Dash, Samuel. *Chief Counsel: Inside the Ervin Committee*. New York: Random House, 1976. The former Chief Counsel of the Senate Investigating committee (known as the Ervin Committee) had an inside view of the early public stage of the Watergate investigation. Dash was a key player when some of the important decisions on how to confront the Nixon administration were first made.

Dean, John W., III. *Blind Ambition: The White House Years*. New York: Simon & Schuster, 1976. Dean, the former counsel to the president, and one of Nixon's first accusers, offers a fascinating tale of a capable, ambitious young man, thrust into the center of power, seduced by the trappings of high office, who let his moral compass slip aside while he played a dangerous power game. Dean was intimately involved in the criminal cover-up and other crimes of Watergate. He testified before the Senate Select Committee as one of the first "higher ups" to implicate the president.

Drew, Elizabeth. *Washington Journal: The Events of 1973–74*. New York: Random House, 1975. A top political journalist, Drew wrote a clear and compelling account of Watergate. She paints in broad strokes and brings in the congressional as well as the executive side of the Watergate scandal.

Ehrlichman, John. *Witness to Power*. New York: Simon and Schuster, 1982. Chief domestic policy adviser to Nixon, Ehrlichman orchestrated the Plumbers' break-in of Daniel Ellsberg's psychiatrist's office and was at the center of the Watergate cover-up. This account of his involvement in Watergate is incomplete but interesting.

Emery, Fred. *Watergate: The Corruption of American Politics and the Fall of Richard Nixon*. New York: Touchstone, 1994. Based on a BBC television program, this recent account of Watergate takes advantage of access to materials only recently released. An excellent updated version of the Watergate scandal.

Ervin, Sam J., Jr. *The Whole Truth*. New York: Random House, 1980. "Senator Sam," the self-deprecating head of the Senate's special investigating committee, pontificates about the Constitution and the crimes of Watergate.

Ford, Gerald R. *A Time to Heal*. New York: Harper and Row, 1979. President Ford's memoirs include information on the final days of the Nixon presidency and the events that led to his pardon of former President Nixon.

Frost, David. *I Gave Them a Sword: Behind the Scenes of the Nixon Interviews*. New York: Morrow, 1978. Shortly after leaving office, Nixon did a series of interviews with British television personality David Frost. This book deal with the events surrounding those interviews and provides a unique glimpse of Nixon shortly after his fall from power.

Genovese, Michael A. *The Nixon Presidency: Power and Politics in Turbulent Times*. Westport, CT: Greenwood Press, 1990. A comprehensive look at the Nixon presidency, this work sees the roots of Watergate growing out of the administration's fears of domestic protest, Nixon's reelection concerns, and Nixon's paranoid psyche.

The Haldeman Diaries: Inside the Nixon White House. New York: Putnam, 1994; and CD-ROM, Cinergi, Graphix Zone. This recent book, and the CD-ROM that goes with it, provides a more personal view of the Nixon White House from the president's former chief of staff. The CD-ROM includes home movies taped by Haldeman covering a wide range of events and ceremonies.

Hougan, Jim. *Secret Agenda: Watergate, Deep Throat and the CIA*. New York: Random House, 1974. A conspiracy theory look at Watergate, this book makes fascinating reading but is farfetched and not supported by serious scholarship.

Hunt, E. Howard. *Undercover: Memoirs of an American Secret Agent.* New York: Berkley, 1974. One of the Watergate burglars, this former CIA agent and spy novel author gives his account of Watergate.

Jaworski, Leon. *The Right and the Power: The Prosecution of Watergate.* New York: Reader's Digest, 1976. The successor to Cox as Special Prosecutor, Jaworski brought the case *U.S. v. Nixon* to the Supreme Court, decided *not* to name the president as an indicted co-conspirator in the Watergate criminal case, and was instrumental in bringing about the demise of the Nixon presidency.

Kissinger, Henry. *The White House Years.* Boston: Little, Brown, 1979.

———. *Years of Upheaval.* Boston: Little, Brown, 1982. Nixon's alter ego on foreign affairs, Kissinger was also instrumental in the early downward drift of the administration by pressuring the president to plug leaks of information. Kissinger's books focus understandably on foreign affairs, but he does shed some light on the events of Watergate.

Kleindienst, Richard. *Justice.* Ottawa, IL: Jameson Books, 1985. Kleindienst, who was attorney general during much of the Nixon administration and whose early investigations into Watergate were careless and incomplete, covers some of the legal questions surrounding Watergate.

Kutler, Stanley I. *The Wars of Watergate: The Last Crisis of Richard Nixon.* New York: Knopf, 1990. An excellent account of Watergate by a distinguished historian, this book is one of the best single-volume versions of what happened in the Watergate crisis.

———. *Abuse of Power.* New York: The Free Press, 1997. As a result of lawsuits filed by Kutler, the Nixon estate was forced to release over 200 hours of Nixon tapes. This book collects the damning, often embarrassing, and ultimately, condemning tapes.

Lasky, Victor. *It Didn't Start with Watergate.* New York: Dial, 1977. A sympathetic, "everybody does it" defense of President Nixon, Lasky attempts to excuse Nixon's behavior by arguing that other presidents engaged in wrongdoing; Nixon got caught, they didn't. Weak.

Liddy, G. Gordon. *Will.* New York: St. Martin's Press, 1980. The infamous G. Gordon Liddy, ultra right-wing tough guy who was involved in the Watergate break-in, gives a bizarre but always interesting account of his life, politics, the drive for power, and Watergate.

Lukas, J. Anthony. *Nightmare: The Underside of the Nixon Years.* New York: Viking, 1973; Penguin Books, 1988. Written by a top political journalist as the Watergate crisis unfolded, Lukas gives a dramatic "I was there" feeling to the reader.

Magruder, Jeb Stuart. *An American Life: One Man's Road to Watergate.* New York: Atheneum, 1974. Initially responsible for running the Committee to Reelect the President, Magruder knew where all the bodies were buried, and in this Watergate memoir, he digs up a few corpses.

Mazlish, Bruce. *In Search of Nixon: A Psychohistorical Inquiry*. Baltimore: Penguin, 1972. A psychohistorical interpretation of Nixon that sees the president as psychologically maladjusted by low self-esteem, self-absorption, and repressed hostility.

McCord, James W., Jr. *A Piece of Tape: The Watergate Story: Fact and Fiction*. Rockville, MD: Washington Media Services, Ltd., 1974. One of the Watergate burglars, McCord wrote Judge Sirica warning that the Watergate scandal went deeper than merely those caught at the Democratic headquarters. His book is an autobiographical description of his role in the Watergate scandal.

Muzzio, Douglas. *Watergate Game: Strategies, Choices, Outcomes*. New York: New York University Press, 1982. Adopting a game-theory approach to the decision-making process of Watergate, Muzzio attempts to use rational decision criteria to understand the many choices made by Nixon and his subordinates.

Nixon, Richard M. *RN: The Memoirs of Richard Nixon*. New York: Grosset and Dunlap, 1978. Richard Nixon's memoirs, sometimes frank, sometimes duplicitous, always revealing are a lengthy self-examination of the totality of his presidency. Nixon does not, in the end, make an especially convincing case for his innocence in the Watergate scandal.

Price, Raymond. *With Nixon*. New York: Viking, 1977. Former Nixon speechwriter and longtime associate takes a personal look at Nixon. Both sympathetic and somewhat critical, Price does an excellent job of describing the "two-Nixons," one good, one bad.

Safire, William. *Before the Fall: An Inside View of the Pre-Watergate White House*. Garden City, NY: Doubleday, 1975. Political journalist and former Nixon administration official, William Safire looks at how the White House operated during the Nixon years. Highly readable and full of insights into how the administration came tumbling down.

Schell, Jonathan. *Time of Illusion*. New York: Random House, 1975. A well-written, impressionistic view of Watergate by a top social commentator, Schell presents a convincing case against President Nixon.

Sirica, John J. *To Set the Record Straight: The Break-in, the Tapes, the Conspirators, the Pardon*. New York: Norton, 1979. One of the key figures in bringing Watergate to the surface, Judge Sirica was not content to rest with the conviction of the burglars. He continued to push the investigation until the cover-up began to crack. Here Sirica tells his side of the Watergate story, focusing on the court proceedings and legal questions.

Sussman, Barry. *The Great Cover-up: Nixon and the Scandal of Watergate*. New York: Signet, 1974. *Washington Post* editor Barry Sussman's overview of the Watergate scandal. An excellent introduction to the crimes and uncovering of Watergate.

"Symposium: United States vs. Nixon." *UCLA Law Review, October, 1974*. An in-depth examination of the Supreme Court case that forced President

Nixon to turn over tape recordings of presidential conversations for use in the criminal trial. This symposium covers some of the key legal questions raised by claims of executive privilege and presidential claims of privacy versus the rights of the state in a criminal trial.

U.S. Department of Justice. Watergate Special Prosecution Force. *Report*. Washington, DC: 1975. The official report of the Special Prosecutor's office on Watergate: some of the insider accounts by Jaworski and others are a better read, but this report presents a compelling case against Nixon.

U.S. House of Representatives. Committee on the Judiciary. *Statement of Information, Hearings, Report*. 93d Congress, 2d session, 1973–1974. The Judiciary Committee, chaired by Peter Rodino, voted affirmatively on Articles of Impeachment. This Committee report details the case against the president.

U.S. Senate Select Committee on Presidential Campaign Activities. *Hearings, The Final Report*. 93d Congress, 2d session, 1973–1974. The Senate "Ervin Committee" held televised hearings, which escalated the Watergate crisis to national attention. This report, done fairly early in the Watergate crisis, is incomplete but fascinating.

White, Theodore H. *Breach of Faith: The Fall of Richard Nixon*. New York: Atheneum, 1975. Noted journalist White provides an elegantly written account of the events that led to the fall of President Nixon. Driven by moral outrage, White presents a devastating case against Nixon.

Woodward, Bob, and Carl Bernstein. *The Final Days*. New York: Simon and Schuster, 1976. *Washington Post* reporters Woodward and Bernstein examine the final days of the Nixon administration. Full of inside stories of intrigue and duplicity, this highly readable account of the fall of Nixon was a best-seller and deservedly so.

MOVIES/CD-ROMS

All the President's Men (1976). A dramatization of the Woodward/Bernstein exposé, this movie is more the story of a mystery unraveled than a study of Nixon himself. Dealing with the break-down of the Nixon cover-up as seen through the eyes of the two *Washington Post* journalists most responsible for uncovering the cover-up, *All the President's Men* (starring Dustin Hoffman and Robert Redford as the journalists) focuses on the role of the press in the Watergate saga.

Nixon (1996). Oliver Stone's tone poem of a movie is a character study of Nixon the man. While taking liberties with historical fact, this movie nonetheless captures the complex, often contradictory elements of Nixon's character. Nixon, played by Anthony Hopkins, is presented as a tortured and troubled man, driven to overcome insecurities that lead to a paranoia that eventually destroys Nixon.

There are a variety of made-for-TV movies, documentaries, and dramatizations dealing with Nixon and Watergate. A&E's *Biography* series has done several very fair, but probing episodes dealing with Nixon. *ABC Video* has produced a tape entitled *Richard M. Nixon: His Life and Times* (1994), that is fair and comprehensive.

Two CD-ROMs are especially noteworthy. Co-released with his film, *Nixon,* Oliver Stone produced a CD-ROM that contains a variety of Watergate-related material, including some of the Watergate transcripts. Also, Nixon's chief-of-staff, H. R. "Bob" Haldeman released a CD-ROM to go along with his book, *The Haldeman Diaries: Inside the Nixon White House* (New York: G. P. Putnam's Sons, 1994).

Index

About the Author

MICHAEL A. GENOVESE is Professor of Political Science and Director of the Institute for Leadership Studies at Loyola Marymount University in Los Angeles. He has written seven books, including *The Nixon Presidency: Power and Politics in Turbulent Times* (Greenwood, 1990), *The Presidency in an Age of Limits* (Greenwood, 1993), and *The Paradoxes of the American Presidency*, co-authored with Thomas E. Cronin (1998). He has won over a dozen university and national teaching awards.